PM Master Prep

EXAM PREPARATION MANUAL

For

Project Management Professional (PMP®)
Certified Associate Project Manager (CAPM®)

A comprehensive guide to passing the PMP® or CAPM® certification exams.
Based on the PMBOK® *Guide* 6th Edition

PM Master Prep™
124 Floyd Smith Office Park Dr. Suite 325
Charlotte, NC 28262
www.PMMasterPrep.com

Printed in the United States of America
Publisher: Lean Sigma Corporation
Library of Congress Control Number: 2018934570
ISBN: 978-0-9963406-5-6

Authors
Michael Parker
William Scott Payne

Other Contributors
Ashley Burnett
Cristina Neagu - Copyeditor

INTRODUCTION

Why You're Here

It's simple: you're here to learn how to pass the PMP® certification exam.

The problem you face is that the exam is difficult, and most course books are long and confusing. Those phone-book-sized training manuals unload page after page of detail on every input, output, and tool and technique of the 49 PMP® processes. Making sense of this flood of information requires that you spend your time memorizing, instead of understanding.

This course is the solution to that problem.

Mastering the PMP exam is not about memorization; it is about making connections.

The *PM Master Prep* course is focused on helping you make those connections. We have created a course to help you learn faster, retain more, and pass the test.

PM Master Prep Helps You *Learn Faster, Retain More, and Pass the Exam*

Our only goal is to help you pass the PMP® exam. We have designed this course in six specific ways to ensure that you do:

1. We teach the PMP® content based on how a normal project is conducted (other courses don't!)
2. We focus on the *why*, not just on the *how*
3. We provide real-life case studies to help you understand and remember key concepts
4. We provide everything you need and nothing you don't
5. We teach you a simple custom method to guarantee you get every EVM question right
6. We give you a 20% discount to our test simulator using the code on the book cover

These six aspects of the course provide you exactly the information and skills you need to answer PMP® questions correctly.

The Power of Teaching the PMP® Content Like a Normal Project

Most PMP® training programs aren't structured in the form of a real project!

It sounds crazy, but it is true. Instead, those courses are organized by knowledge area. This means they explain everything related to scope all at once, then schedule, then cost, and so on. This method creates confusion by forcing you to constantly jump around in the project life cycle. Worst of all, when you get to the end of the course, you are not at the end of a project—you covered the information related to the end of the project during the first chapter.

Why do they do this? Easy: it is how the *PMBOK®* is organized. The *PMBOK®* is where the test information comes from. We love the *PMBOK®*, but we believe the best way to learn the content is in a logical project-focused arrangement.

PM Master Prep teaches by process group, not knowledge area.

As we stated earlier, PMP® mastery is based on making connections, not memorization. That is why our decision to teach you the PMP® content by process group is significant. You will learn later that there are five process groups that group project activities to methodically achieve project objectives.

Teaching concepts by process groups helps you grasp the purpose and intent of each process and its outputs. Understanding the purpose of each process and how it links to other processes is what you need to answer questions correctly. This way we avoid discussing project activities such as managing project work or closing a project before we've discussed planning the project.

Throughout this book we will cover every process by traversing down each column of the table, starting at the top of the Initiating process group followed by the Planning process group and ending with the Closing process group.

	Initiating	Planning	Executing	Monitoring and Controlling	Closing
4. Integration Mgt.	4.1 Develop Proj. Charter	4.2 Develop Project Management Plan	4.3 Direct/Manage Proj. Work 4.4 Manage Proj. Knowledge	4.5 Mon./Control Proj. Work 4.6 Perf. Int. Change Control	4.7 Close Project or Phase
5. Scope Mgt.		5.1 Plan Scope Mgt. 5.2 Collect Requirements 5.3 Define Scope 5.4 Create WBS		5.5 Validate Scope 5.6 Control Scope	
6. Schedule Mgt.		6.1 Plan Sched. Mgt. 6.2 Define Activities 6.3 Sequence Activities 6.4 Est. Durations 6.5 Develop Schedule		6.6 Control Schedule	
7. Cost Mgt.		7.1 Plan Cost Mgt. 7.2 Estimate Costs 7.3 Determine Budget		7.4 Control Costs	
8. Quality Mgt.		8.1 Plan Quality Mgt.	8.2 Manage Quality	8.3 Control Quality	
9. Resource Mgt.		9.1 Plan Resource Mgt. 9.2 Est. Activity Resources	9.3 Acquire Resources 9.4 Develop Team 9.5 Manage Team	9.6 Control Resources	
10. Comm. Mgt.		10.1 Plan Comm. Mgt.	10.2 Manage Comm.	10.3 Monitor Comm.	
11. Risk Mgt.		11.1 Plan Risk Mgt. 11.2 Identify Risks 11.3 Qual. Risk Analysis 11.4 Quant. Risk Analysis 11.5 Plan Risk Responses	11.6 Implement Risk Responses	11.7 Monitor Risks	
12. Proc. Mgt.		12.1 Plan Proc. Mgt.	12.2 Conduct Proc.	12.3 Control Proc.	
13. Stakeholder Mgt.	13.1 Identify Stakeholders	13.2 Plan Stakeholder Engmt.	13.3 Manage Stakeholder Engmt.	13.4 Control Stakeholder Engmt.	

Understanding *Why* Matters

Real PMP® mastery is achieved when you understand *why* a process is completed, not just *how*. We ensure you get that perspective by providing high-level summaries of the objectives, key outputs, and points of focus at the beginning of each process group and individual process.

Case Studies Help You Strengthen Your PMP Test-taking Skills

We have crafted and weaved a unique real-life story throughout the course. It's the story of a young project manager, John, learning and using PMP® concepts to complete a project. The story unfolds in 25 short case studies spread throughout the course.

Following John through his struggle to complete a project helps you understand the PMP® concepts, why they are used, and what they are intended to accomplish. This "real-life" perspective will cement your understanding of how process elements interact and contribute to a successful project.

Each case study is followed by questions that challenge you to interpret the story. This strengthens your learning and your ability to answer the long-form PMP® questions you will face on the exam.

Master Points Distill Exactly What You Need to Know

Our Master Points are a collection of over 175 focused statements that help distill and link key concepts. Master Points emphasize key concepts and help you make the necessary connections.

Master Points are more than merely facts. They are short messages that make links between processes, provide greater perspective, and deepen your understanding of important topics.

Master Points are distributed throughout the book. We recommend that you repeatedly read the Master Points while you study.

Master Points are statements distilling key concepts and highlighting important points.

Custom Method to Get Every EVM Question Right

Many people find the math-focused earned value management (EVM) questions on the PMP® exam challenging. The difficulty of learning and remembering the correct equation creates fear and stress in exam takers. Fear and stress hurt your ability to be relaxed and confident on the test.

We have created a method that will eliminate your fear of EVM questions, and instead make you wish they were the only questions on the test.

You will get every EVM question right on the exam if you follow the simple process we have created.

This course will teach you to use a simple template to organize the equations and answer any EVM question on the exam.

PM Master Prep	Earned Value Management Template

BAC		Total budget
PV		Work that should be done
EV		What is done
AC		Actual spend

SV = EV – PV	CV = EV – AC
SPI = EV / PV	CPI = EV / AC

EAC = BAC / CPI
Est. to Complete = EAC - AC
Variance at Complete = BAC – EAC

Find Your Weaknesses and Eliminate Them with a 20% Discount to Our Online Exam Simulator using the code on book cover

Fine-tune and solidify your mastery of the PMP concepts with our online PMP Exam Simulator. The simulator offers you the ability to take full practice exams or focused quizzes related to every knowledge area and process group. Each test draws questions randomly from a pool of over 1,200 questions. The Exam Simulator has the same number, style, and category of questions as a real exam, as prescribed by "PMI's Exam Content Outline," so that you get a good idea about the actual exam. You can see your results by process group and review previous test results with test question explanations.

Access the simulator by visiting our website, www.pmmasteprep.com.

PMP Exam Simulation

Time limit: 03:49:08

1. Question

A structured review of the procurement process is performed by reviewing the procurements from the Plan Procurement Management through the Control Procurements to identify what went well and what did not. What do you call such a review?

- Procurement audit
- Performance review
- Procurement review
- Negotiated settlement

2. Question

In which process is the bidder conference held?

- Close Procurements
- Plan Procurement Management
- Conduct Procurements
- Control Procurements

PMP Exam Simulation

Results

13 of 200 questions answered correctly

Your time: 00:01:59

You have reached 13 of 200 point(s), (6.5%)

Average score	21.5%
Your score	6.5%

Categories

Closing Process Group	**14.29%**
Executing Process Group	**3.23%**
Initiating Process Group	**7.69%**
Monitoring & Controlling Process Group	**10%**
Planning Process Group	**4.17%**

maximum of 200 points

24. Question

Power, urgency, and legitimacy are attributes of which stakeholder classification model?

- Power/interest
- Influence/impact
- Power/influence
- Salience

Correct

Correct. The salience model describes classes of stakeholders based on their power (ability to impose their will), urgency (need for immediate attention), and legitimacy (their involvement is appropriate).

25. Question

Which tool or technique measures the performance of the project?

- Pareto chart
- Resource leveling
- Earned value management
- Parametric measuring

Incorrect

Earned value management is used to measure the performance of the project

PMP® AND CAPM®
EXAM OVERVIEW

PMP® and CAPM® Exam Overview

PMP® and CAPM® certifications are the gold standard for project management, and they are administered by the Project Management Institute (PMI). The PMI distributes industry-recognized certifications for project managers.

The certifications are obtained by passing multiple-choice-question exams. The minimum requirements to be eligible to take the exams are education, project management experience, and project management education. Applications confirming eligibility must be approved by the PMI. Continuing education is required to maintain the PMP® certification.

ELIGIBILITY AND REGISTRATION

To be eligible for the PMP® or CAPM® credential, you must meet specific education, experience, and training requirements.

PMP® Minimum Requirements

Education	Project Management Experience	Project Management Education
Bachelor's Degree	4,500 hours	35 hours
High School Diploma	7,500 hours	35 hours

CAPM® Minimum Eligibility Requirements

Education	Experience
High School Diploma	1,500 hours of professional experience
OR	
High School Diploma	23 hours of project management education

Documenting Project Experience

Before applying to take the exam, document your project management experience, ensuring that you have the minimum required hours. All project management experience must have been accrued within the eight consecutive years prior to your application.

We have provided a template to document your project experience: https://pmmasterprep.com/tools-templates

Grand Total Project Hours: 0

Project #1

Your Name		Organization Address		Contact Name	
Your Title		Organization City		Contact Title	
Your Organization		Organization State		Contact Email	
Your Project Role		Organization Zipcode		Contact Phone	

Project Title	Description	Start Date	End Date	Duration Months	Initiating Hours	Planning Hours	Executing Hours	Mntr & Control Hrs	Closing Hours	Total Hours
		Dec-14	Jun-15	5.6	0	0	0	0	0	0

Project #2

Your Name		Organization Address		Contact Name	
Your Title		Organization City		Contact Title	
Your Organization		Organization State		Contact Email	
Your Project Role		Organization Zipcode		Contact Phone	

Project Title	Description	Start	End	Duration	Initiating	Planning	Executing	Monitoring	Closing	Total Hours
				0.0	0	0	0	0	0	0

Project Management Education Requirement

By completing our online PM Master Prep course requirements, you can earn the required 35 professional development units (PDUs) needed to take the PMP® exam. When you complete all online requirements, the system will present you with an official letter available within your account.

Applying to Be Eligible to Take the PMP® or CAPM® Exam

Applications are submitted on the PMI website (https://www.pmi.org) and require the payment of an application fee. Applications are evaluated and approved or rejected within 5 days. The application fee is determined by PMI member status. Referenced below there are differing fees for PMI members, type of exam, and method of testing (computer- or paper-based). The PMI membership fee is $129 annually. Students or retirees have discounted membership fees. Once your application is approved, you have one year to take the exam.

PMP® and CAPM® Exam Fees

Exam Type	PMI Member Status	Exam Fee
PMP Computer-based	Member	$405
PMP Computer-based	Non-member	$555
PMP Paper-based	Member	$250
PMP Paper-based	Non-member	$400
CAPM Computer-based	Member	$225
CAPM Computer-based	Non-member	$300
CAPM Paper-based	Member	$225
CAPM Paper-based	Non-member	$300

PMI Audits

All applications are subject to auditing. PMI audits approximately 10% of all applications. If you are selected for an audit, you will be notified by email and may be asked to provide supporting documentation to validate your education, project management experience, or project management education.

Responses to an audit must be submitted within 90 days. The PMI will review and approve or reject your application within 5–7 days. Once your application is approved, you have one year to take the exam. If your application is rejected, your application fee will be refunded.

Maintaining Your Certification

Once you pass your exam, you must complete additional requirements to maintain your certification. Below is a table showing these requirements.

Certification Maintenance

Certification	Maintenance Requirement	Time Period
PMP	60 PDU credits	Every 3 years
CAPM	Retake and pass CAPM exam	Every 5 years

PMP® AND CAPM® EXAM STRUCTURE

The PMP® and CAPM® exams consist of multiple-choice questions testing comprehension of information included in the *PMBOK® Guide*. The exams are graded using psychometric analysis, requiring a score of approximately 61% to pass. The exams are scored based on correct answers. There is no penalty for incorrect answers.

Exam Structure

PMP Exam	CAPM Exam
200 Multiple-choice Questions	150 Multiple-choice Questions
175 Scoreable Questions	135 Scoreable Questions
25 Unscored Questions	15 Unscored Questions
4 Hours to Complete the Exam	3 Hours to Complete the Exam

Exam Question Format

The PMP® and CAPM® exam questions are often formulated as short paragraphs that require careful reading and interpretation to answer correctly.

EXAMPLE

An application enhancement project has reached the end of the design phase 10 days earlier than planned and 20% under the planned expense. Next, the development phase is to start, followed by multiple testing iterations. The design team and development team are not colocated. What is the first thing the project manager should do?

a. Validate scope
b. Control quality
c. Perform team building
d. Hire additional developers

This book is designed specifically to prepare you for this type of question as well as others. You will find over 25 case studies that explain key concepts as a continuous story, which will prepare you to answer questions of this nature.

PMP® Exam Content Focus

The PMP® exam question content is distributed across the five process groups defined by PMI's "Exam Content Outline." These five process groups will be defined in depth later. The following table shows PMP® exam question proportions by process group.

PMP® Exam Content Outline

Process Group	Proportion of Exam	Questions
Initiating	13%	26
Planning	24%	48
Executing	31%	62
Monitoring and Controlling	25%	50
Closing	7%	14

CAPM® Exam Content Focus

The CAPM® exam question content is distributed across the chapters of the *PMBOK® Guide*, as indicated in the following table.

CAPM® Exam Content Outline

PMBOK Guide Chapter	Proportion of Exam	Questions
1	6%	9
2	6%	9
3	7%	10-11
4	9%	13-14
5	9%	13-14
6	9%	13-14
7	8%	12
8	7%	10-11
9	8%	12
10	10%	15
11	8%	12
12	4%	6
13	9%	13-14

STYLES OF EXAM QUESTIONS

The PMP® exam uses six main question types to test your project management skills and knowledge:

1. Situational
2. Interpretation
3. Formula
4. Definition
5. Knowledge
6. Ethics and professional conduct

Situational Questions

Situational questions are longer questions formulated to challenge your decision-making skills in "real-life" project management situations. As these questions may offer multiple correct answers, you must select the best response.

<u>EXAMPLE</u>

> You are a new project manager and have been assigned to estimate a project's costs. You go to a senior project manager who has been working in the company for 10 years and ask his advice. He recommends that you increase your cost estimate by 25% since management always cuts the project budget by 25% before approving a project. What should you do?
>
> a. Inflate each task's cost estimate by 25%.
> **b. Present the actual cost estimate with a brief explanation of the impact of a budget cut on the project.**
> c. Add a contingency reserve equal to 25% of the costs.
> d. Present the actual cost estimate along with a letter stating that you will not manage the project if the budget is not approved as is.

Interpretation Questions

Interpretation questions require that you analyze the given facts and make the correct assessment or reach the correct conclusion. The challenge with these questions is to apply project management principles to the facts presented. These questions may also provide a graph or performance metric.

<u>EXAMPLE</u>

> Your project has a CPI value greater than 1.0. What does this indicate?
>
> **a. Actual costs are less than earned value**
> b. Actual costs are equal to earned value
> c. Actual costs are greater than earned value
> d. There is not enough information to reach a conclusion

Formula Questions

Formula questions require that you calculate the correct answer using data drawn from the information provided. The challenge is to remember the formulas and how to use them properly. In the Cost Management: Monitoring and Controlling chapter, this book provides you with an approach to ensuring accurate responses to these questions.

EXAMPLE

An equipment repair project has an actual total cost of $300,000 against a total budget of $400,000. The project is 75% complete. What is the earned value?

a. 0.75
b. $100,000
c. $300,000
d. Answer cannot be determined from the information provided

Definition Questions

Definition questions ask you to select the correct name of the concept, tool, or process described. These are the simplest form of question you will face. They will often include wording such as "is known as."

EXAMPLE

What technique uses the values of parameters from previous similar projects for estimating the same parameter or measure for a current project?

a. Reserve analysis
b. Three-point estimating
c. Parametric estimating
d. **Analogous estimating**

Knowledge Questions

Knowledge questions test your knowledge of foundational *PMBOK® Guide* structure and project management concepts. The exam details factual knowledge of process groups, knowledge areas, and process components. Read the question carefully to determine exactly what is being asked!

EXAMPLE

> In which knowledge area is the project charter developed?
>
> a. Project Scope Management
> b. Project Cost Management
> **c. Project Integration Management**
> d. Project Stakeholder Management

Ethics and Professional Conduct Questions

Ethics and professional conduct questions test your ability to select the approach that best follows the PMI *Code of Ethics and Professional Conduct*. There are four foundational values that will be of primary interest:

1. Responsibility
2. Respect
3. Fairness
4. Honesty

It is important that during your exam (and in your career), you never compromise any legal or regulatory requirements and always consider cultural, societal, and country-based norms.

EXAMPLE

> You are the project manager of a large ship construction project in a foreign country. The VP of your primary welding contractor meets you for lunch and offers you a complimentary weekend vacation package at a local resort. Your company has no official policy on accepting gifts, and the VP stated that the previous project manager enjoyed a similar package last year. What is the best way to handle the offer?
>
> a. Accept the package and pay the taxes on the value of the package
> b. Accept the package, to not potentially offend regional customs
> **c. Politely turn down the vacation package**
> d. Refuse the package and report the VP to the local PMI chapter for an ethics violation

Passing the PMP® Exam

PMP® Test-taking Environment

Understanding the test-taking environment and preparing for it will help you succeed on exam day. Testing is often provided by a third party, so before test day, find out where the test center is located. Testing will take place in a quiet room, with others taking the same or other exams. Security in and out of the test room is taken seriously, and you should be prepared to respect all test center rules. Attempting to simulate this environment while preparing for the exam will help you feel more comfortable on the big day.

In terms of materials, most test centers will not allow you to bring any support materials including cell phones, keys, or other items into the exam room. In most cases, you will be expected to use the paper and pencils provided by the test center. However, we recommend that you bring a pencil and calculator—just in case your test center allows them.

PMP® Test-taking Approach

Following a test-taking approach helps you methodically work through the test in a disciplined and organized manner. As soon as you begin the exam, immediately write down the PM Master Prep EVM template and key equations. The EVM template and method will be explained in detail in the Monitoring and Controlling Process Group chapter.

Work the questions that come easiest to you first, then spend more time on the more difficult questions. You will be able to mark them for review and follow-up. The test is long, and working easy to hard will give you confidence and help you build momentum. As you are taking the exam, monitor the pace at which you're competing questions. You have 4 hours (240 minutes) to complete 200 questions. This allows you 1.2 minutes per question. However, you should aim to complete one question per minute. This way, you will have 40 minutes to review questions you're unsure of and take needed breaks.

Strategies for Getting the Right Answer

Employing strategies increases your odds of selecting the correct answer. Be methodical and read the questions carefully. Eliminate the obvious wrong answers to increase your probability of choosing the correct answer. Don't leave any question unanswered! There is no penalty for incorrect answers. Even if you don't know the correct answer to a question, guess, as there is still a 25% chance of guessing correctly.

Succeeding on Exam Day

Increase your ability to succeed on exam day by removing stress, being prepared, and following the strategies provided throughout this book. Be sure to arrive early; don't run the risk of being late. Bring the required forms of identification and, just in case, your own pencil, paper, and calculator (don't expect them to be allowed in the test room, however).

Pay attention to the instructions provided in the exam room. Normally a short explanation will be provided as to how to use the test taking software and hardware. You will also be told how to request assistance and take breaks. If you have any questions, don't hesitate to ask for additional clarification.

PMBOK® Guide Overview

ABOUT THE PMBOK® GUIDE

The **PMP® exam** is driven primarily from information contained within PMI's *A Guide to the Project Management Body of Knowledge*, known as the *PMBOK® Guide*. The *PMBOK® Guide* is the accumulation of foundational knowledge from the project management profession, including both traditional and innovative practices.

Some people say that the *PMBOK® Guide* is a tough read, but we love it, because it's long (756 pages, to be exact), dense, and detailed. In addition to having detailed descriptions, the book is packed with tables and diagrams. So, why don't we recommend you only read the *PMBOK® Guide*? Because it's long, dense, and detailed. Have you read and memorized many 756-page books lately? Our book distills the lengthy *PMBOK® Guide* into a form that is easy to understand, logical, and relatable.

The *PMBOK® Guide* is constantly evolving (currently on the 6th edition).

PROJECT PROCESSES

The *PMBOK® Guide* organizes all the work within a project into 49 distinct **processes**. Each process is focused on producing multiple deliverables or outcomes, referred to as **outputs**. The source materials and information that feed into a process are known as the **inputs**. Each process uses **tools and techniques** to translate inputs into outputs.

The inputs, tools and techniques, and outputs (ITTO) for each process are depicted in the table below. These tables are referred to as ITTO tables in the *PMBOK® Guide*. We provide the ITTO tables for each process after the summary of the individual process sections throughout this book.

5.1 Plan Scope Mgt.	Inputs	Tools and Techniques	Outputs
	Project charter **Project management plan** • *Quality management plan* • *Project life cycle description* • *Development approach* **EEFs** **OPAs**	**Expert judgement** • *Data analysis* • *Alternatives analysis* **Meetings**	**Scope mgt. plan** **Requirements mgt. plan**

A process is not a solitary activity, isolated from all other processes and only completed once. Instead, processes are linked by the outputs they produce. This book highlights that outputs from one process often feed into multiple processes as inputs.

This linked nature of processes creates a dynamic and iterative project environment. For this reason, the outputs from one process can have cascading effects on previous and future processes. As you study each process, challenge yourself to think about what other processes the outputs flow into and which process would be affected.

> Processes are often <u>iterative</u>. They are used and reused as the project evolves.

PROCESS GROUPS AND KNOWLEDGE AREAS

All 49 processes are logically grouped within and across five process groups and 10 knowledge areas. The process groups are organized by the processes required to produce specific objectives. Knowledge areas distribute the processes within each process group by the category of knowledge that the process relates to.

Processes are not evenly distributed across process groups or knowledge areas. The dispersion of processes across process groups and knowledge areas is shown in the following table. The following table is used to guide the flow of this book. Each chapter will start with a picture of the table, with the area of focus highlighted, helping you understand where you are in the overall project.

Process Groups (5)

Knowledge Areas (10)	Initiating	Planning	Executing	Monitoring & Controlling	Closing
4. Integration Mgt.	4.1 Develop Proj. Charter	4.2 Develop Project Management Plan	4.3 Direct and Manage Proj. Work 4.4 Manage Project Knowledge	4.5 Monitor and Control Proj. Work 4.6 Perform Int. Change Control	4.7 Close Project or Phase
5. Scope Mgt.		5.1 Plan Scope Mgt. 5.2 Collect Requirements. 5.3 Define Scope 5.4 Create WBS		5.5 Validate Scope 5.6 Control Scope	
6. Schedule Mgt.		6.1 Plan Sched. Mgt. 6.2 Define Activities 6.3 Sequence Activities 6.4 Est. Durations 6.5 Develop Schedule		6.6 Control Schedule	
7. Cost Mgt.		7.1 Plan Cost Mgt. 7.2 Estimate Costs 7.3 Determine Budget		7.5 Control Costs	
8. Quality Mgt.		8.1 Plan Quality Mgt.	8.2 Manage Quality	8.3 Control Quality	
9. Resource Mgt.		9.1 Plan Resource Mgt. 9.2 Estimate Activity Resources	9.3 Acquire Resources 9.4 Develop Team 9.5 Manage Team	9.6 Control Resources	
10. Communications Mgt.		10.1 Plan Communications Management	10.2 Manage Communications	10.3 Monitor Communications	
11. Risk Mgt.		11.1 Plan Risk Mgt. 11.2 Identify Risks 11.3 Qual. Risk Analysis 11.4 Quant. Risk Analysis 11.5 Plan Risk Responses	11.6 Implement Risk Responses	11.7 Monitor Risks	
12. Procurement Mgt.		12.1 Plan Procurement Management	12.2 Conduct Procurements	12.3 Control Procurements	
13. Stakeholder Mgt.	13.1 Identify Stakeholders	13.2 Plan Stakeholder Engagement	13.3 Manage Stakeholder Engmt.	13.4 Control Stakeholder Engmt.	

Process Groups

Projects progress from Initiating to Closing by completing the processes within each process group. Each process group is designed to progressively deliver project objectives. Initiating is focused on establishing official authorization of the project. Planning focuses on defining the project scope, objectives, plans that will govern the project, and the course of action for proceeding. Executing is where the actual work is completed. Monitoring and Controlling is designed to track, regulate, and review process completion and to identify, evaluate, and implement any changes that are needed. The Closing process group formally completes the project.

> Project groups can overlap. Sequential completion is not mandatory.

As with processes, it is incorrect to think of process groups as solitary. Projects do flow logically from Initiating to Closing, but it is not required that all the processes within each process group be completed before work within the next process group begins. Additionally, processes within previous process groups are often reused as the project evolves.

> Project groups are **not** the same as project phases.
> A project can have multiple phases. Each phase follows **every** process group.

Knowledge Areas

Each of the 10 knowledge areas defines a specific category of project management knowledge. Detailed descriptions of how the knowledge area and the processes within them relate to each process group are provided within each chapter.

4. Integration Management
5. Scope Management
6. Schedule Management
7. Cost Management
8. Quality Management
9. Resource Management
10. Communications Management
11. Risk Management
12. Procurement Management
13. Stakeholder Management

4. Project Integration Management

Integration management is the "glue" that holds all project work together. The aim of all processes within this knowledge area is to identify, unify, and coordinate the various processes into a successful project. Develop Project Charter is the first process in this effort, and Close Project or Phase is the last. Additionally, these are the first and last processes completed, and they formally authorize and end a project, respectively. Integration Management processes are part of every process group, and they include the actual processes where work is directed, managed, and monitored, and where change is controlled. The key outputs of this knowledge area are:

- Project charter
- Assumption log
- Project management plan
- Deliverables
- Change requests
- Work performance data
- Issue log
- Work performance reports
- Approved change requests

TAILORING CONSIDERATIONS

On their own, all projects are different, but even more so when coupled with specific enterprise environmental factors and organizational influences. As a result, project managers may need to tailor how Project Integration Management processes are applied throughout the project. Considerations for such customizations may include the following:

Project and Developmental Life Cycles

Project managers should consider the most appropriate approach to project implementation regarding predictive or adaptive approaches. Additionally, different development approaches (incremental, iterative, hybrid) should be considered based on the specific needs of the project. The unique aspects of a project and the organization in which it is being delivered may call for adaptations of such things as **change**, **governance**, **knowledge management**, and overall **management**. Although Integration Management processes are very prescriptive, determining the extent to which they are used should be based on the needs of the project relative to the organization's demands and expectations.

AGILE CONSIDERATIONS AND EMERGING PRACTICES

Project management methodologies are evolving to incorporate new practices such as agile and other iterative techniques. Along with these emerging practices is the expansion of the role of the project manager. It is becoming more common for project managers to be called on to develop the business case and benefits management plan, which historically have been the responsibility of management. The project manager is becoming more integrated into the key activities and conversations at senior levels. These trends suggest a project manager's interpersonal and team skills must be acute, because in agile projects, these skills will be needed to engage the project team in a more collaborative and iterative fashion while consistently engaging sponsors and stakeholders for feedback and re-scoping. Using an agile approach means the project manager must continue to conduct the activities and responsibilities outlined in the Integration Management processes, but will also need to build and maintain a collaborative decision-making environment that will support the agile approach.

5. Project Scope Management

Project Scope Management includes the processes required to ensure that the project comprises all the deliverables and only the work required to produce those deliverables. Scope is about defining baselines, requirements, the work necessary to meet requirements, and controlling and validating deliverables. The key outputs of Scope Management are:

- Scope management plan
- Scope statement
- Scope baseline
- Accepted deliverables
- Requirements management plan
- Requirements documentation
- Requirements traceability matrix
- Work performance information

TAILORING CONSIDERATIONS

Tailoring considerations for Scope Management activities should include thoughtful adaptations for how the project should **manage knowledge** depending on the organization's formal or informal requirements management systems. **Validation and control** activities will also depend on the formality of an organization's policies and procedures.

AGILE CONSIDERATIONS AND EMERGING PRACTICES

Projects with agile life cycles are intended to respond to high levels of change, and they require consistent stakeholder engagement. The scope of an agile or adaptive project will be decomposed into a set of requirements, sometimes referred to as a product **backlog**. At the beginning of an iteration, the team works on the highest-priority items on the backlog list. The processes of Collect Requirements, Define Scope, and Create WBS are repeated for each iteration. Consistent customer and stakeholder engagement ensures that timely feedback on deliverables is received and that the product backlog reflects their current needs.

With requirements gaining more attention in the field of project management, organizations are recognizing how business analysis can be used as a competitive advantage. As a result, business analysis activities are becoming more common before a project is even initiated. These activities are focused on identifying business needs and recommending viable solutions for meeting those needs. With this in mind, project managers need to consider the business analyst as a key collaborator and seek to fully comprehend the business analyst's role to increase the likelihood of project success.

> In agile or adaptive projects, the scope is defined and redefined throughout the project. Requirements constitute the backlog.

6. Project Schedule Management

Project Schedule Management includes the processes required to manage the project schedule. This knowledge area is concerned with developing the schedule management plan and the schedule baseline. The schedule management plan establishes the criteria and activities for developing, monitoring, and controlling the schedule. The schedule baseline is composed of logically sequenced activities, resource estimates, duration estimates, and derived probability distributions for project durations. Once the schedule baseline is approved, changes to it should only be made through approved change requests. The key outputs of the Schedule Management knowledge area are:

- Schedule management plan
- Activity list
- Activity attributes
- Milestone list
- Schedule baseline
- Change requests
- Project schedule network diagrams
- Duration estimates
- Project schedule and calendars
- Work performance data
- Schedule forecast

TAILORING CONSIDERATIONS

How a project life cycle is intended to be executed will have a significant impact on the defined approach for schedule management. Other considerations for tailoring are **resource availability**, **project dimensions**, and **technology support**.

AGILE CONSIDERATIONS AND EMERGING PRACTICES

Adaptive planning defines a plan, but recognizes that priorities and requirements will change, and the plan must reflect the need to be adaptable and receive iterative changes. The following two key emerging practices facilitate adaptive scheduling methods:

- **Iterative scheduling with a backlog** is a form of rolling-wave planning based on adaptive life cycles. Requirements are defined and prioritized before execution and then developed using time-boxed periods of work. This approach is effective when multiple teams can work concurrently on a large number of features with interconnected dependencies. This not only enables but also encourages changes throughout the development life cycle.
- **On-demand scheduling** is used in a Kanban system and is based on the theory-of-constraints and pull production scheduling. It limits a team's work in progress (WIP) by balancing demand with the team delivery throughput. On-demand scheduling does not rely on a schedule, but rather pulls work from a backlog as resources are available. It is often used in projects that have operational environments where tasks may be relatively similar in size and scope or can be bundled by size and scope.

Using agile approaches creates shorter development cycles with reviews and adaptations before initiating the next cycle. This allows for rapid feedback and the ability to incorporate changes for future development cycles. Despite the reality that the project manager's role does not change given the project approach, the project manager should be familiar with such techniques in order to apply these adaptive principles effectively.

> Iterative scheduling with a backlog is a form of rolling-wave planning based on adaptive life cycles.

7. Project Cost Management

Project Cost Management includes the processes concerned with planning, estimating, budgeting, financing, funding, managing, and controlling costs to increase the probability of completing the project within budget. It is important to consider the effect of decisions during the project on ongoing operations after the project. To consider life-cycle cost, the project manager should analyze the value or the benefit-cost ratio over the entire life cycle of the project, as well as considering a holistic perspective of design, production, service, maintenance, usage, and disposal.

Cost Management has a strong connection to Time Management and Risk Management. The project manager should always consider risk-related costs from Risk Management activities. The key outputs of the Cost Management knowledge area are:

- Cost management plan
- Cost estimates
- Basis of estimates
- Cost baseline
- Change requests
- Project funding requirements
- Work performance information
- Cost forecasts

TAILORING CONSIDERATIONS

Because each project is unique, Cost Management processes may need to be tailored to meet specific needs. Some key considerations for tailoring are the **use of agile** methodologies and how this will impact cost estimations and **earned value management**. The existence, or lack of, formal cost estimating policies and procedures will also affect a project's **estimating and budgeting** approach.

AGILE CONSIDERATIONS AND EMERGING PRACTICES

Among some of the newer emerging practices in the project management profession is the expansion of earned value management concepts. Earned schedules (ES) has surfaced as an adaptation to the schedule variance (SV) measure to include ES - AT (actual time) where a calculated result greater than 0 indicates the project is ahead of schedule, and a value less than 0 indicates the project is behind schedule. The schedule performance index (SPI) can also be adapted with this approach using ES/AT to indicate the project's efficiency of executing the work. Similar to the existing SPI result interpretation, a value greater than 1 indicates an efficiency better than project schedule, while a value less than 1 indicates an efficiency leaving the project behind schedule.

> Earned schedule (ES) and actual time (AT) offer an emerging variant to the schedule variance (SV) calculation where SV = ES - AT.

8. Project Quality Management

Project Quality Management refers to designating project quality standards, detailing compliance, and using the principles of continuous improvement. Quality management planning addresses the deliverables and management of the project. Product quality is conformance to the requirements and fitness of use. Project quality is the degree to which the project realizes requirements. The key outputs of the Quality Management knowledge area are:

- Quality management plan
- Quality metrics
- Quality control measurements
- Change requests
- Verified deliverables
- Work performance information

There are a few key quality-related concepts that must be understood throughout the Quality Management processes. First, quality and grade are not the same thing. Quality is the degree to which the characteristics of the product fulfill requirements. Grade, on the other hand, is a category of the product having the same functional use but different technical requirements. Anytime a product fails to meet requirements, it is of poor quality and is problematic. However, producing a low-grade product is not necessarily a problem as long as the product meets its lower technical requirements.

In terms of assessing and addressing quality, prevention is always preferred over inspection. It is better to design quality into the process of producing the product rather than finding quality issues at an inspection stage. In reality, the cost of preventing defects is far less than the cost of correcting defects after production.

Cost of quality (COQ) includes all costs incurred over the life of the product by investment in preventing defects, inspecting for defects, and correcting defects. Failure costs are generally categorized as internal (found by the project team) or external (found by the customer). Failure costs are also referred to as cost of poor quality. Organizations should choose to invest in defect prevention because of the benefits over the life of the product. Methods commonly used to address cost of poor quality are noted here in increasingly effective quality management:

- **Let the customer find the defects** is usually the most expensive approach, leading to warranty claims, issues, recalls, rework, and reputation damage.
- **Detect and correct** is an approach that entails inspection and correction before the product reaches the customer. The costs here are confined to "internal" cost of poor quality and are related to inspection and rework.
- **Quality assurance** entails using quality inspection and correction on the process which produces the defective product.
- **Incorporate quality** into the planning and designing of the product.
- **Create a culture** throughout the organization of being aware and committed to quality processes and products.

TAILORING CONSIDERATIONS

A key consideration for tailoring a project's quality management processes is how the organization addresses quality management through **continuous improvement**, **auditing**, and compliance to the **standards and regulatory requirements** expected of the organization and its products.

AGILE CONSIDERATIONS AND EMERGING PRACTICES

In order to adequately manage quality during the incremental and frequent delivery cycles of an agile project, smaller-batch systems aim to uncover defects earlier in the project, when overall costs of change in processes or procedures will be lower.

The use of continuous improvement is an important emerging practice (it is not necessarily new, but is becoming more applicable to all industries and hence all types of projects and organizations). **Continuous improvement** incorporates several effective quality management methodologies, such as plan-do-check-act (PDCA), total quality management (TQM), six sigma, and lean six sigma. These practices are used to improve both the quality of project management and that of the final product. Effective implementation of continuous improvement can lead an organization to the higher-order quality management status mentioned earlier, whereby the organization can create a culture of quality awareness and commitment.

> Implementation of continuous improvement can help organizations create a culture of quality awareness and commitment.

9. Project Resource Management

Project Resource Management includes the processes used to identify, acquire, and manage the resources needed for the successful completion of the project. These processes help ensure that the right resources will be available to the project at the right time and place. Resource Management includes both physical resources (equipment, materials, facilities, etc.) and human resources, such as personnel with varied skills needed for various activities throughout the project. The key outputs of this knowledge area are:

- Resource management plan
- Team charter
- Resource requirements
- Basis of estimates
- Resource breakdown structure
- Change requests
- Physical resource requirements
- Project team assignments
- Resource calendars
- Team performance assessment
- Work performance information

TAILORING CONSIDERTATIONS

A few tailoring considerations related to project resources that a project manager should be sensitive to are the diversity background of the team, their location, and how they may be acquired for the project. This also applies to physical resources in terms of location and acquisition. The uniqueness of the project and its life cycle approach may require team resources to be trained, and organizational resources may dictate alternative methods of team development.

AGILE CONSIDERATIONS AND EMERGING PRACTICES

Regardless of which project life cycle approach is used, project management styles have been shifting away from a command-and-control structure and toward a more collaborative and supportive management approach. This helps empower teams by delegating decision making to them.

Projects with high variation, such as adaptive or agile projects, benefit greatly from high collaboration and supported team infrastructures. They achieve greater flexibility, improved communications, increased innovation, and accelerated integration into their work activities.

The increased use of agile approaches has led to the rise of **self-organizing teams**, where the team functions without central control.

Globalization, the scarcity of specialized skills, and the availability of communication technology such as audio conferencing, web-based meetings, and video conferencing have enabled **virtual team** capabilities and changed how a project manager facilitates team management and development.

10. Project Communications Management

Project Communications Management ensures the timely and appropriate planning, collection, creation, distribution, storage, management, control, monitoring, and the ultimate disposition of project information. The project manager needs to facilitate the flow of knowledge between stakeholders. The key outputs of this knowledge area are:

- Communications management plan
- Project communications
- Work performance information
- Change requests

TAILORING CONSIDERATIONS

Communications management is highly impacted by factors such as the physical location of team members and the availability of certain communication technology. The project manager will need to be aware of these factors to tailor project communications for greater effect and success.

AGILE CONSIDERATIONS AND EMERGING PRACTICES

Due to their iterative nature, agile projects will create greater demands on the frequency of project communications. Project managers must consider the project life cycle approach when developing the communications plan. Some emerging trends in project communications facilitate communication through the use of **increased use of social computing** in the form social media services and personal electronic devices.

11. Project Risk Management

Project Risk Management involves taking smart chances. This knowledge area includes the processes of conducting risk management planning, identifying risk, analyzing risk, planning risk responses, and controlling risk.

There are two types of risks: risks with positive effects (opportunities) and risks with negative effects (threats). The so-called known-unknowns are risks that the project team has already identified, while the unknown-unknowns are risks that have not been identified. Project Risk Management answers the question, "What might stop us?"

Risks also exist at two levels within every project. **Individual risks** are uncertain events or conditions that if they occur have a positive or negative effect on project objectives. **Overall project risk** is the effect of uncertainty on the project as a whole, representing positive or negative risk exposure of the project outcome.

PMI's *Practice Standard for Project Risk Management* emphasizes that to increase a project's probability of success, the organization should recognize the value of performing risk management. There needs to be collective commitment and individual responsibility for the organization to perform risk management. The key outputs of the Risk Management knowledge area are:

- Risk management plan
- Risk register
- Risk report
- Change requests
- Work performance information

TAILORING CONSIDERATIONS

Some of the factors that should be considered when tailoring risk management practices are project size, complexity, and importance. A **project's size** in terms of budget, schedule, or duration will give good reason to plan risk management to the uniqueness of the project. **Project complexity** can be greater on projects with high levels of innovation or significant technology interfaces.

While all projects are important or they would not be undertaken, some can be considerably more important if they are aligned with the strategic direction of the organization or are necessary to sustain business.

AGILE CONSIDERATIONS AND EMERGING PRACTICES

Agile or adaptive projects have higher variability and thus are inherently susceptible to more risk and uncertainty. Project managers need to be aware of the project approach when planning and managing risk.

One of the growing trends in risk management that may need to be considered in a risk management plan is the recognition of **non-event risks**. Most projects focus on the risks that are uncertain future events, but there are also two types of non-event risks that may creep into a project:

- **Variability risk** is a type of risk that is uncertainty related to characteristics of planned events, activities, or processes. Examples might include higher or lower product defect rates or even weather conditions during construction phases of projects.
- **Ambiguity risk** is a type of risk that is uncertainty about what might happen in the future in areas such as compliance and regulatory requirements or external technology developments.

Emergent risks are also being recognized with a growing awareness of "unknowable-unknowns," which are risks that can only be recognized after they have occurred. Emergent risks can't necessarily be predicted and planned for, but **"project resilience"** strategies can be incorporated into projects to help minimize the impact of these risks. Some strategies are

- Budget and schedule contingency
- Flexible project processes
- Empowered project teams that are trusted to respond and adapt
- Review frequency can be increased to help identify warning signs of emerging risks

Emergent risks (unknowable-unknowns) are only recognized after they occur. Projects can deal with them by developing project resilience.

12. Project Procurement Management

Project Procurement Management includes the processes necessary to purchase or acquire products, services, or results needed from outside the project team. It designates the approach, selecting the contract type, developing bid documents, determining source selection criteria, negotiating a contract, managing contractual relationships, and reporting performance. The key outputs of this knowledge area are:

- Procurement management plan
- Procurement strategy
- Bid documents
- Procurement statement of work
- Source selection criteria
- Make-or-buy decisions
- Independent cost estimates
- Change requests
- Selected sellers
- Agreements
- Closed procurement
- Work performance information

TAILORING CONSIDERATIONS

The unique needs of projects play a role in procurement based on things such as the location of sellers and whether or not they are in the same time zone or country. Tailoring project needs based on procurement complexity is also a consideration. A project may need multiple sellers or a series of different contracts at key milestones throughout the project. It is the project manager's responsibility to determine the specific needs of the project and ensure the availability of contractors is consistent with the work requirements of the project.

AGILE CONSIDERATIONS AND EMERGING PRACTICES

Some contractors or sellers may not be acclimated to agile or adaptive project life cycles. The project manager will need to ensure that collaboration and team work is a high priority at these times.

Project managers must also be aware of trends and emerging practices related to procurement. For example, online tools are now available that give buyers a central point where procurements can be advertised, which also provide sellers a single place to find procurement documents.

Changing contract processes are also a big shift over the past few years. Many projects are global in scale, requiring the adherence to internationally recognized standards for contract forms, claims, and other administrative assets. These global projects also put heavy emphasis on the planning and management of **logistics and supply chain**.

13. Project Stakeholder Management

Stakeholder Management identifies people, groups, or organizations that could impact or be impacted by the project. Stakeholder Management analyzes stakeholders' expectations and impact. Stakeholders are continuously engaged by communication. The project manager must manage stakeholder issues, conflict management, and stakeholder engagement, and always keep stakeholder satisfaction as a key objective. The key outputs of the Stakeholder Management knowledge area are:

- Stakeholder register
- Change requests
- Stakeholder engagement plan
- Work performance information

TAILORING CONSIDERATIONS

The unique aspects of a project require the project manager to deal with **stakeholder diversity** so that the project manager may recognize the different communities and cultures represented by various stakeholders. **Stakeholder complexity** should also be addressed depending on the breadth of communities a stakeholder participates in. The more complex information, or misinformation, a stakeholder receives from their community can play a role in how a project manager engages stakeholders.

AGILE CONSIDERATIONS AND EMERGING PRACTICES

The volatility of a project should dictate how a project manager engages stakeholders and how the team is managed and developed. Adaptive teams engage with stakeholders directly. Many times, in these types of projects, clients, users, and developers exchange information and collaborate in a dynamic co-creative process that leads to higher stakeholder involvement.

As the field of project management continues to expand, the definition of a "stakeholder" is broadening to include parties external to the organization conducting the project. Groups such as regulators, environmentalists, financial organizations, media, and lobby groups may be identified as stakeholders if they are affected by the work and have a vested interest in the outcome of the project.

Remembering Process Groups and Knowledge Areas

The focus of your study should not be solely to memorize the location of each process within the process groups and knowledge areas. Succeeding on the exam requires that you understand what each process is designed to accomplish and how it interacts with other processes.

If you are not familiar with the process groups and knowledge areas, we have provided you with a mnemonic device that will help you quickly learn and remember them.

			"I"	"P"	"E"	"M/C"	"C"
			I	**Pass**	**Every**	**Management Course**	**Comfortably**
			Initiating	**Planning**	**Executing**	**Monitoring & Controlling**	**Closing**
"IM"	**I'm**	4. Integration Mgt.	4.1 Develop Project Charter	4.2 Develop Project Mgt. Plan	4.3 Direct and Manage Prj. Work 4.4 Manage Project Knowledge	4.5 Monitor & Control Prj. Work 4.6 Perform Int. Change Control	4.7 Close Project or Phase
"S"	**Sure**	5. Scope Mgt.		5.1 Plan Scope Mgt. 5.2 Collect Requirements 5.3 Define Scope 5.4 Create WBS		5.5 Validate Scope 5.6 Control Scope	
"S"	**Scott**	6. Schedule Mgt.		6.1 Plan Schedule Mgt. 6.2 Define Activities 6.3 Sequence Activities 6.4 Est. Activity Durations 6.5 Develop Schedule		6.6 Control Schedule	
"C"	**Can**	7. Cost Mgt.		7.1 Plan Cost Mgt. 7.2 Estimate Costs 7.3 Determine Budget		7.4 Control Costs	
"Q"	**Quote**	8. Quality Mgt.		8.1 Plan Quality Mgt.	8.2 Manage Quality	8.3 Control Quality	
"R"	**Really**	9. Resource Mgt.		9.1 Plan Resource Mgt. 9.2 Est. Activity Resources	9.3 Acquire Resources 9.4 Develop Team 9.5 Manage Team	9.6 Control Resources	
"C"	**Complicated**	10. Communications Mgt.		10.1 Plan Communications Mgt.	10.2 Manage Communications	10.3 Monitor Communications	
"R"	**Rhymes**	11. Risk Mgt.		11.1 Plan Risk Mgt. 11.2 Identify Risks 11.3 Perform Qual. Risk Analysis 11.4 Perform Quant. Risk Analysis 11.5 Plan Risk Responses	11.6 Implement Risk Responses	11.7 Monitor Risks	
"P"	**Positively**	12. Procurement Mgt.		12.1 Plan Procurement Mgt.	12.2 Conduct Procurements	12.3 Control Procurements	
"S"	**Stunningly**	13. Stakeholder Mgt.	13.1 Identify Stakeholders	13.2 Plan Stakeholder Engmnt.	13.3 Manage Stakeholder Engmt.	13.4 Monitor Stakeholder Engmt.	

Project Management Overview

Project Management Foundations

What is a Project?

A project is a temporary endeavor taken to create a unique product, service, or result. The temporary nature means that a project exists during a finite span of time, with a clearly defined beginning and end. Projects also drive change and create or enable value creation. Value can be tangible or intangible. Additionally, successful organizations focus their projects to assist in achieving their overall strategic goals.

> No two projects are identical.
> Project managers must **tailor** their approach to meet unique situations.

Project Creation Criteria

The need for a project is driven by four major factors. Responding positively to these factors is critical to an organization's ongoing success.

1. Meet regulatory, legal, or social requirements
2. Satisfy stakeholder requests or needs
3. Create, improve, or fix products, processes, or services
4. Implement or change business or technological strategies

Business Documents

After identifying the need for a project, a business case and benefits management plan are developed to evaluate the economic feasibility of a potential project. These documents help to define and evaluate the expected impact of the project and are used as key inputs for developing the project charter in Develop Project Charter (4.1).

Business Case

The business case states the project objectives and projected benefits.

The development of this document is often led by the project sponsor and is used to determine if the expected outcomes exceed the required investment. This cost-benefit analysis creates a go/no-go decision point prior to starting to develop a project charter.

Creating the business case is the first step in defining exactly what the project is intended to produce and how it will benefit the company.

Project Benefits Management Plan

The project's benefits management plan is a detailed definition of how and when project benefits would be delivered and measured. As with all project plans, this document is intended to be iteratively developed. As additional information is uncovered and developed, the plan is revised and improved.

> The business case and project benefits management plan are **source** inputs;
> they feed directly into Develop Project Charter (4.1).

Project Charter

The project charter is the project's foundational document, defining key components and formally authorizing the project's existence. The charter creates a shared vision and clear expectations by defining the purpose, projected schedule, costs, risks, and scope boundaries. The project charter is developed by the project sponsor, often assisted by the project manager.

A project is not official until it has been authorized by the project sponsor. An authorized project charter is a major output of the Initiating process group, formally granting the project manager the authority to apply resources to project activities.

> Develop Project Charter (4.1) is the first process to be completed in the Initiating process group.

Project Management Plan
1. Scope mgt. plan 2. Requirements mgt. plan 3. Schedule mgt. plan 4. Cost mgt. plan 5. Quality mgt. plan 6. Resource mgt. plan 7. Communications mgt. plan 8. Risk mgt. plan 9. Procurement mgt. plan 10. Stakeholder mgt. plan 11. Change mgt. plan 12. Configuration mgt. plan 13. Scope baseline 14. Schedule baseline 15. Cost baseline 16. Perf. measurement baseline 17. Project life-cycle description 18. Development approach

Project Management Plan

The project management plan translates the project charter into actionable plans for how the project will be planned, executed, monitored, and controlled.

The project management plan is composed of multiple subsidiary plans and project baselines (scope, schedule, cost). Each knowledge area has a specific subsidiary project plan that defines how the work within the knowledge area processes will be managed. Additionally, the specific focus of Planning is to integrate the work of all processes in a functional and productive manner.

Project Success Measures

While framing a project and evaluating the business case, it is essential to define in clear, objective terms the criteria by which a project's success will be measured.

In haste to deliver value, many project managers fail to spend the time and thought necessary to complete this task, or they only define the project's success criteria in pure financial terms.

A project can have both financial and non-financial benefits, and both areas should be fully evaluated. Well-defined project success criteria help to align expectations for how the project will be evaluated.

> Project success measures answer three questions:
> What does success look like? | How will success be measured? | What factors impact success?

Project Management Data and Information

Project status and success are informed by collecting, analyzing, and presenting project data through project processes. The data and information are defined in three formats: work performance data, information, and reports, within the *PMBOK® Guide*. You will see all three as inputs and outputs of many processes in the Planning, Executing, and Monitoring and Controlling process groups.

The relationships between data, information, and reports are logical, each feeding the next to translate detailed project information into clear summaries used to monitor the status and track project progress and identify issues.

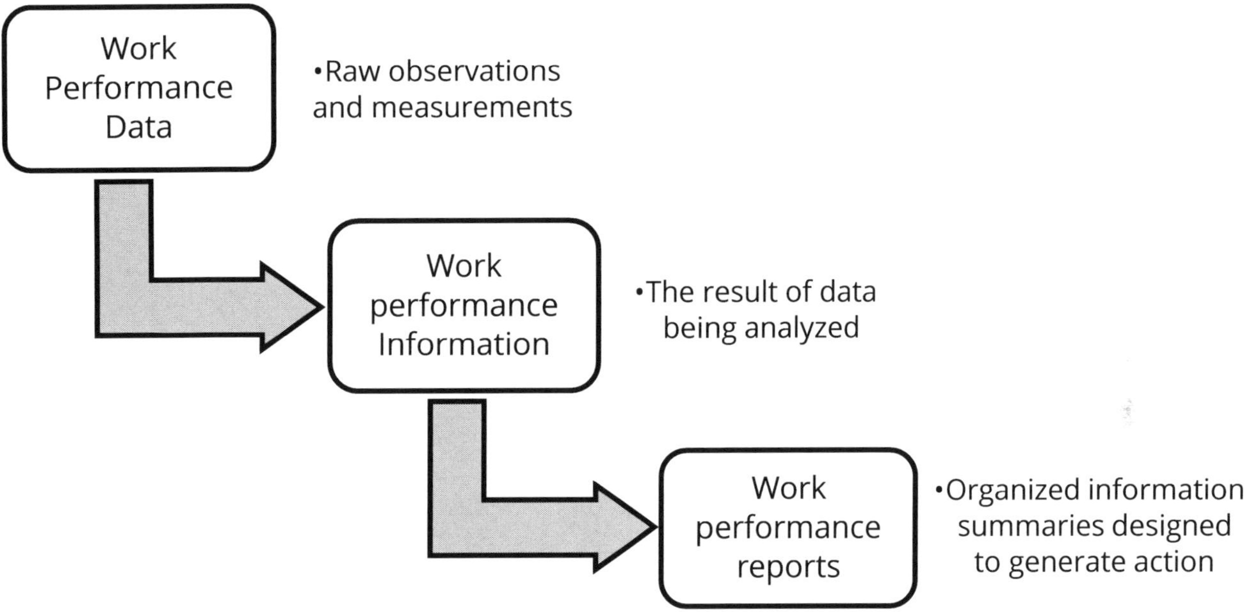

Project vs. Operations Management

Project and operations management are distinct activities, with different roles. While operations management is focused on operating the existing processes and procedures at maximum efficiency, project management is focused on improving existing processes and products, or creating new ones.

Daily operation is outside of the scope of a project, but project management can often complement operations management by serving to improve the current way of doing things.

Operations management and project management are different!
Operations management = Ongoing operation of existing production
Project management = Short-term effort to achieve defined goals

Organizational Project Management

Organizations have many projects underway at the same time, each delivering unique benefits. Successful organizations often group projects into portfolios and programs that support the organization's overall strategic goals. The portfolio and program framework provides a method of aligning multiple projects that serve higher-level goals in different ways.

Aligning and managing the projects into portfolios and programs helps the organization understand which projects are being executed to support the organization's vision and where opportunities and weaknesses may exist. The structure of the projects, programs, and portfolios is often depicted in an organizational-chart-type format. A visual format makes it easy to see how each project feeds into and supports the various programs and portfolios. Additionally, distinct roles (portfolio and program managers) are established to assist in the successful completion of the projects.

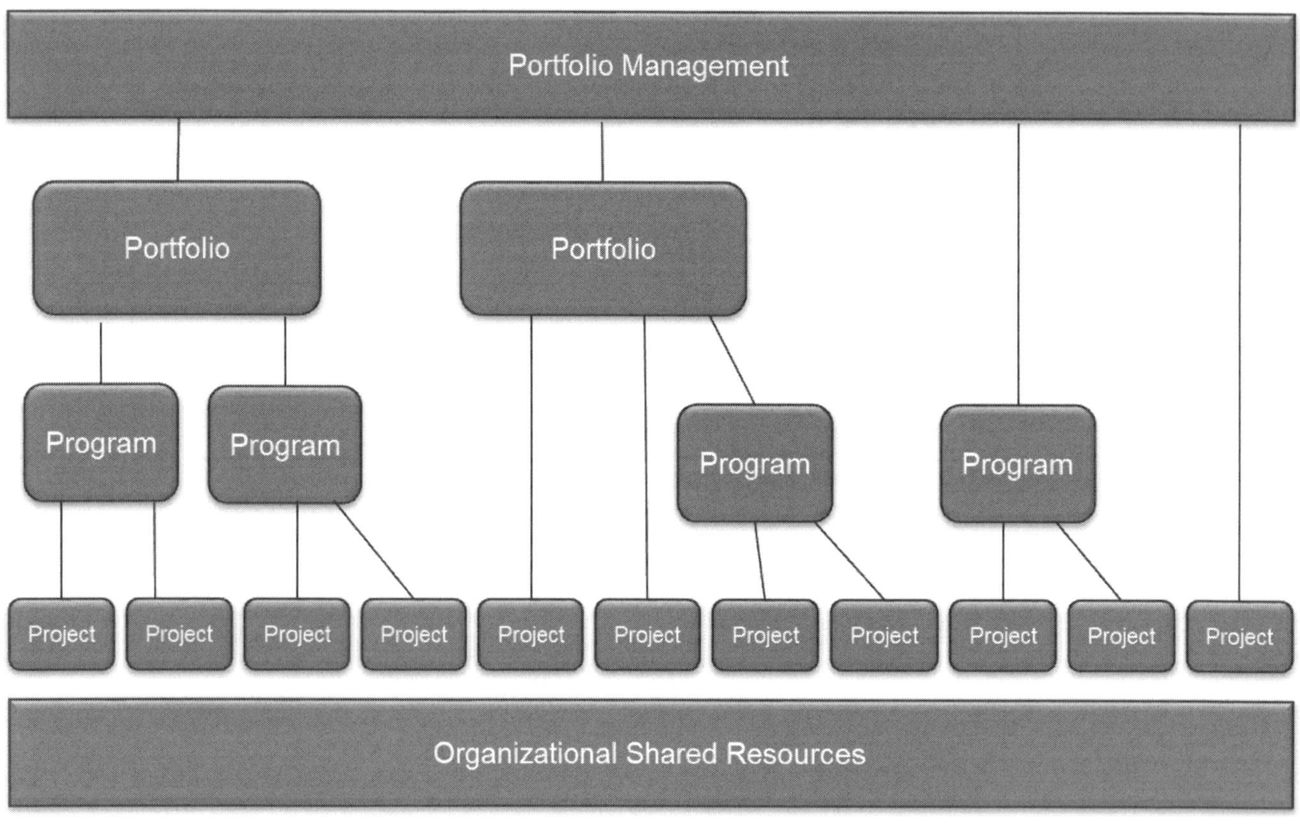

Portfolio vs. Program Management

Portfolio and program management both serve critical roles in helping guide the execution of projects to positively impact an organization's strategic goals.

Portfolio managers have the highest level of oversight and direction. They ensure that the strategic objectives are supported by selecting the right programs and projects, prioritizing them, and providing sufficient resources. A portfolio manager may be responsible for managing one or multiple programs and potentially individual projects.

Program managers are closer to the projects than portfolio managers, but they are not managing the individual project work. Individual project work is managed by the project manager. To support the project manager in delivering the results needed, the program manager allocates resources across projects, resolves issues, and provides guidance.

> Portfolio and program management are different!
> Portfolio management = Select the "right" programs or projects
> Program management = Ensure projects are completed the "right" way

Case Study: "Getting Thrown into the Fire"

"So, this is our savior? Maybe I should be tuning up my resume." The comment hit John like a ton of bricks. Worst of all, it had come from the VP of Operations. John had heard stories of the VP being a hard-charging, no-nonsense leader, but he had never experienced it firsthand. Now, 13 words into his first meeting with the man known as "Action Jackson," John worried that today may be his last at Alliance International.

"John, I'll get right to it. You're here because we have a big problem that we need you to fix." John sat with focused intensity, quietly nodding along as he pulled in every word, nervously unsure what exactly he was being asked to do.

Next to John sat Sara—the project guru, a rising star in the organization, and the person John most wanted to become. Over the past five years, it seemed that every project she led was a smashing success. During her time as a project manager she worked in various departments, quickly turning meandering efforts into focused projects that delivered high returns. In addition to notoriety, her success brought opportunity. She was recently promoted and was now responsible for overseeing a large group of projects.

"As you should know, we are in the process of expanding, making big pushes to grow our current capabilities. Our problem is that we just got informed that there are new regulations taking effect next year that could impact a new line we have rolling out next year."

The VP slid a diagram across the table. It looked like an organizational chart, but where John expected to see individuals' names he saw project names. "This is every project that matters. In addition to my normal job, it's my responsibility that everything on here gets done. Sara is accountable for this section." He took out a pen and circled boxes making up about one-third of the paper. "Your project is going to be in here. All of those projects support the same goal in different ways."

"I need you to lead the effort to ensure that the new line doesn't violate the new regulations, and if it does, you need to get the designs modified to conform and make sure manufacturing is ready. The design work is pretty much done, but manufacturing isn't scheduled to start for a while. This is a big responsibility; can you handle it?"

John nodded, confirming that he understood, but before he could respond, the VP continued: "Look, John, I can't stop everyone while we make sense of the regulations. I need them pushing forward on other things. It is your job to pull a team together and to clean up any issues that we may have."

True to his nickname, the VP pushed on, "As of this moment, you are officially leading this project. Sara will give you the project specifics and introduce you to Lloyd. He is the manager of the Project Management Office. He helps keep us aligned on the best ways to do things. Now if you could see yourself out, I have another meeting."

CASE STUDY QUESTIONS: "GETTING THROWN INTO THE FIRE"

What is the main factor that drove the need for John's project?

a. Create, improve, or fix a product, process, or service
b. Meet regulatory, legal, or social requirements
c. Satisfy stakeholder requests or needs
d. Implement or change business or technological strategies

In terms of the projects within Alliance, what role does the VP serve?

a. Portfolio manager
b. Program manager
c. Project sponsor
d. Project champion

In terms of the projects within Alliance, what roles does Sara serve?

a. Portfolio manager
b. Program manager
c. Project sponsor
d. Project champion

Case Study Answers: "Getting Thrown into the Fire"

What is the main factor that drove the need for John's project?

a. Create, improve or fix a product, process, or service
b. Meet regulatory, legal, or social requirements
c. Satisfy stakeholder requests or needs
d. Implement or change business or technological strategies

In terms of the projects within Alliance, what role does the VP serve?

a. Portfolio manager
b. Program manager
c. Project sponsor
d. Project champion

In terms of the projects within Alliance, what roles does Sara serve?

a. Portfolio manager
b. Program manager
c. Project sponsor
d. Project champion

PROJECT ENVIRONMENT

Factors Impacting Projects

Project managers must understand the key factors influencing their project and navigate the environment to ensure project success. The *PMBOK® Guide* defines two major categories of factors as enterprise environmental factors (EEF) and organizational process assets (OPA).

Both EEF and OPA are terms that capture a wide variety of factors which can have positive or negative impacts on a project. It is essential to understand the difference between what is defined as an EEF versus an OPA. EEFs are conditions that are not under the project team's control, while OPAs are organization-specific factors. You will see EEFs and OPA consistently used as inputs and outputs to processes throughout this book.

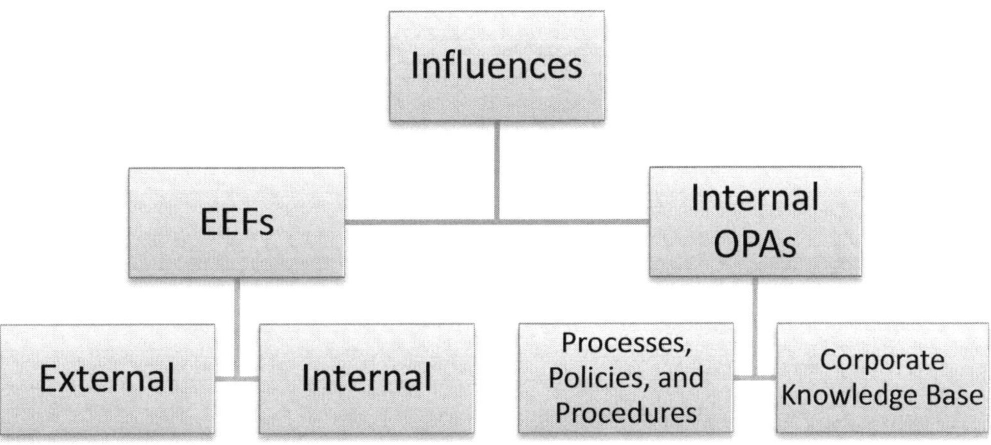

A large percentage of project processes have OPAs and EEFs as inputs.

Enterprise Environmental Factors (EEFs)

Enterprise environmental factors are defined as conditions outside the control of the project team that impact the project. These factors could be either internal or external to the organization. Examples of common internal EEFs include organizational cultures, the geographic distribution of facilities and resources, and established IT software. Common external EEFs are market conditions, legal restrictions, commercial databases, and financial considerations (for example, exchange rates, interest rates, tariffs).

Organizational Process Assets (OPAs)

Organizational process assets are defined as the plans, processes, and knowledge bases internal to the organization that impact the project. The two categories of OPAs are processes, policies, and procedures and corporate knowledge bases. Examples of processes, policies, and procedures include guidelines, standards, templates, and change control procedures. Common corporate knowledge bases include past project files and data repositories holding lessons learned, issue logs, or financial data.

Impact of Organizational Structures

An organization's structure directly impacts the project manager's role and authority, the availability of resources, and the way the budget is managed. The following table summarizes the differences between the six most common organizational structures.

Organizational Structure Types	Project Characteristics					
	Project Manager's Role	Project Manager's Authority	Resource Availability	Work Groups Arranged by:	Who Manages the Project Budget?	Project Management Administrative Staff
Functional (Centralized)	Part-time; may or may not be a designated job role	Little or none	Little or none	Job being done (e.g., engineering, manufacturing)	Functional manager	Part-time
Matrix Strong	Full-time; designated job role	Moderate to high	Moderate to high	By job function, with project manager as a function	Project manager	Full-time
Matrix Balanced	Part-time; embedded in the function as a skill	Low to moderate	Low to moderate	Job function	Mixed	Part-time
Matrix Weak	Part-time; done as part of another job	Low	Low	Job function	Functional manager	Part-time
Project Oriented	Full-time; designated job role	High to almost total	High to almost total	Project	Project manager	Full-time
Hybrid	Mixed	Mixed	Mixed	Mix of other types	Mixed	Mixed

The six structures can be grouped into three major types: projectized, matrix, and functional.

Projectized and functional structures are in sharp contrast. Projectized organizations are arranged by projects, not functional departments, while functional organizations are the exact opposite. The three types of matrix organizations span the difference between functional and projectized, offering a variety of differences.

Most notably, the difference in a project manager's authority across all types is significant. For example, when operating within a functionalized organization, the project manager holds very little formal authority, and therefore must rely on a relationship and negotiations with a functional manager. Remember to consider the type of organization when exam questions ask you to suggest the most appropriate action a project manager should take in a given situation.

Project Management Office (PMO)

Project management offices (PMOs) are established to provide support and guidance to projects. There are three main types of project management offices: supportive, controlling, and directive. Their levels of control and roles differ significantly.

Supportive

- Low level of control over projects
- Consultative role providing training, templates, best practices, and lessons learned

Controlling

- Medium level of control
- PMO defines specific frameworks and methods to use

Directive

- High level of control
- Project managers are assigned to and report to the PMO

Project Roles

The successful development and execution of a project requires more parties than solely the project manager and sponsor.

Portfolio Managers

Portfolio managers are higher-level members of an organization that select the right programs and projects which will support an organization's overall goals.

Program Managers

Program managers support project managers by ensuring that sufficient resources are available to a project, and that large conflicts and disputes are mitigated promptly, so that project success is not negatively impacted.

Project Sponsor

The project sponsor provides the resources for the project. Additionally, the sponsor often defines the need for the project and the high-level schedule, cost, and scope expectations and constraints. Throughout the project the sponsor is often a key resource used to assist political navigation within the organization and to resolve significant conflicts.

Project Manager

The project manager is ultimately responsible for leading the team to complete the project's objectives. The project manager is formally enabled to allocate resources to a project when the project charter is authorized.

Project Coordinators

Coordinators are not commonly used in most organizational structures, the exception being the occasional use in weak matrix and functional structures. Project coordinators have much less authority than project managers in that coordinators are not authorized to make decisions regarding the project.

Stakeholders

A stakeholder is any person that is involved or impacted, either positively or negatively, by a project. In addition to developing the charter, the focus of the Initiating process group is to identify and understand the stakeholders impacted by a project. Stakeholders can be excellent sources of institutional knowledge and expertise. Project managers must focus heavily on managing stakeholder engagement throughout the five process groups.

Functional Managers

Functional managers own specific departments and resources within an organization. Project managers must interact with and seek the help of functional managers to obtain project personnel and resources. Functional managers can provide expert judgement during multiple processes.

Case Study: "Understanding the Organization"

As John leaned back in his chair and took a deep breath, the gravity of his new job sunk in. Last week, he was just a manager in the Quality department, relishing the opportunities when he was pulled into to help on projects where his skills could be of use. Now he was also a project manager assigned to lead a project in the Engineering department—a project that really mattered to the company. Wow!

This realization excited him. Leaning forward he said to himself, "This type of opportunity doesn't come around often; I have to find a way to make this project a success." As he opened his computer he started populating a mental list of what could help or hurt his chances of success. On the positive side, the project was interesting, management had pledged their support, and there seemed to be resources he could lean on. Just then he typed in his password to log into the company's project management hub. The site had templates, procedures, and a section holding lessons learned documents for over 100 projects.

"No reason to recreate the wheel; I'll use this stuff as much as possible."

His confidence continued to grow as he remembered that Lloyd, the manager of the project management office, had told him that he'd be happy to coach him on how to use the templates and provide him advice on how to navigate the organization. Never one to turn down help, John had scheduled a quick session for Monday.

While he was searching through the site, a comment Sara made popped in his head and dragged on his confidence like an anchor. While she conveyed that he would have a moderate amount of authority, she had made it very clear that he wouldn't have full control over the budget or the employees on his team. She emphasized that his ability to develop strong relationships with the managers of his team members would be extremely important.

He knew he had the skills and passion to lead, but he hadn't met the managers he would be working with. What if they didn't have the same desire to make the project successful? How would he get the work done? Feeling his heart rate starting to increase, he took another deep breath. No need to worry about that yet. First things first: get ready for the meeting with Lloyd.

Case Study Questions: "Understanding the Organization"

What type of organizational structure does Alliance operate with?

a. Project-oriented
b. Strong matrix
c. Balanced matrix
d. Weak matrix

What type of project management office does Alliance have?

a. Supportive
b. Controlling
c. Directive
d. Hybrid

What type of inputs would the documents in the project management hub be considered?

a. Organizational process assets (OPAs)
b. Enterprise environmental factors (EEFs)
c. Project charter documents
d. Business documents

CASE STUDY ANSWERS: "UNDERSTANDING THE ORGANIZATION"

What type of organizational structure does Alliance operate with?

a. Project-oriented
b. Strong matrix
c. Balanced matrix
d. Weak matrix

What type of project management office does Alliance have?

a. Supportive
b. Controlling
c. Directive
d. Hybrid

What type of inputs would the documents in the project management hub be considered?

a. Organizational process assets (OPA)
b. Enterprise environmental factors (EEF)
c. Project charter documents
d. Business documents

Role of a Project Manager

Project Manager's Core Competences

PMI's talent triangle defines the three competences project managers must use to successfully lead the team in delivering the intended objectives.

Technical Project Management

Project managers use technical project management to select and apply the correct processes to meet the unique challenges faced. This method is known as project tailoring.

Leadership

Project managers need to guide and motivate the team through complicated situations. Success requires the use of negotiation, resilience, and problem solving.

Strategic and Business Management

Project managers need to be able to navigate the project to continually support the strategic direction of the organization.

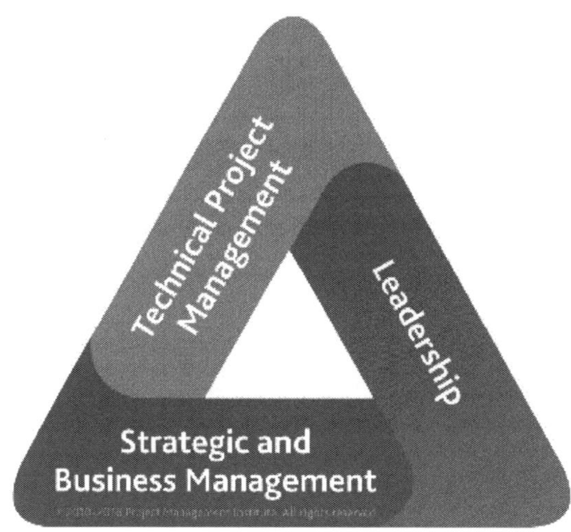

Leadership Styles

There is no one perfect way to lead a project. Many successful project managers have different leadership styles. The six distinct leadership styles referenced on the PMP® exam are laissez-faire, transactional, servant leadership, transformational, charismatic, and interactional. Analyze and remember the characteristics of each style, as the exam will often challenge your ability to identify them.

Laissez-faire

Project managers with this leadership style follow a hands-off approach. Laissez-faire leaders are available for advice when requested, but otherwise they allow the team to make their own decisions.

Transactional

Focused on facts and results, transactional leaders drive their teams in a logical and analytical approach. Transactional leaders emphasize management by exception and use data to help inform decisions.

Servant Leadership

Servant leaders place others first and focus on relationships and development. Proponents of lean methodologies often adopt servant leadership styles.

Transformational

Inspiring and empowering, transformational leaders focus on encouragement of innovation and experimentation.

Charismatic

Charismatic leaders are hard to miss; they exhibit high levels of energy, appear confident, and hold strong convictions.

Interactional

Interactional leaders are jacks of all trades, combining aspects of transactional, transformational, and charismatic leadership styles.

Tailoring the Project

All projects are different. Project managers must tailor their project to succeed in the face of unique constraints and opportunities. Tailoring involves organizing the total project life cycle by defining the distinct project phases, and selecting the correct mix of processes and tools and techniques that will best produce the desired results.

While every project is unique, past project experiences should be used. Expertise and knowledge on the tailoring approach can be drawn from project team members, the sponsor, PMO, and industry best practices.

Designing the Project Life Cycle

The project manager is responsible for tailoring the project to meet the unique demands faced. Critical to this task is crafting the overall project life cycle.

A project's life cycle is the total time that is required to complete a project. The following image illustrates the project life cycle.

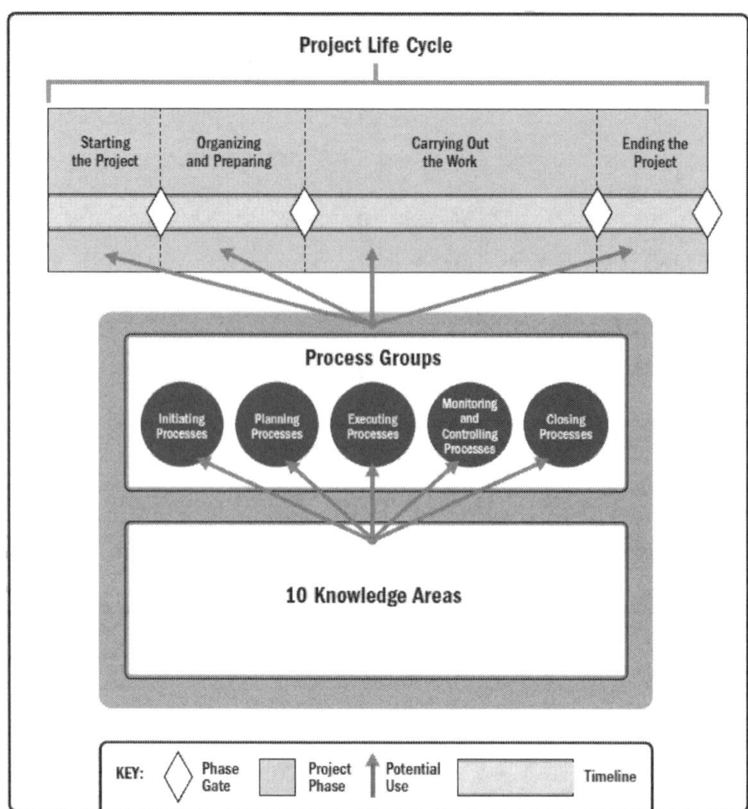

Some people confuse the concepts of project life cycle with the process groups focused on throughout the *PMBOK® Guide*. These concepts are related, but not identical, and the key to understanding the difference is the project phase.

As the image above shows, a project could have multiple phases within the total life cycle. Each phase is designed to deliver one or more distinct deliverables. For example, a project to develop a new product may include distinct phases for design, build, and test. While each phase is designed to deliver unique deliverables, all phases are similar in that the same process group structure (Initiating to Closing) is followed to complete them.

> **Products and projects have different life cycles!**
> Product = Total product life (concept to retirement)
> Project = Defined length of the project

Projects transition from phase to phase with the use of phase gate reviews, held at the end of each project phase. These provide the opportunity to evaluate actual vs. expected progress. Go or no-go decisions are taken based on the results. These reviews are also commonly called stage gates or kill points.

Life Cycle Management Approaches

Critical to the design of the project life cycle is the selection of the project life cycle management approach. The three most common approaches are predictive, adaptive, and iterative. These approaches differ in how and when scope, time, and cost are defined and managed.

Often organizations have established approaches to life cycle management. Project managers should aim to understand the standard approach used within their organization and model their projects accordingly.

Predictive Life Cycles

The predictive approach, also known as waterfall, is the traditional project management method. The total scope, time, and cost are defined very early in a waterfall project. Any future changes require significant analysis and are managed carefully.

Adaptive Life Cycles

In contrast, the newer approach, known as adaptive or agile, defines the scope early and uses a more flexible approach to managing a project. This approach is most commonly used in software development, where functionality is progressively delivered in short cycles. Projects are initiated with a clear vision of the final product, but during each cycle a small set of features are developed and reviewed. The cycles are finite in length, typically two to four weeks. In each new cycle, a small number of features are added. This approach allows the project team to react to a changing environment.

Iterative Life Cycles

Projects with iterative life cycles also define the scope early, but use an iterative approach to define cost and schedule. As the project progresses, the budget and schedule can be modified as a clearer and deeper understanding of project realities is obtained.

> Projects can have multiple phases.
> All process groups are completed within each.

Importance of Project Integration

If there is one lesson to take away from this book, it is the importance of project integration. Project integration is essential to successfully manage a project in complicated and changing environments. For this reason, the first knowledge area defined in the *PMBOK® Guide* is Project Integration Management.

Additionally, the questions on the PMP® exam are not focused solely on individual processes, but many require a deeper analysis and understanding of how all processes work together and interact to drive home success.

The analogy that comes to mind is that of an orchestra. All the individual musicians are critical and unique, much like the 49 processes defined in the *PMBOK® Guide*. However, if each played off their "own sheet of music," the results would make Bach roll over in his grave. The brilliance comes from the orchestra conductor guiding all the musicians together to play at the correct time. Project integration aims to achieve a similar effect with the project processes.

The project manager is responsible for acting as the conductor of the project, using the project integration processes to define the plan for each knowledge area and ensure that it is followed.

Case Study: "Designing the Path"

John had downloaded the charter and stakeholder register templates. As he started to fill in the details, his brain jumped forward and questions piled up: What were his next steps? How would he get the team together, and would he be able to lead them? Shouldn't he be directing people to do things? With questions came insecurities. John eagerly unloaded these in his meeting with Lloyd.

"It feels different being at the helm of a project. Maybe I was naïve, but on my past projects, it always felt like the project manager had all the answers."

"What you're feeling is normal. You're making a big jump: team member to project manager. It may have felt like every project manager knew all the answers, but they often didn't. Don't worry, you will be successful if..." Lloyd paused to see if John was truly paying attention. He was. Lloyd continued, "you stay disciplined yet flexible."

Lloyd had a calm and relaxed, yet confident manner. Sitting in Lloyd's office, John felt that this was equal mentoring and therapy session. "Disciplined yet flexible? I don't know what you mean."

"Let's start with flexible. As a project manager, you must understand the deliverables and then structure your project in strategic phases to achieve them. Additionally, there are lots of processes to choose from, but every phase doesn't require them all. You must pick the unique mix of processes the team completes and build in strategic gate checks to evaluate if you were successful."

"So, is every phase totally unique?"

"No. Every phase doesn't require every process, but it does follow the same flow of process groups. This is where discipline comes into play."

John had begun taking notes. As Lloyd continued, John followed along, writing the words Initiating, Planning, Executing, Monitoring and Controlling, and Closing along the left side of his paper. "John, I want you to refresh yourself on these process groups and the processes within each. Remember these process groups aren't totally sequential. It isn't mandatory that one finishes before the next starts—no, instead they overlap and are interrelated."

Lloyd could see that the complexity of this realization had not yet crystalized in John's mind. He continued explaining in an effort to help. "Many of the processes interact and build on each other. Because of this, when something in the project changes, you must loop back and adjust. This is not a bad thing; instead, it is reality and the major part of all successful projects. Remember 'disciplined yet flexible'."

"So, what do I do first to be disciplined yet flexible?"

"You are making the correct first steps now. Continue moving through Initiating, and get serious about Planning. Don't focus too heavily on Execution this early. Instead, establish a clear foundation and build buy-in with your stakeholders. Execution will come in time. Be patient but push forward." John left Lloyd's office with a new perspective. He would trust the process and stick to the principles of a great project.

Case Study Questions: "Designing the Path"

Lloyd recommends that all project managers must understand their projects and select the ideal mix of processes that best supports their success. What is this approach called?

e. Phase analysis
a. Phase gating
b. Project life cycle analysis
c. Tailoring

After the meeting, John is advised by a younger project manager that the best way to speed up an early phase of a project is to skip the Monitoring and Controlling process group. Would you support John in following this advice?

a. No; every process group serves a distinct purpose in each phase and must be used
b. No; early phases require the use of all process groups, but later phases do not require Initiating
c. Yes; John must tailor the project to fit its unique needs
d. Yes; process groups are not mandatory

Case Study Answers: "Designing the Path"

Lloyd recommends that all project managers must understand their projects and select the ideal mix of processes that best supports their success. What is this approach called?

a. Phase analysis
b. Phase gating
c. Project life cycle analysis
d. **Tailoring**

After the meeting, John is advised by a younger project manager that the best way to speed up an early phase of a project is to skip the Monitoring and Controlling process group. Would you support John in following this advice?

a. **No; every process group serves a distinct purpose in each phase and must be used**
b. No; early phases require the use of all process groups, but later phases do not require Initiating
c. Yes; John must tailor the project to fit its unique needs
d. Yes; process groups are not mandatory

Case Study: "First Challenge: To Compromise or Not?"

John's peace and confidence in following the "disciplined yet flexible" approach to project management lasted one and a half days.

The VP had called Friday morning. Not recognizing the number, John had answered unprepared for what awaited him.

"Have you found anything yet? What kind of changes are we making? I just spoke to the Engineering manager. He said they haven't started working on redesigns. Why haven't you gotten his guys moving? What are you waiting on?"

John had counted four questions. He was unsure if he had an acceptable answer to any of them. Instead, he attempted to explain the process.

"Sir, it may appear we aren't moving quickly, but I can assure you things are progressing well. We are moving in the right direction. We are getting into Initiating and going to start some of the processes in the Planning process group soon."

John was cut off before he could continue. "Planning? I don't want plans. I want results." John could feel the displeasure dripping from the VP's words. "I know Lloyd is filling your head with all that 'disciplined but flexible' stuff, but save that for the next project. This project is way too important to spend the time going through each process group. I want to make myself clear now. Act fast, work quickly, and get results. If you don't, our next conversation will not be as cordial."

Throughout the weekend, the VP's call to "act fast...work quickly" rang in John's head. This approach matched with his own initial instincts, but it was in direct conflict with what Lloyd had advised. John felt stuck.

After two days of contemplation, John believed he had found a middle ground: a way he could satisfy both the VP's need for fast results and Lloyd's discipline. He would get a few engineers working now and then he would finish the charter once time freed up. As he began making calls to engineers he reaffirmed himself, "this one little compromise won't hurt." In the back of his mind he hoped he was right.

CASE STUDY QUESTIONS: "FIRST CHALLENGE: TO COMPROMISE OR NOT?"

What approach should John have taken in response to the VP's request?

a. Accept his direction: make some progress, complete the charter later
b. Refuse and ask to be removed from the project manager position
c. Explain the necessity of the charter and enlist Lloyd and Sara for assistance
d. Report the VP to the local PMI chapter for an ethics violation

In defending the necessity and value of project initiation, what two documents would you explain will be created during the Initiating process group?

a. Approved project charter and stakeholder register
b. Project charter and scope baseline
c. Project charter and team assignments
d. Business documents and project charter

Case Study Answers: "First Challenge: To Compromise or Not?"

What approach should John have taken in response to the VP's request?

a. Accept his direction: make some progress, complete the charter later
b. Refuse and ask to be removed from the project manager position
c. Explain the necessity of the charter and enlist Lloyd and Sara for assistance
d. Report the VP to the local PMI chapter for an ethics violation

In defending the necessity and value of project initiation, what two documents would you explain will be created during the Initiating process group?

a. Approved project charter and stakeholder register
b. Project charter and scope baseline
c. Project charter and team assignments
d. Business documents and project charter

INITIATING PROCESS GROUP

Initiating Process Group Summary

The Initiating process group contains two important processes that work together to define, authorize, and ultimately "initiate" a project:

- Develop Project Charter (*PMBOK Guide*® 4.1)
- Identify Stakeholders (*PMBOK Guide*® 13.1)

Objectives

From a big-picture perspective, the objectives of the Initiating process group are simple:

1. Define the project
2. Obtain project approval
3. Identify and start to understand the stakeholders

Key Outputs

To achieve the three objectives listed above, the project sponsor, key stakeholders, and project manager will collaborate and use relevant inputs and tools and techniques to generate a few key outputs that will serve as the foundation for the project:

- Project charter
- Assumption log
- Stakeholder register

Because project management is an iterative process, circumstances during a project such as a procurement agreement, may require the further identification of new or different stakeholders. When a process such as Identify Stakeholders is revisited later in the project, changes may warrant **change requests** and updates to the project management plan, as well as other **project documents updates**, for example, to the assumption log, issue log, and risk register.

DEVELOP PROJECT CHARTER (*PMBOK GUIDE®* 4.1)

Summary

The Develop Project Charter process is where the idea of a project becomes a reality.

The Develop Project Charter process focuses on developing and gaining sponsor approval of the project charter. A project charter is the foundational document of a project. It directly links the project to strategic objectives defined by the organization.

The key outputs of the Develop Project Charter process are the project charter and assumption log. Important: Without an approved project charter, there is no project! Therefore, the project charter is the first necessary output for all project management processes.

Develop Project Charter I.T.T.O.

4.1 Develop Project Charter	Inputs	Tools and Techniques	Outputs
	Business documents • *Business case* • *Benefits management plan* **Agreements** **EEFs** **OPAs**	**Expert judgement** **Data gathering** • *Brainstorming* • *Focus groups* • *Interviews* **Interpersonal and team skills** • *Conflict management* • *Facilitation* • *Meeting management* **Meetings**	**Project charter** **Assumption log**

Key Outputs

PROJECT CHARTER

A project charter formally documents the high-level details of a project as well as several key elements that structure and organize the formation of a project. Some of the information in a project charter may not be accurate; it's the first formal documentation of an effort to produce something by way of a project. The charter should include information such as the following:

- Project name and title
- Project sponsor
- Project manager
- Project purpose
- Key requirements
- Estimated costs
- Estimated duration
- Initial scope
- Known risks
- Known constraints

Once approved by the project sponsor, the charter authorizes the existence of the project. Without approval from a sponsor, there is no project.

Project Charter				
Project Name:				
Sponsor Name:			Project Recipient:	
Manager Name:			Date:	
Project Function	Project Summary	Project Requirements	Estimated Expenses	Possible Liabilities

Summary Milestones	Completion Date

	Project Goals	Achievement Standard	Approval Signature
Scope			
Duration			
Price			
Quality			
Other			

Approval Signatures			
Sponsor Signature:		Manager Signature:	
Sponsor Name:		Manager Name:	

ASSUMPTION LOG

The assumption log is used to record all assumptions and constraints known at any point during the project. Initially, during the Develop Project Charter process, it is important to declare and document as many known assumptions and constraints as possible. These will become barriers or obstacles if not adequately addressed.

> The project manager should be identified and assigned as early as possible, preferably during charter development.

Key Inputs

The need for a project to be initiated and the development of a charter that documents this need can be initiated and supported by many sources. These sources are the inputs to the Develop Project Charter process.

BUSINESS CASE

A business case helps to define the objectives, purpose, and assumptions of a project. It is used prior to starting a project to determine if the benefits of achieving the objectives are worth the required investment. Project sponsors may initiate the development of a business case to study the economic feasibility of a project intended to address any of the following:

- Market demand
- Organizational need
- Customer request
- Technological advance
- Legal or compliance requirement
- Ecological requiremen

> The business case helps create the charter by determining if the expected outcomes justify the required investment.

AGREEMENTS

Agreements help to define the initial intentions for a project and can be used to help frame charter details. They can be the catalyst for the need of a project due to **service level agreements (SLA)** with customers. Agreements exist in various forms and may include the following:

- Contract (commonly used when a project is being performed for an external customer)
- Memorandum of understanding (MOU)
- Letter of agreement or Letter of intent
- Verbal agreement, email agreement, other written agreements

ENTERPRISE ENVIRONMENTAL FACTORS (EEFs)

EEFs must be evaluated and addressed in the development of a project charter. There may be several factors at play that will affect the project, such as **government regulations** or new or changing **legal requirements**. Other factors could be the following:

- Industry standards
- Market conditions
- Organizational culture
- Organizational governance frameworks
- Stakeholders' expectations

ORGANIZATONAL PROCESS ASSETS (OPAs)

OPAs are the tangible internal assets that should be used throughout a project. For any good charter development, the following things will be considered:

- Organizational policies, processes, procedures
- Portfolio, program, and project governance
- Internal reporting methods
- Internal tools, templates, and other resources
- Historical information and lessons learned repository

Key Tools and Techniques

Along with the information and business need driving the development of the project charter, there are important methods necessary in gathering and processing the intellectual assets to produce an approved project charter.

EXPERT JUDGEMENT

Gathering or bringing to bear specialized information and specific knowledge or skills is necessary to make good business decisions.

DATA GATHERING

There are various ways a project manager can gather the necessary information and data to develop the project charter. A project manager may use methods such as

- Brainstorming
- Focus groups
- Interviews

Because project managers are engaging people and organizational assets to deliver the charter, good **interpersonal and team skills** are also important to *how* project managers engage with others and facilitate interactions. These skills include

- Conflict management
- Facilitation
- Meeting management

> Charter development is a collaboration effort led by the project manager or sponsor to deepen the understanding of project's purpose, objective, and benefit.

Case Study: "Getting the Charter Authorized"

John believed that his decision to act and charge ahead would pay dividends. He now had two engineers analyzing the current designs. It was only a matter of time before they called with good news. Later that day John did receive a call. But it was from Sara.

"John, I just bumped into an old engineer buddy. He said you are asking him to look over some drawings." As Sara spoke, John began to feel his hands sweat. Her tone was not as upbeat as usual; it was more direct. "I like the enthusiasm, but I would recommend you focus on being methodical. Your first task is to get the project authorized and start getting everyone on board. I haven't seen your approved charter. Don't jump into action. If you do, you will regret it."

The call was short but clear. She did not approve of his approach. Sara had been successful, and he didn't want to upset her. In his haste to get things moving he had forgotten to finish the charter. He kicked himself. Before hanging up he had apologized and committed to Sara that he would stop the engineers from continuing their review, and have an approved charter on her desk as soon as possible. Pulling up the half-completed charter John focused his attention on three sections: "Key Members," "Statement of Work," and the "Business Case."

He penciled in the obvious ("Project Title," "Project Manager") and paused as he contemplated the "Sponsor." The VP was obviously pushing this project and Sara was responsible for making sure this and other projects were successful. Lloyd would be critical to helping John navigate the project to a successful completion and the legal and procurement departments had resources he would lean on for their expertise. Additionally, Sara had mentioned that Lawrence was the director of the engineering department that owned the designs in question and would be the final say on resources and spending. After evaluating all parties, John wrote in the name of the sponsor and moved on.

John logically broke down the statement of work into the business need and product scope description. The VP made it clear that the project materialized because of the new regulations. That seemed like the "Business Need." Complementing the business need was the product scope, the first draft being "ensure that the line design meets all regulatory standards and delivers the maximum value." John felt it was a good start but not perfect. The statement evolved as the day proceeded.

To attack the business case John leveraged the assistance of a business analyst. The two incorporated existing data on profit projections with the research they had discovered on fines and violations. The data provided an interesting story. The risk of penalty was something that could not be ignored.

John and the analyst also documented the assumptions and constraints and defined a high-level schedule. With a strong draft completed, John and the analyst looked at each other. John said, "I think it's ready for prime time. I'm booking a meeting with the sponsor."

During the meeting John found that the depth of information helped to explain the project and clarify expectations. The sponsor redlined the document and provided feedback that John used to improve the charter, all while sitting in the sponsor's office. After 30 minutes and two revisions, John left the sponsor's office. He found the analyst and smiled. John slapped the charter on the analyst's desk and said, "He signed the charter. It's official. We are in the game."

Case Study Questions: "Getting the Charter Authorized"

Who is the project sponsor and why?

a. The company's VP. He initially gave the direction to start the project.
b. Lawrence. He is the director of the Engineering department that owns the designs and controls the resources to fund the project.
c. Sara. She is responsible for the successful completion of all the projects in the program.
d. The controller. He has the final say on large expenditures of resources to fund the project.

The charter template is considered what type of input?

a. Work performance information
b. Framing document
c. Enterprise environmental factor (EEF)
d. Organizational process asset (OPA)

The regulations are considered what type of input?

a. Agreements
b. Work performance data
c. Enterprise environmental factors (EEF)
d. Organizational process assets (OPA)

Case Study Answers: "Getting the Charter Authorized"

Who is the project sponsor and why?

a. The company's VP. He initially gave the direction to start the project.
b. Lawrence. He is the director of the Engineering department that owns the designs and controls the resources to fund the project.
c. Sara. She is responsible for the successful completion of all the projects in the program.
d. The controller. He has the final say on large expenditures of resources to fund the project.

The charter template is considered what type of input?

a. Work performance information
b. Framing document
c. Enterprise environmental factor (EEF)
d. Organizational process asset (OPA)

The regulations are considered what type of input?

a. Agreements
b. Work performance data
c. Enterprise environmental factors (EEF)
d. Organizational process assets (OPA)

IDENTIFY STAKEHOLDERS *(PMBOK® GUIDE* 13.1)

Summary

The Identify Stakeholders process identifies, analyzes, and classifies all stakeholders that could impact or be impacted by the project. Stakeholders can exert positive or negative influences over a project and project deliverables. Each stakeholder's level of interest, involvement, and potential impact is documented on the stakeholder register. It is critical to identify all stakeholders (positive and negative) as early as possible. Once stakeholders are identified, the team can then develop the appropriate focus of engagement for each stakeholder.

Identify Stakeholders I.T.T.O.

13.1 Identify Stakeholders	Inputs	Tools and Techniques	Outputs
	Project charter **Business documents** • *Business case* • *Benefits management plan* **Project management plan** • *Communications mgt. plan* • *Stakeholder mgt. plan* **Procurement documents** • *Change log* • *Issue log* • *Requirements documentation* **Agreements** **EEFs** **OPAs**	**Expert judgement** **Data gathering** • *Questionnaires and surveys* • *Brainstorming* **Data analysis** • *Stakeholder analysis* • *Documents analysis* **Data representation** • *Stakeholder mapping and representation* **Meetings**	**Stakeholder register** **Change requests** **Project mgt. plan updates** • *Requirements mgt. plan* • *Communications mgt. plan* • *Stakeholder engmt. plan* **Project documents updates** • *Assumption log* • *Issue log* • *Risk register*

Key Outputs

STAKEHOLDER REGISTER

The stakeholder register is a document used to record information on every stakeholder. Stakeholders are identified and input into the stakeholder register with pertinent information about each person, their function, title, level of interest in the project, and level of influence on the project. This register should also include contact information.

Using the stakeholder register, project teams can plan appropriate ways to engage stakeholders based on relevant identifying information. This identification and prioritization process is critical to a project's success.

> Stakeholder identification and analysis helps the team design ways to appropriately engage each stakeholder.

Key Inputs

PROJECT CHARTER

Early in the project, the project charter and business case can be used to identify the initial stakeholder list. As the project develops, additional inputs such as the **communications plan** and **stakeholder engagement plan** will help improve the stakeholder list and bolster the stakeholder register. As the project continues, issues and changes may introduce new stakeholders, which may be identified through project documents such as the change log and issue log.

Through processes such as procurement, where a project may be seeking to acquire resources necessary to meet objectives and requirements, **agreements** could become a source of new or changing stakeholders, which may prompt updates to the stakeholder register.

 Initially, the charter and business case are sources of stakeholder identification. Later, agreements or issues may prompt stakeholder updates.

Key Tools and Techniques

DATA GATHERING

The Identify Stakeholders process may require input from various sources and people. **Questionnaires** and **surveys** can be distributed and conducted via one-on-one interviews, focus group sessions, or mass information collection techniques to identify stakeholders.

Brainstorming is another method of eliciting information from groups or individuals such as team members or subject matter experts.

DATA ANALYSIS

Identifying stakeholders is only the initial task of the Identify Stakeholders process. Assessing the stakeholders' level of influence, engagement, and interest requires analysis. **Stakeholder analysis** performed to obtain this information may be displayed graphically through data representation techniques.

DATA REPRESENTATION

Stakeholder mapping can help classify stakeholders based on their interest and influence. The use of mapping techniques such as a **power-interest grid** (shown below) can provide a graphical display of where stakeholders are perceived to be relative to their power and interest in the project.

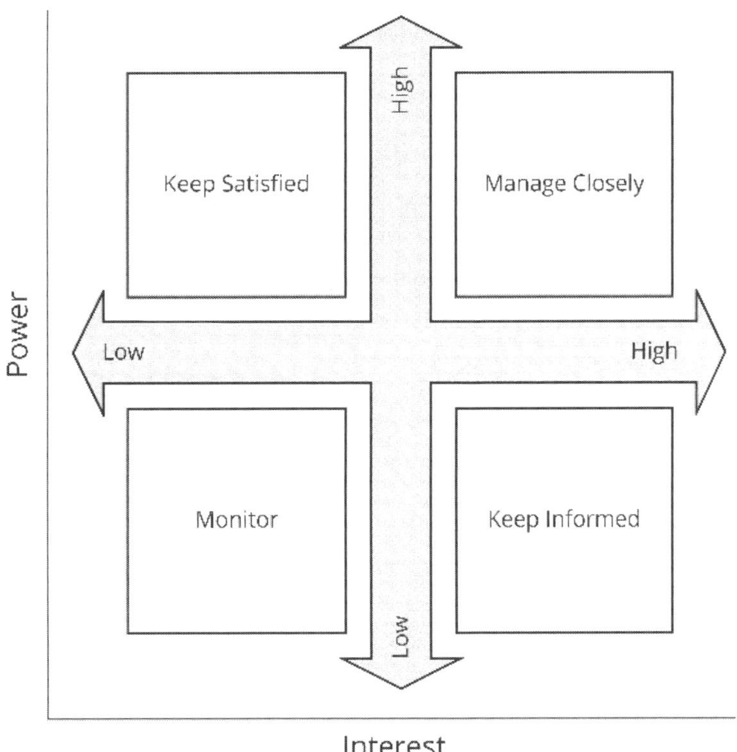

Other graphical representations that have similar characteristics are

- Power-influence grid
- Influence-impact grid
- Salience model

> Identifying, categorizing, and prioritizing stakeholders will help the project team define appropriate engagement levels.

CASE STUDY: "UNDERSTANDING WHO IS AFFECTED"

"The list looks pretty good, but I think you should definitely add Sam from Procurement, and what about Olivia from Quality Assurance?" John had heard this same type of comment four times over the last two days. After obtaining the sponsor's approval of the charter, John began the task of building a list of project stakeholders. As he added Sam and Olivia, he remarked that it really did feel as though he was literally "building" the list person by person. Every time he shared the list with a new stakeholder the list inevitably grew.

What started as a few names and basic details (name, position, contact information) quickly grew into a detailed list with descriptive information. Sara had stressed the importance of this list when he hand-delivered a copy of the approved charter. She explained that it was essential to understand the stakeholder landscape and referred to it as the stakeholder register. As stakeholders were suggested, John followed up with simple questions aimed at understanding each one's perspective on the project.

Having fleshed out the list into a well-developed register, John met again with the sponsor. Prepared with a basic classification model, John led with a simple and direct request: "I would like your assistance in analyzing each stakeholder, namely by their level of concern with the project's outputs and their level of authority in the organization. I aim to use this understanding to develop strategies that will help us build support and lower the risk of issues."

Working methodically, they analyzed and classified everyone, placing them on the classification grid and defining a perceived level of engagement. John made sure to record the detailed information on the register. Moving through the list, John quickly realized how valuable the sponsor's experience was. He understood how the corporate history and individual stakeholder personalities played into the situation, and he was able to identify opportunities to build strategic coalitions to mitigate risk.

Leaving the sponsor's office, John felt confident: He was beginning to better understand what he would need to do to help make this project a success.

CASE STUDY QUESTIONS: "UNDERSTANDING WHO IS AFFECTED"

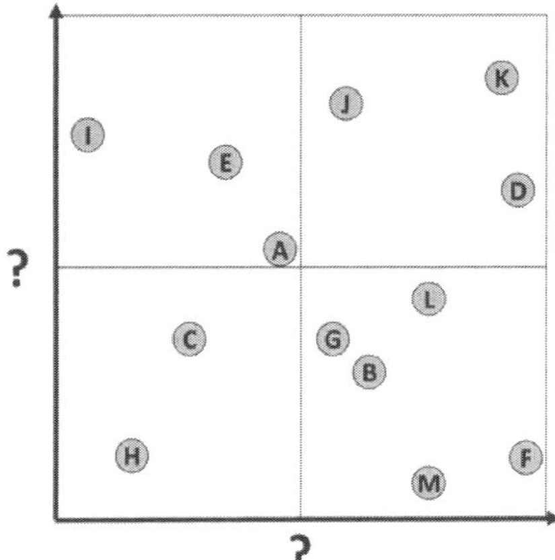

What type of classification model did John use to assist in analyzing stakeholders?

a. Salience model
b. Power-interest grid
c. Power-influence grid
d. Impact-influence grid

In the grid, which quadrant represents the greatest risk?

a. Lower left quadrant
b. Upper left quadrant
c. Upper right quadrant
d. Lower right quadrant

What was the primary output created through the Identify Stakeholders process?

a. Signed project charter
b. Assumption log
c. Stakeholder register
d. Stakeholder engagement plan

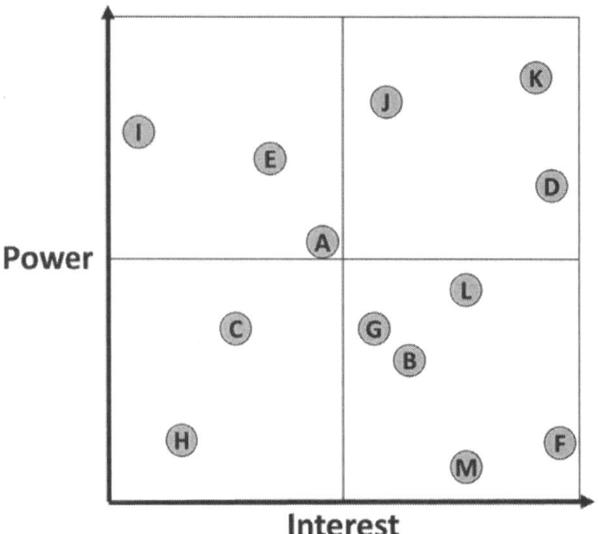

What type of classification model did John use to assist in analyzing stakeholders?

a. Salience model
b. Power-interest grid
c. Power- influence grid
d. Impact- influence grid

In the grid, which quadrant represents the greatest risk?

a. Lower left quadrant
b. Upper left quadrant
c. Upper right quadrant (high power–high interest)
d. Lower right quadrant

What was the primary output created through the Identify Stakeholders process?

a. Signed project charter
b. Assumption log
c. Stakeholder register
d. Stakeholder engagement plan

PLANNING PROCESS GROUP

Planning Process Group Summary

The processes and activities of the Planning process group focus on developing the project management plan and the documents that will be used to execute the project. As the project progresses, more planning will certainly take place as new or changed information and circumstances inform the project management plan.

Objectives

The ultimate objective of the Planning process group is creating a documented and informed project management plan. This plan will consider all aspects of scope, time, cost, quality, risk, resources, communication, procurement, as well as ownership and accountability. When planning a project, the project manager needs to answer the following questions in detail:

- Where are we going?
- How do we get there?
- Do we have enough of the right resources?
- What might deter us?

Key Outputs

The Planning process group is the most comprehensive of the five process groups. It is home to 24 of the 49 processes (or about half of them), which generate many outputs. The nucleus of all outputs is the project management plan. Twelve subsidiary plans and four baselines are the primary components of the project management plan. Every knowledge area except the Integration knowledge area generates a subsidiary management plan (scope, cost, schedule, risk, etc.). The project management plan is composed of the following:

- Scope mgt. plan
- Requirements mgt. plan
- Schedule mgt. plan
- Cost mgt. plan
- Quality mgt. plan
- Resource mgt. plan
- Communications mgt. plan
- Risk mgt. plan
- Procurement mgt. plan
- Stakeholder mgt. plan
- Change mgt. plan
- Configuration mgt. plan
- Scope baseline
- Schedule baseline
- Cost baseline
- Perf. measurement baseline
- Project life-cycle description
- Development approach

Many other outputs will be generated in this process group, but they will be discussed in detail later. The important take-away here is that the Planning process group creates these plans and baselines, and then as each of them is created, it "re-informs" the overall plan through project documents updates, change requests, and work performance information.

DEVELOP PROJECT MANAGEMENT PLAN (*PMBOK® GUIDE* 4.2)

Summary

The project management plan is the "mother of all plans," defining how the project and all elements will be executed, managed, and controlled. The project management plan integrates 12 subsidiary plans and four baselines. The project baselines will become approved versions of the scope, schedule, and cost management plans. To maintain discipline, the baselines once approved can only be changed using the Integrated Change Control process.

> The project management plan uses the Change Control process to react to the realities of a constantly changing project environment.

At this point in the project, the project management plan is merely a "shell." It likely only contains or references the project charter, business documents, and the stakeholder register. At this stage, none of the working components of the plan has been generated yet. They will be generated as the project progresses through the Planning process group.

> The Develop Project Management Plan process only initiates the creation of a comprehensive plan. It will be updated and revisited often during the project.

Develop Project Management Plan I.T.T.O.

	Inputs	Tools and Techniques	Outputs
4.2 Develop Project Mgt. Plan	**Project charter** **Outputs from other processes** **EEFs** **OPAs**	**Expert judgement** **Data gathering** • *Brainstorming* • *Checklists* • *Focus groups* • *Interviews* **Interpersonal and team skills** • *Conflict management* • *Facilitation* • *Meeting management* **Meetings**	**Project management plan**

Key Outputs

PROJECT MANAGEMENT PLAN

The project management plan is an all-encompassing entity. It will contain many subsidiary plans that are produced by executing other Planning processes. The project management plan will be populated, updated, and revisited in an iterative manner as the outputs of other processes are created. The following are the components that this plan will incorporate:

Project Management Plan	Project Documents	
Scope mgt. plan	Activity attributes	Project team assignments
Requirements mgt. plan	Activity list	Quality control measurements
Schedule mgt. plan	Assumption log	Quality metrics
Cost mgt. plan	Basis of estimates	Quality report
Quality mgt. plan	Change log	Requirements documentation
Resource mgt. plan	Cost estimates	Req. traceability matrix
Communications mgt. plan	Cost forecasts	Resource breakdown structure
Risk mgt. plan	Duration estimates	Resource calendars
Procurement mgt. plan	Issue log	Resource requirements
Stakeholder mgt. plan	Lessons learned register	Risk register
Change mgt. plan	Milestone list	Risk report
Configuration mgt. plan	Physical resource requirements	Schedule data
Scope baseline	Project calendars	Schedule forecasts
Schedule baseline	Project communications	Stakeholder register
Cost baseline	Project schedule	Team charter
Perf. measurement baseline	Project schedule network diagram	Test and evaluation documents
Project life-cycle description	Project scope statement	
Development approach		

Key Inputs

PROJECT CHARTER

Initially, the project charter will be the foundational input to opening the project management plan. This is the starting point supplying high-level information on the project vision, purpose, scope, schedule, and primary requirements.

OUTPUTS FROM OTHER PROCESSES

As the project matures and processes are completed, outputs from those processes will continuously feed into the overall project management plan.

EEFs AND OPAs

At any point in the project (beginning, middle, or end), enterprise environmental factors and organizational process assets will influence the project and should be incorporated into the project management plan.

Key Tools and Techniques

Developing the project management plan is an ongoing activity that will require skills and expert judgement from numerous disciplines. Incorporating this type of information will be achieved through data gathering techniques such as **brainstorming** during group sessions, as well as **interviews** with subject matter experts. This engagement and collaboration will test the interpersonal and team skills of any project manager who will be charged with **facilitation** and effective **meeting management**.

> A project kick-off meeting is a common practice to clearly communicate project objectives and build team and stakeholder buy-in.

CASE STUDY: "THE IMPORTANCE OF PLANS"

"Lloyd! I have great news! The charter was approved, and I've defined the key stakeholders."

Lloyd smiled as he listened, patiently allowing John to expound on his progress. "The best thing is that in meeting some of the stakeholders I think we uncovered some low-hanging fruit. I went ahead and got the team working on the ideas." It was obvious that John was both proud of his progress and eager for approval. Not looking to kill his enthusiasm but seeing the need to provide guidance, Lloyd responded in a measured and encouraging tone: "That is positive, but let's think this through. I know you think you see opportunity and that running forward feels like the best action, but be careful. Your focus right now should be on planning." Undeterred, John pressed forward confidently: "Don't worry, we drew up a simple plan for attacking the low-hanging fruit. I just want to get some results quickly."

Lloyd's measured advice clearly did not hit home. Maybe John was a young "Action Jackson Jr." in the making, more inclined to push forward than calculate. Being more forceful, Lloyd tried a different approach: "Have you defined all the requirements? How are you going to define success? How about scope, schedule, and cost baselines? Do you have those? Have you decided how to estimate, monitor, and control costs? What's the plan for measuring quality? How about risk? Oh, and schedule? What's your policy for planning, developing, and controlling schedule?" John paused, caught off guard partially by the questions and more by the disapproving tone.

Seeing the impact, Lloyd pushed on: "There is no one perfect way to run a project, but one thing I can assure you of is that if you try to take shortcuts, you set yourself up for failure. There are a variety of different knowledge areas that affect every project: scope, cost, schedule, risk, etc." Lloyd emphasized these by counting them off with his fingers. "Within each area there are big gaps of unknowns. These things will flare up and cause you problems. You have to plan for these." Lloyd paused to emphasize the importance of the next point and went in for the kill: "What you need to be doing now is spending the time on planning how you will execute, monitor, and control each of these areas. Call these your subsidiary plans. All those plans roll up together with the baselines I mentioned earlier into something we call the project management plan."

"The project management plan is the basis for all your project work. The great thing is that we have templates you can follow and a lot of examples from other projects. Read through some of those and build off their experience." Lloyd could almost see the wheels turning in John's head. The logic made sense, but John's enthusiasm had dropped. Looking dejected, John thanked Lloyd for his guidance and started to turn away. "Keep your head up, be methodical, and trust the process. Come see me again when you have your project management plan fleshed out. And John...don't underestimate the power of good plans."

Case Study Questions: "The Importance of Plans"

Lloyd explained to John that the project management plan consolidates all subsidiary plans and project baselines. Which of the following is not one of the three project baselines?

a. Scope baseline
b. Schedule baseline
c. Benefits baseline
d. Cost baseline

Once John establishes a project baseline, by what is the only means the baseline can be modified?

a. Baselines can be modified as needed if the changes are recorded in the change log
b. Verification from the project sponsor
c. Change request approved through the Perform Integrated Control process
d. Project manager has the authority to modify baselines

Project manager has the authority to modify baselinesAfter meeting with Lloyd, John is eager to build out the project management plans. He plans that his first step will be to bring together a small group of stakeholders to discuss the project management approach and the integration of the different components with the project management plan. Which data gathering technique is John planning to utilize?

a. Brainstorming
b. Checklists
c. Focus groups
d. Interviews

CASE STUDY ANSWERS: "THE IMPORTANCE OF PLANS"

Lloyd explained that the project management plan consolidates all subsidiary plans and project baselines. Which of the following is not one of the three project baselines?

a. Scope baseline
b. Schedule baseline
c. Benefits baseline
d. Cost baseline

Once John establishes a project baseline, by what is the only means the baseline can be modified?

a. Baselines can be modified as needed if the changes are recorded in the change log
b. Verification from the project sponsor
c. Change request approved through the Perform Integrated Control process
d. Project manager has the authority to modify baselines

After meeting with Lloyd, John is eager to build out the project management plans. He plans that his first step will be to bring together a small group of stakeholders to discuss the project management approach and the integration of the different components with the project management plan. Which data gathering technique is John planning to utilize?

a. Brainstorming
b. Checklists
c. Focus groups
d. Interviews

PLAN SCOPE MANAGEMENT (*PMBOK® GUIDE* 5.1)

Summary

Defining high-level requirements in the charter and communicating with the stakeholders often brings along a new challenge. Everyone has an opinion and desire for what the project should accomplish. This input is valuable, but the project can't deliver everything. Instead, the project manager must lead the team through a process of selecting the correct mixture of charter-defined requirements and those of various stakeholders. The final mixture of requirements is then formatted into a clear and concise definition of what the project will deliver, known as the scope baseline. The scope baseline is the major output of the four scope management processes in the Planning process group.

The scope baseline is a combination of three essential documents: the project scope statement, work breakdown structure (WBS), and WBS dictionary. The other supporting outputs of the scope management processes in Planning are the scope management plan, requirements management plan, requirements documentation, and requirements traceability matrix.

The **scope management plan**, produced as the output of the Plan Scope Management process, defines the method by which the scope baseline (described above) will be produced and managed.

> Project scope defines all the necessary work that is required to complete the project.

Plan Scope Management I.T.T.O.

5.1 Plan Scope Mgt.	Inputs	Tools and Techniques	Outputs
	Project charter **Project management plan** • *Quality management plan* • *Project life cycle description* • *Development approach* **EEFs** **OPAs**	**Expert judgement** **Data analysis** • *Alternatives analysis* **Meetings**	**Scope mgt. plan** **Requirements mgt. plan**

Key Outputs

SCOPE MANAGEMENT PLAN

The scope management plan is the first building block within the project management plan. Developing the scope management plan should start as soon as the project charter is approved.

The scope management plan clarifies the approach that will be followed in the next three scope processes to create the scope baseline and WBS. Each of the three additional scope management processes progressively accomplishes work contributing to these outputs, as described next.

- Collect and document all requirements from stakeholders (5.2 Collect Requirements)
- Select the correct requirements and create a detailed project description (5.3 Define Scope)
- Break down the project deliverables into manageable work components (5.4 Create WBS)

Defining the approach to creating the scope baseline is not enough. The scope management plan also defines how the scope will be managed throughout the project and how completed deliverables will be formally accepted. Placing controls on how scope changes will be made helps to prevent scope creep, one of the biggest killers of projects. Scope creep is the expansion of work beyond the approved project boundaries. Scope creep is every project manager's sworn enemy.

REQUIREMENTS MANAGEMENT PLAN

Often called the business analysis plan, the requirements management plan is the next building block of the project management plan. A long list of detailed requirements will be created as the next three processes unfold. The requirements management plan defines how the requirements will be planned, tracked, and reported.

Key Inputs

PROJECT CHARTER

The project charter is the starting point for both the requirements and scope management plans. The high-level information contained therein helps frame the appropriate approaches taken in creating the plans. Specifically, the assumptions, constraints, and primary requirements will be of highest value.

PROJECT MANAGEMENT PLAN

The **project life cycle description** and **development approaches** defined in the project management plan directly impact the method by which the scope and requirements will be developed. The life cycle descriptions define the project phases, while the development approach impacts how the scope and deliverables will be developed.

In projects using a predictive approach, all project deliverables and scope are defined at the beginning of the project, and scope changes are managed progressively using the Integrated Change Control process. However, in projects that use an agile approach, smaller groups of deliverables are defined over multiple iterations. Additionally, all project management plans are living documents. When the initial versions of the scope and requirements management plans are created, other plans may not exist yet. However, the development of other plans, such as the **quality management plan**, often produces additional information and realizations that make it necessary to refine the scope and resource management plans.

EEFs AND OPAs

In developing the scope and requirements management plans, it often helps to understand the **organization's culture** (EEFs) and to reference **lessons learned** (OPAs) from past projects to inform the best approaches to follow.

Key Tools and Techniques

EXPERT JUDGEMENT AND DATA ANALYSIS

Expert judgement and data analysis are used to better understand the project and develop more thorough plans by pulling together and evaluating best practices and lessons learned.

COLLECT REQUIREMENTS (*PMBOK GUIDE*® 5.2)

Summary

The goal of the Collect Requirements process is to create a detailed list of potential project requirements.

A project requirement is a condition or capability that must be present in the project's finished product. In other words, requirements describe *what* will be produced, not *how* it will be produced.

Collect Requirements is the first of three processes (5.2, 5.3, 5.4) that transform high-level requirements into a clear objective scope defining the bounds of the project. The requirements documentation and requirements traceability matrix created in this process are the foundation on which the scope statement (in 5.3 Define Scope) and scope baseline (in 5.4 Create WBS) will be built.

As mentioned previously, stakeholders have their own desires for what they would like the project to produce. The project manager's role in this process is to compile, analyze, and record the requirements. This task requires significant interaction with stakeholders and presents an ideal opportunity to start developing relationships.

The Collect Requirements process uses analysis and decision-making techniques to evaluate and prioritize requirements. However, not all the requirements defined in this process may be included in the actual project. The final selection of requirements occurs in the next process, Define Scope (5.3).

> A requirement is a condition or capability that **MUST** be present in the finished product to satisfy a business need.

Collect Requirements I.T.T.O.

5.2 Collect Requirements	Inputs	Tools and Techniques	Outputs
	Project charter **Project management plan** • *Scope mgt. plan* • *Requirements mgt. plan* • *Stakeholder engagement plan* **Project documents** • *Assumption log* • *Lessons learned register* • *Stakeholder register* **Business documents** • *Business case* **Agreements** **EEFs** **OPAs**	**Expert judgement** **Data gathering** • *Brainstorming* • *Interviews* • *Focus groups* • *Questionnaires and surveys* • *Benchmarking* **Data analysis** • *Document analysis* **Decision making** • *Voting* • *Autocratic decision making* • *Multicriteria decision analysis* **Data representation** • *Affinity diagrams* • *Mind mapping* **Interpersonal and team skills** • *Nominal group technique* • *Observation and conversation* • *Facilitation* **Context diagrams** **Prototypes**	**Req. documentation** **Req. traceability matrix**

Key Outputs

REQUIREMENTS DOCUMENTATION

The full list of requirements compiled in this process is organized in two distinct documents: requirements documentation and requirements traceability matrix.

The requirements documentation serves to clearly define all potential project requirements needed for creating the scope baseline in process Create WBS (5.4). It should be clear how each requirement relates to and addresses the business needs of the project.

Six requirement categories are often used to classify, organize, and document each project requirement:

1. Business
2. Stakeholder
3. Solution
4. Transition or readiness
5. Product
6. Quality

Each of these requirement types is drawn from a unique perspective.

1. Business requirements are high-level needs, often listed in the charter, defining why the project is undertaken.
2. Each stakeholder defines requirements that serve their individual and department needs.
3. Solution requirements describe the traditional "feature, functions, and characteristics" of a product, service, or result often thought of when requirements are discussed. Solution requirements can be both functional and nonfunctional. Functional requirements describe what the project should execute, while nonfunctional requirements describe the general qualities the product must embody (for example, reliability, safety, and performance).
4. Transition requirements describe temporary capabilities that the project needs to move from the current to a desired state.
5. Product requirements set the conditions the project must meet, such as milestones, cost constraints, and contractual obligations.
6. Quality requirements define the conditions and criteria needed to confirm the successful completion of a project deliverable or project requirement.

> Requirement documentation details how each requirement supports the project's business need.

REQUIREMENTS TRACEABILITY MATRIX

The requirements traceability matrix organizes the requirements in a visual manner that links each requirement to the individual deliverables that satisfy it. The deliverable information is created through a technique called decomposition in Create WBS (5.4).

Attributes are recorded for each requirement, allowing each to be easily identified (by a unique identifier) and providing detailed descriptions of each.

The requirements traceability matrix is used throughout the project, specifically, to track the status and completion of deliverables and to manage changes to the product scope. As each deliverable is verified (in 8.3 Control Quality) and formally accepted (in 5.5 Validate Scope), the requirements traceability matrix is updated. The concepts of deliverable verification and acceptance will be explained in detail later.

> The requirements traceability matrix is used to track the status of requirements throughout the project.

Key Inputs

PROJECT MANAGEMENT PLAN

Scope, **requirements**, and **stakeholder management plans** are key inputs informing the approach to collect requirements and define the scope. More specifically, the requirements management plan defines the approach to be followed in collecting, documenting, and analyzing the project requirements.

PROJECT CHARTER

The high-level requirements defined in the project charter are the starting place for requirement development.

PROJECT AND BUSINESS DOCUMENTS

Stakeholders often contribute to requirement development. The **stakeholder register** lists the individuals who can help create, evaluate, and prioritize the full list of requirements.

As the list is completed, the **assumption log** provides context that could impact the requirements developed, and the **lessons learned register** provides best practices for completing the Collect Requirements process.

AGREEMENTS

If agreements are involved, they must be evaluated, as they contain project and product requirements.

Key Tools and Techniques

DATA GATHERING

Several data gathering techniques can help project managers draw requirements from stakeholders:

- Brainstorming
- One-on-one interviews (formal or informal)
- Focus groups
- Questionnaires and surveys
- Benchmarking

For many project managers, a **stakeholder workshop** is a cost- and time-effective method for developing and evaluating a large number of requirements. In such a workshop—commonly managed by **facilitators**—stakeholders work together to develop, evaluate, and prioritize requirements at one time.

> A trained facilitator is often used in the Collect Requirements process to get requirements from stakeholders and others with expert judgement.

DATA ANALYSIS

In addition to stakeholders, **document analysis** provides fertile opportunities for uncovering additional project requirements. The documents that may be analyzed include the following:

- Agreements
- Business plans
- Current process flows
- Policies and procedures
- Regulatory documentation
- Problem or issue logs

DATA REPRESENTATION

The goal of this process is for the team (project team and stakeholders) to create a detailed list of prioritized requirements that will be used in the Define Scope process. Data representation techniques are used to organize and present the requirements visually, helping the team to gain different perspectives.

Affinity diagrams classify requirements into distinct groups for review and analysis.

Mind mapping is used when multiple independent brainstorming sessions have been conducted. The results of these sessions are combined into one shared map, which is used to identify similarities and differences, and potentially develop additional requirement ideas.

Context diagrams are scope models that portray the total product scope by visually representing how business systems, people, and other systems interact.

<u>DECISION MAKING</u>

Multiple decision-making techniques are used to come to an agreement on the list of requirements and prioritize them.

Project managers who choose **autocratic decision-making** decide for the entire group.

Multicriteria decision-analysis uses systematic ranking criteria to evaluate and rank requirements.

Voting is also commonly used to gain consensus on and prioritize requirements. The three major voting approaches are defined below:

- Unanimity—decision is achieved when everyone agrees on a single course of action
- Majority—decision is achieved when more than 50% of voters agree
- Plurality—decision is achieved by the largest voting bloc, even if a majority is not achieved

The **nominal group technique** is a structured, four-step, brainstorming and voting method used to determine the most important ideas for further brainstorming.

The four-step process is as follows:

1. A question or problem is presented to the group, and everyone silently records their ideas.
2. The facilitator records all ideas on a flip chart.
3. Each idea is discussed until everyone fully understands it.
4. A round of voting is conducted. Everyone ranks each idea on a scale of 1 to 5. The highest-ranked ideas are selected for further brainstorming. Multiple voting rounds are conducted to constantly improve the ideas selected.

> Prototyping a model of the potential product and providing it for review can be a fast and inexpensive method of obtaining feedback on requirements.

The last few weeks had been difficult. Both Sara and Lloyd had disciplined John for the decisions he had made. The feedback was tough and hard to hear, but John ultimately knew that they were right. He wasn't following the process and instead was attempting to find shortcuts.

After deep reflection, John realized his approach compromised the project's long-term success, and he decided to change. He vowed not to pursue any shortcuts and instead was now focusing his energy on two activities: fully developing all the subsidiary plans and bringing all stakeholders into alignment on the project fundamentals and the plans for moving forward.

His return to the fundamentals had begun to show positive results. In completing the overall project management and scope management plans, he quickly realized that most of the stakeholders were open to the prospect of improvement and eager to help.

Excited by this success and appetite to continue making progress, John scheduled a three-hour group meeting with all project stakeholders. The instructions were simple: "Bring your ideas for the most important requirements of the project."

Fueled with coffee and donuts, the team started like a rocket. John had obtained a trained facilitator from the PMO office. The facilitator was leading the meeting and everyone was offering requirement ideas, jotting them down on sticky notes and slapping them on a white board. During the session John worked one on one with the stakeholders to help them improve their ideas, ensuring every requirement was clear and quantifiable.

After one and a half hours, the wall looked wild—sticky notes everywhere. John wondered how he would make sense of them all. Detecting his worry, the facilitator leaned over and whispered to John, "Don't look so confused. We are almost there. All we must do is organize these into groups. Let's let them take a swing at it."

With that, the facilitator turned his back to the team and started moving notes around. He motioned for the team to stand up and help, telling them to group similar requirements together. Over the next 30 minutes, order began to appear. When it was all done, the team had organized all the requirements into three categories. Surprisingly, during the effort, a few requirements were discarded and a few new ones popped up.

The facilitator started clapping and remarked, "Good work! Now vote on which requirements are most important to the project. Put these on the highest-value ideas." He handed five small red stickers to every stakeholder. It took 15 minutes for everyone to vote, and afterwards the consensus of the room was obvious. Some requirements obtained no stickers, most gathered a few, but a core group was covered in red.

CASE STUDY QUESTIONS: "THE ART OF GATHERING REQUIREMENTS"

Which tool and technique did the facilitator use to help gather and develop requirements?

a. Interview
b. Brainstorming
c. Focus group
d. Mind mapping

Which tool and technique was used to organize the requirements generated?

a. Affinity diagram
b. Mind mapping
c. Context diagram
d. Chartering

Which tool and technique was used to rank the requirements?

a. Autocratic decision making
b. Multicriteria decision analysis
c. Nominal group technique
d. Voting

On which document should John record the requirements?

a. Project charter
b. Requirements traceability matrix
c. Assumption log
d. Business case

CASE STUDY ANSWERS: "THE ART OF GATHERING REQUIREMENTS"

Which tool and technique did the facilitator use to help gather and develop requirements?

a. Interview
b. Brainstorming
c. Focus group
d. Mind mapping

Which tool and technique was used to organize the requirements generated?

a. Affinity diagram
b. Mind mapping
c. Context diagram
d. Chartering

Which tool and technique was used to rank the requirements?

a. Autocratic decision making
b. Multicriteria decision analysis
c. Nominal group technique
d. Voting

On which document should John record the requirements?

a. Project charter
b. Requirements traceability matrix
c. Assumption log
d. Business case

DEFINE SCOPE (*PMBOK GUIDE*® 5.3)

Summary

The Collect Requirements process developed and prioritized an extensive list of product requirements. Significant effort was made to understand each stakeholder's unique vision of requirements. The Define Scope process builds on the work done in the Collect Requirements process to prune that list into the essential requirements that the project will deliver. This process uses that final list of requirements to craft a clear description of the project scope, known as the project scope statement. This is the key output of Define Scope.

> A well-defined scope statement creates clear boundaries, reducing scope creep.
> Scope creep: Expansion of project work beyond the project boundaries

Define Scope I.T.T.O.

5.3 Define Scope	Inputs	Tools and Techniques	Outputs
	Project charter **Project management plan** • *Scope mgt. plan* **Project documents** • *Assumption log* • *Requirements documentation* • *Risk register* **EEFs** **OPAs**	**Expert judgement** **Data analysis** • *Alternatives generation* **Decision making** • *Multicriteria decision analysis* • *Facilitation* **Product analysis**	**Project scope statement** **Project doc. updates** • *Assumption log* • *Req. documentation* • *Req. traceability matrix* • *Stakeholder register*

Key Outputs

PROJECT SCOPE STATEMENT

The project scope statement is a detailed definition of the project and product scope, major deliverables, assumptions, and constraints. This statement clearly defines what is in the scope of the project and what is excluded.

The scope statement is a great centering tool, aligning the team and all stakeholders behind the product characteristics (product scope); the verifiable products, results, and capabilities to be produced (deliverables); and the criteria that must be met before deliverables are accepted (acceptance criteria).

Details from the scope statement will be used in Create WBS (5.4) to produce the scope baseline. The bounds defined in the scope statement will be used to evaluate all future change requests to determine if project boundaries are being violated.

The project scope statement includes the product scope; however, project and product scope differ in what they describe.

- Project scope describes the work performed to deliver a product, service, or result.
- Product scope describes the features and functions of the actual product, service, or result.

Additionally, the completion of each type of scope is measured against different standards:

- Project scope is measured against the project management plan.
- Product scope is measured against the product requirements.

> Project scope and product scope are different!
> Product scope is included **within** the project scope.

PROJECT DOCUMENTS UPDATES

Commonly, the **assumption log**, **requirements documentation**, **requirements traceability matrix**, and **stakeholder register** must be updated to reflect additional project details discovered in the creation of the scope statement.

Key Inputs

PROJECT CHARTER AND PROJECT DOCUMENTS

The project and requirement information in the **charter** and the **requirements documentation**, **assumption log, and risk register** provide the details needed to create the scope statement.

Key Tools and Techniques

Transforming the information in the charter and project documents requires expert judgement to conduct analysis, provide perspective, and share lessons learned.

EXPERT JUDGEMENT

Expert judgement is used to analyze project documents and requirements and select the project specifications used to build the scope statement.

DATA AND PRODUCT ANALYSIS

Decision making is supported through both data and product analysis.

Alternatives analysis is a data analysis method in which multiple potential approaches to meet each requirement and achieve each objective are proposed and evaluated.

Product analysis is used to define products and services by systematically asking questions about the desired product or service and crafting answers to describe its use and characteristics. When needed, the answer is further decomposed until the required level of detail is obtained.

DECISION MAKING

Multicriteria decision analysis is a common technique used to analyze scope characteristics against a set of defined criteria.

CREATE WBS (*PMBOK GUIDE®* 5.4)

Summary

The Create WBS process is the final scope process in the Planning process group. This process builds on the project scope statement, created in Define Scope (5.3), to package the scope baseline. The scope baseline is one of the three foundational baselines (scope, cost, schedule) guiding the project. The scope baseline is composed of three documents: scope statement, work breakdown structure (WBS), and work breakdown structure dictionary.

The WBS translates the project scope statement into actionable work that must be delivered. Completion of the Create WBS process requires that the scope baseline be approved by the project sponsor. Once approved, the scope is cemented, and any changes to the scope baseline require the use of the Integrated Change Control process.

> Three documents make up the scope baseline:
> (1) scope statement, (2) work breakdown structure (WBS), and (3) WBS dictionary.

Create WBS I.T.T.O.

5.4 Create WBS	Inputs	Tools and Techniques	Outputs
	Project management plan • *Scope mgt. plan* **Project documents** • *Project scope statement* • *Requirements documentation* **EEFs** **OPAs**	**Expert judgement** **Decomposition**	**Scope baseline** **Project documents updates** • *Assumption log* • *Req. documentation*

Key Outputs

<u>SCOPE BASELINE</u>

As mentioned earlier, the scope baseline is a combination of three documents: scope statement, work breakdown structure, and WBS dictionary.

The scope baseline establishes the standard by which work completion is compared throughout the project. The act of evaluating and formally accepting deliverables against the acceptance criteria defined in the scope statement of the scope baseline occurs in the Monitoring and Controlling process group, as follows.

After each deliverable is produced, it is first evaluated for correctness in the Control Quality (8.3) process. Once deemed correct in terms of quality, the deliverable is considered a verified deliverable. It then passes to the Validate Scope (5.5) process as an input. The customer or sponsor inspects the verified deliverable, comparing it against the acceptance criteria defined in the **scope statement** of the scope baseline. If the deliverable meets the criteria, it becomes an accepted deliverable and formal documentation is sent to the Close Project or Phase (4.7) process.

Work Breakdown Structure (WBS)

The work breakdown structure is a decomposition of the total scope to be carried out by the team to accomplish the project objectives and create the deliverables. The WBS is an organized visual display of all the product and project work. The document is organized from top to bottom, progressively translating higher-level scope or deliverables into smaller, manageable work. Each level down of the WBS represents a definition of project work in an increasing level of detail.

The lowest level of work in the WBS is referred to as the **work package**. To assist in organization, each work package is labeled with a unique identifier. This method of numbering creates a structured code of accounts. The work packages are summed into control accounts, allowing for cost performance to be monitored throughout the project.

> "Work" refers to the deliverables produced,
> **NOT** the activities that produce the deliverables.

Work Breakdown Structure Dictionary

The work breakdown structure dictionary provides the supporting information needed to understand the WBS components. Detailed information is recorded on the delivery, activity, and schedule of every component of the WBS:

- Code of account identifier
- Description of work
- Responsible organization
- Schedule milestones
- Resources required
- Cost estimates
- Quality requirements
- Acceptance criteria

> Most of the detailed information in the WBS dictionary
> is created by other processes and added later.

<u>PROJECT DOCUMENTS UPDATES</u>

Finalizing the scope baseline and obtaining approval creates clarity in assumptions and requirements that must be updated in the **assumption log** and **requirements documentation**.

Key Inputs

<u>SCOPE MANAGEMENT PLAN</u>

The scope management plan defines how the WBS will be created from the project scope statement.

<u>PROJECT DOCUMENTS</u>

The **scope statement** and **requirements documentation** provide the foundation to create a WBS and finalize the scope baseline. The scope statement defines the work that will be performed and work that is excluded. The requirements documentation describes how each requirement meets the project's business need.

Key Tools and Techniques

DECOMPOSITION

The WBS is created from the project scope statement using decomposition. Through this technique, the scope is subdivided into progressively smaller and more manageable parts. The goal is to break the work down to a level where cost and duration can be effectively managed. The bottom level of work is known as the **work package**. The specific level of decomposition differs based on the size and complexity of a project.

> The **work package** is the lowest level of the WBS and the smallest amount of work for which cost and duration can be estimated and managed.

There are multiple approaches to decomposing the WBS:

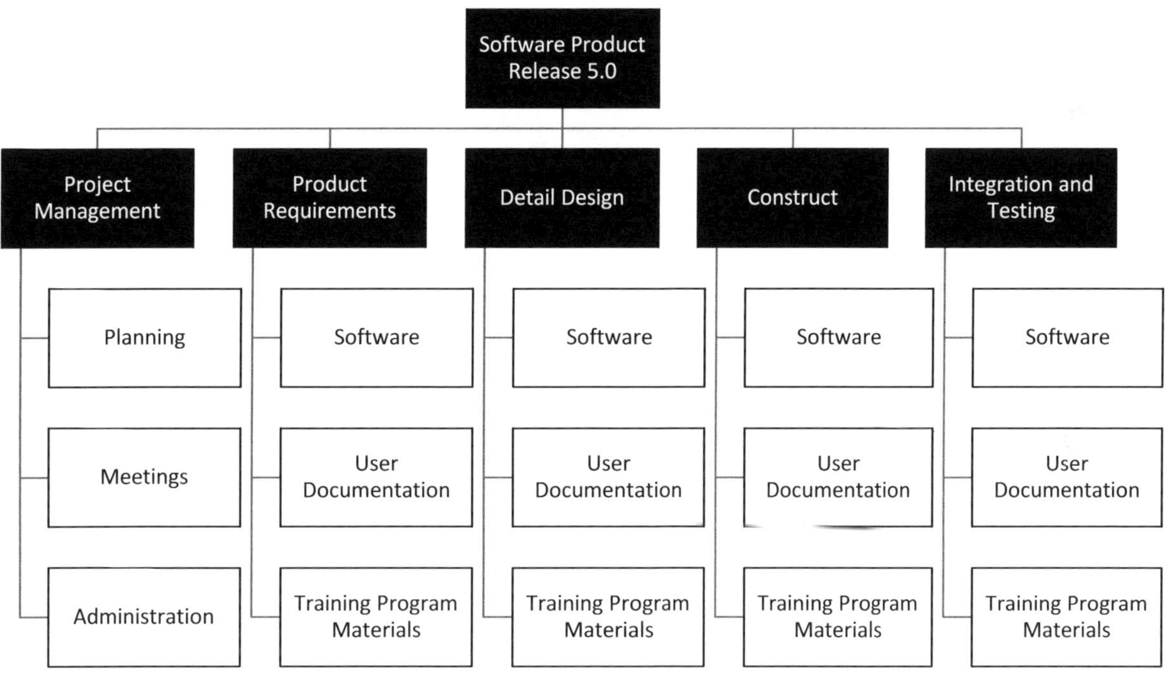

- Top-down
- Bottom-up
- Organizational-specific guidelines or WBS templates

Regardless of the technique used to create the WBS, the components should represent verifiable products, services, or results. In verifying the completion of the WBS, the project manager must confirm that the lower-level components are necessary and sufficient to deliver the higher-level components. The WBS diagram shown below is organized by project phase.

> The WBS should follow the **100% rule**: the total of all work at the lowest level (work packages) should roll up so that nothing is left out and no extra work is performed.

Case Study: "Translating Deliverables into Manageable Components"

John smiled as he finished typing a short email, "Just got agreement for the scope baseline. Thank you for your help!", and hit send.

The email was to the facilities engineering manager. The reason for the smile was that before the requirements collection workshop, the manager was a resistant stakeholder with high influence. He was upset that the project might cause his department more work, but now he was a leading supporter. What a change a month had made!

At the end of the workshop, John had noticed a slight change when the manager approached him and said, "This was actually pretty helpful. Getting everyone together and hearing their perspectives helped me see the bigger picture. Maybe I was wrong. Come by and see me next week."

John jumped to seize the opportunity, extending the request for the manager to get involved in the next Scope Management processes: "After we get out of here, we still have a lot of work to do. I'd love you and your team's help in refining the scope statement and the work breakdown structure."

Early the following week, John met with the manager and reviewed the drafts of the project scope statement, WBS, and WBS dictionary that his team had created. Surviving a strong barrage of questions, John was able to explain the purpose of each document and the assistance he needed.

Surprisingly, the manager was willing to help. He lent experienced engineers to help the team decompose the work for the work breakdown structure. Even more surprisingly, he became an ally, accompanying John to meetings with other stakeholders to review the scope baseline and negotiate support for the project.

The email was to share the good news that the sponsor had given his support for the scope baseline documents. John hoped he could keep this trend of good news going as he dove into the next challenge of developing the schedule.

Case Study Questions: "Translating Deliverables into Manageable Components"

The facilities engineering manager's attitude towards the project changed. Which document should John update to reflect this change?

a. Assumption log
b. Stakeholder assessment matrix
c. Project management plan
d. Project charter

Which three documents make up the scope baseline?

a. Project charter, scope statement, project management plan
b. Scope management plan, scope statement, WBS
c. Scope statement, WBS, WBS dictionary
d. Scope statement, WBS, assumption log

Which technique did John and team use to methodically subdivide the scope into progressively smaller and more manageable parts?

a. Benchmarking
b. Decomposition
c. Multicriteria decision making
d. Data analysis

Throughout the Create WBS process John directed the team to break down the work to a level where cost and duration could be effectively managed. Which term is used to describe this lowest level of the WBS?

a. Work plan
b. Work product
c. Work package
d. Work point

Once approved, which process must be used to evaluate and approve any requests to change the scope baseline?

a. 5.1 Plan Scope Management
b. 4.6 Perform Integrated Change Control
c. 5.4 Create WBS
d. 4.5 Monitor and Control Project Work

CASE STUDY ANSWERS: "TRANSLATING DELIVERABLES INTO MANAGEABLE COMPONENTS"

The facilities engineering manager's attitude towards the project changed. Which document should John update to reflect this change?

a. Assumption log
b. Stakeholder assessment matrix
c. Project management plan
d. Project charter

Which three documents make up the scope baseline?

a. Project charter, scope statement, project management plan
b. Scope management plan, scope statement, WBS
c. Scope statement, WBS, WBS dictionary
d. Scope statement, WBS, assumption log

Which technique did John and team use to methodically subdivide the scope into progressively smaller and more manageable parts?

a. Benchmarking
b. Decomposition
c. Multicriteria decision making
d. Data analysis

Throughout the Create WBS process John directed the team to break down the work to a level where cost and duration could be effectively managed. Which term is used to describe this lowest level of the WBS?

a. Work plan
b. Work product
c. Work package
d. Work point

Once approved, which process must be used to evaluate and approve any requests to change the scope baseline?

a. 5.1 Plan Scope Management
b. 4.6 Perform Integrated Change Control
c. 5.4 Create WBS
d. 4.5 Monitor and Control Project Work

PLAN SCHEDULE MANAGEMENT (*PMBOK GUIDE*® 6.1)

Summary

Plan Schedule Management (6.1) is the first of five schedule management processes in the Planning process group. This process is critical in that it defines how the project schedule will be developed, monitored, and controlled. The plan created is known as the schedule management plan, and it is a subsidiary plan of the overall project management plan.

The next four processes (6.2 to 6.5) use the schedule management plan to progressively translate the deliverables defined in the scope baseline into a logically sequenced work schedule of specific actions. The team will complete these actions to produce the deliverables defined.

The nature of the project environment should be considered when planning the project management approach and selecting the scheduling method to use.

Predictive Projects

Projects with lower levels of expected change often use the critical path approach to develop a complete schedule at the beginning of the project. Any changes that are needed during the project are evaluated as change requests in the Perform Integrated Change Control (4.6) process.

Adaptive or Agile Projects

In comparison, adaptive or agile projects often have a high degree of expected change. In these projects, the schedule is developed in shorter incremental portions. Short cycles of work, rapid feedback, and analysis are used to adapt the schedule as the project evolves.

> The critical path method and agile are two major scheduling approaches.

Plan Schedule Management I.T.T.O.

6.1 Plan Schedule Mgt.	Inputs	Tools and Techniques	Outputs
	Project charter **Project management plan** • *Scope mgt. plan* • *Development approach* **EEFs** **OPAs**	**Expert judgement** **Data analysis** **Meetings**	**Schedule mgt. plan**

Key Outputs

SCHEDULE MANAGEMENT PLAN

The schedule management plan is the only output of this process. The plan describes how the schedule will be developed, monitored, and controlled to ensure timely project completion. In addition to defining the sequence of activities, the schedule management plan establishes the following:

- **Project schedule model development**—method and tool used in creating the schedule model
- **Level of accuracy**—acceptable range in determining activity duration estimates
- **Units of measure**—units to quantify each resource (hours or days, time, tons, or cubic yards)
- **Project schedule model maintenance**—process to update and record progress
- **Rules of performance measurement**—EVM techniques to use
- **Reporting formats**—method and frequency of schedule reporting

Key Inputs

PROJECT CHARTER

The charter is the foundational reference used to develop the schedule management plan, because the charter contains the high-level requirements and milestone dates.

PROJECT MANAGEMENT PLAN

Additionally, the project management plan contains the **scope management plan** and the intended **development approach** (predictive vs. agile). The declared approach to how the project will function will be a critical input to developing the project schedule.

EEFs AND OPAs

Enterprise environmental factors and organizational process assets provide the foundation on which the schedule management plan is built.

- Enterprise environmental factors (EEFs) include the following:
    - Scheduling software—influences the method of scheduling and reporting
    - Standard estimating data—internal or commercial databases provide information to form scheduling
    - Team resource, skill, and physical resource availability
- Organizational process assets (OPAs) can help with the following:
    - Templates
    - Schedule development, management, and control policies (formal or informal)
    - Historical information and lessons learned
    - Monitoring and reporting tools

Key Tools and Techniques

Expert judgement from individuals with specialized expertise, experience with scheduling, or both can be used to produce a good schedule. Additionally, **data analysis** can generate the means or alternate methods for determining the best scheduling plan possible with the information available.

DEFINE ACTIVITIES (*PMBOK GUIDE®* 6.2)

Summary

The Define Activities process is the first step in transforming the scope into the detailed schedule of actions the project team will complete.

The list of activities defined as an output of this process will be used by later schedule processes to create the

- Project schedule network diagram in Sequence Activities (6.3)
- Duration estimates in Estimate Activity Durations (6.4)
- Project schedule and schedule baseline in Develop Schedule (6.5)

Additionally, a document detailing activity attributes and a milestone list are created during the Define Activities process. These two documents define the activities at a greater depth and frame the unique schedule constraints that the project must operate within.

> The Define Activities process describes the actions that deliver the deliverables defined by Create WBS (5.4).

Define Activities I.T.T.O.

6.2 Define Activities	Inputs	Tools and Techniques	Outputs
	Project charter **Project management plan** • *Schedule management plan* • *Scope baseline* **EEFs** **OPAs**	**Expert judgement** **Decomposition** **Rolling wave planning** **Meetings**	**Activity list** **Activity attributes** **Milestone list** **Change requests** **Project mgt. plan updates** • *Schedule baseline* • *Cost baseline*

Key Outputs

ACTIVITY LIST

The activity list displays all the specific actions that must be performed to produce the work packages defined in the WBS. When defining the activities, the goal is to provide a description sufficient to ensure that the team can understand the work. Specific ID numbers are assigned to activities so they can be organized and tracked.

> **Activity** is a distinct, scheduled portion of work to be performed.

ACTIVITY ATTRIBUTES

Activity attributes extend the description of activities defined in the list, providing details of the effort type required and where it will be performed. The following information is included:

- WBS ID (linking activity to WBS)
- Activity name and description
- Predecessor and successor activities
- Leads and lags
- Resource requirements

> Activity attributes <u>evolve</u> and <u>deepen</u> in description as the project progresses.

<u>MILESTONE LISTS</u>

The **milestone list** frames schedule constraints affecting the project. Each milestone defined must be categorized as mandatory (contractually obligated) or optional (based on historical information). The significant dates and events and their categorizations help provide the team with the context necessary to design a schedule that will meet the project and organizational demands.

> Milestones have **zero** duration! They define a point in time, not an activity.

<u>CHANGE REQUESTS</u>

Change requests may be required to evaluate and adjust the project to any additional work uncovered while decomposing work packages into activities. Once a baseline has been approved, all changes to add work not originally defined must be made using a change request.

> All change requests are evaluated using the
> Perform Integrated Change Control (4.6) process.

Key Inputs

<u>PROJECT MANAGEMENT PLAN</u>

The schedule management plan and scope baseline set the parameters on how the schedule will be developed and what work it needs to accomplish. The **schedule management plan** defines the schedule methodology that will be used and the level of detail necessary to manage the work. The team uses the WBS, deliverables, constraints, and assumptions defined in the **scope baseline** to drive the creation of the appropriate activities.

<u>EEFs AND OPAs</u>

The EEF and OPA factors affecting a project provide the structure on which the schedule is built and displayed and the details that help fully decompose the activities.

- **EEFs**
  - Project management information systems
  - Published commercial data

Project management information systems are used to gather, integrate, and disseminate the schedule network diagram produced as an output. Published commercial data is often used to provide details needed to better understand potential work activities.

- **OPAs**

- Lessons learned repository
- Templates
- Formal or informal policies

Lessons learned repositories often contain historical activity lists that can provide insight into how previous projects delivered similar work packages. Using templates helps to standardize activity lists in an organized format and reduce the time needed to create the lists. The formal or informal policies define schedule methodologies to follow.

Key Tools and Techniques

EXPERT JUDGEMENT AND DECOMPOSITION

Expert judgement is used in **decomposing** work packages into activities.

Decomposition is a technique for subdividing the scope and deliverables into small, manageable activities. The involvement of team members and experts in this process is essential.

ROLLING WAVE PLANNING

Rolling wave planning is an iterative technique to define activities where the near-term work is planned in detail, while further work is planned at a high level. This method allows the team to focus on the activities most critical to current progress, and provides flexibility to adjust activities in the future.

SEQUENCE ACTIVITIES (*PMBOK GUIDE®* 6.3)

Summary

The Sequence Activities process organizes the list of activities created in Define Activities (6.2) into a schedule network diagram that graphically shows the order in which work will be completed.

This schedule network diagram will be used by the later schedule processes to define

- Duration estimates in Estimate Activity Durations (6.4)
- Project schedule and schedule baseline in Develop Schedule (6.5)

Sequence Activities I.T.T.O.

	Inputs	Tools and Techniques	Outputs
6.3 Sequence Activities	**Project mgt. plan** • *Schedule mgt. plan* • *Scope baseline* **Project documents** • *Activity attributes* • *Activity list* • *Assumption log* • *Milestone list* **EEFs** **OPAs**	**Precedence diagramming method** **Dependency determination and integration** **Leads and lags** **Project mgt. information system**	**Project schedule network diagrams** **Project doc. updates** • *Activity attributes* • *Activity list* • *Assumption log* • *Milestone list*

Key Outputs

PROJECT SCHEDULE NETWORK DIAGRAM

The **project schedule network diagram** displays the sequence in which the team must complete the activities to produce the deliverables. The diagram is a visual representation of the logical relationships of all activities from start to finish.

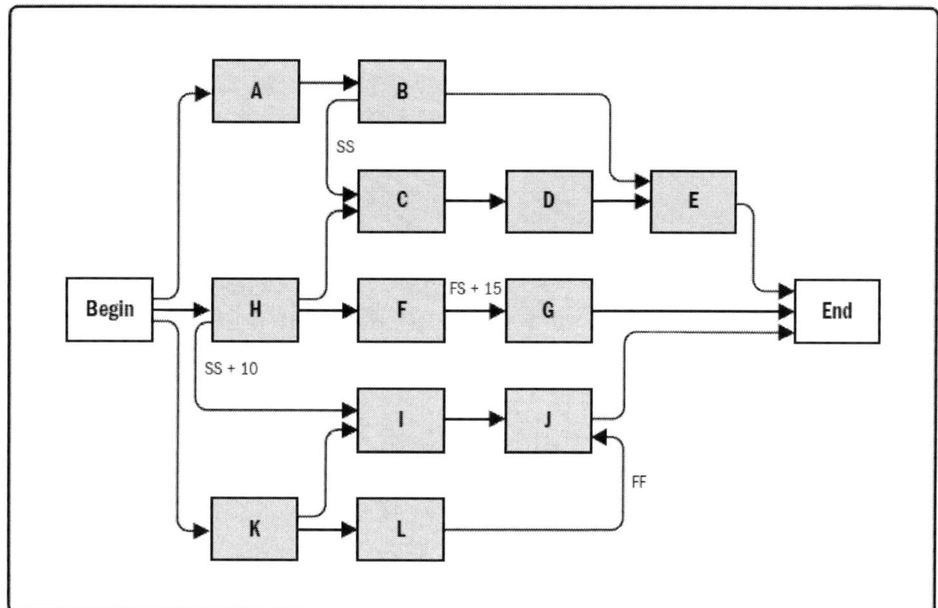

These diagrams can be created manually or by using project management software. However, regardless of the method used, the sequence of events is affected by the constraints and contingencies between activities.

PROJECT DOCUMENTS UPDATES

Project documents may be updated based on additional information uncovered while developing the project schedule network diagram:

- Activity list
- Activity attributes
- Assumption log
- Milestone list

These four documents are the same documents described in the Key Input section below.

Key Inputs

PROJECT MANAGEMENT PLAN

As similarly used in the Define Activities (6.2) process, the schedule management plan and scope baseline set the parameters on how the schedule will be developed and what work it needs to accomplish.

PROJECT DOCUMENTS

Project documents provide the details and unique project conditions that directly influence the sequence by which activities will be organized.

- **Activity list**—high-level description of every activity
- **Activity attributes**—dependency and constraint relationships between activities
- **Assumption log**—assumptions and constraints that limit options and create risks
- **Milestone list**—dates that the project must deliver

EEFs AND OPAs

The EEFs and OPAs affecting a project provide the tools with which to build the network diagram and the details that help define the relationships between activities.

- **EEFs**
  - Project scheduling software
  - Project management information system (PMIS)

The project scheduling software is used to build a network diagram, and the PMIS is used to distribute the information.

- **OPAs**
  - Lessons learned repository
  - Templates

Lessons learned repositories include historical sequence and dependency relationships between activities. Templates can provide a defined network diagram format to use.

> The software used to build a network diagram is an **EEF**.
> The process that defines how to use the software is an **OPA**.

Key Tools and Techniques

Transforming the activity list into a project schedule network diagram requires an understanding of the logical dependencies and lead vs. lag relationships between activities. A project management information system is used to display the entire network of activities in a visual format that is easy to understand.

PRECENDENCE DIAGRAMMING METHOD

The **precedence diagraming method** is used to construct a schedule by linking all activities by the sequence in which they must be performed.

All logical relationship between activities can be categorized into one of four relationship types:

- Finish-to-start (FS)
  - Successor cannot start until predecessor has finished
- Finish-to-finish (FF)
  - Successor cannot finish until predecessor has finished
- Start-to-start (SS)
  - Successor cannot start until predecessor has started
- Start-to-finish (SF)
  - Successor cannot finish until predecessor has started

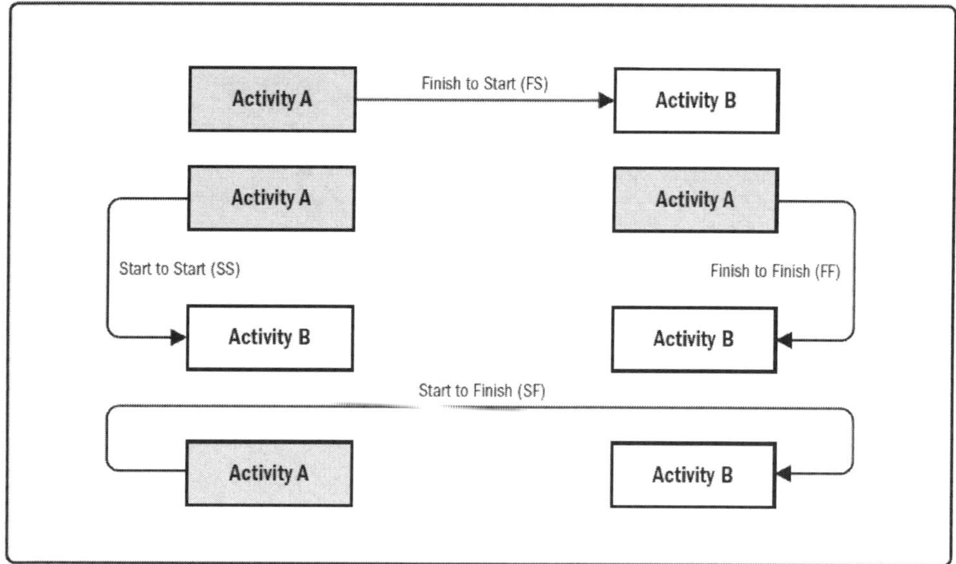

Finish-to-start (FS) is the **most common** relationship;
start-to-finish (SF) is the **least common**.

DEPENDENCY DETERMINATION AND INTEGRATION

Dependency determination and integration helps define the schedule's flexibility by defining the nature of the dependency between activities.

The four attribute types, defined below, describe the nature of dependencies between attributes. Each dependency could be described by a combination of mandatory vs. discretionary and external vs. internal attributes.

- Mandatory
- Discretionary
- External
- Internal

Mandatory dependencies are required by the nature of the work, or are legally or contractually required. In contrast, discretionary dependencies are not mandatory but preferred, usually based on best practices.

The external vs. internal designations are related to the level of control the project team holds. External dependencies are those relationships between project and non-project activities that are outside the control of the project team. Internal dependencies describe the relationships between project activities that are within the team's control.

The activity list and activity attributes **must** be updated as dependencies are better defined.

LEADS AND LAGS

Lead and lag define the start time of each activity in reference to the activities that occur directly before (predecessor) and after (successor), respectively. **Lead** is the amount of time a successor activity can be advanced with respect to a predecessor. **Lag** is the amount of time a successor activity can be delayed with respect to a predecessor.

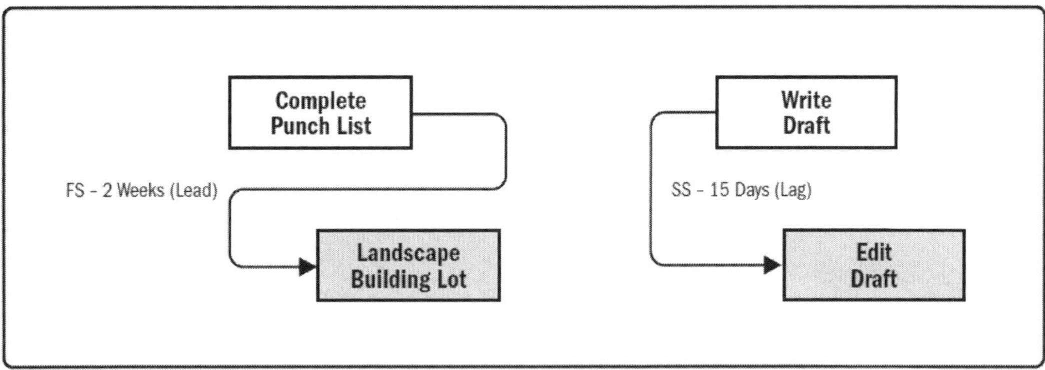

Lead moves a successor **LEFT** (earlier); lag moves it **RIGHT** (later).

PROJECT MANAGEMENT INFORMATION SYSTEM

Scheduling software used to record the schedule network diagram is held within a project management information system (PMIS). The PMIS converts dependency and lead and lag information into the graphical project schedule network diagram. Using scheduling software can help reduce the time to develop and adjust the network diagram.

ESTIMATE ACTIVITY DURATIONS (*PMBOK GUIDE*® 6.4)

Summary

Estimate Activity Durations brings depth and perspective to the project schedule network diagram by defining the amount of effort and resources each activity demands. This process uses estimating techniques to produce duration estimates for each activity that will be used by the Develop Schedule (6.5) process to create the project schedule and schedule baseline. In addition to the estimated amount of resources required, the team must also evaluate the availability and skills of the resources needed.

> Duration estimates are calculated in terms of the number of work periods needed to complete an activity.

Estimate Activity Durations I.T.T.O.

6.4 Estimate Activity Durations	Inputs	Tools and Techniques	Outputs
	Project management plan • *Schedule mgt. plan* • *Scope baseline* **Project documents** • *Activity attributes* • *Activity list* • *Assumption log* • *Lessons learned register* • *Milestone list* • *Project team assignments* • *Resource breakdown structure* • *Resource calendars* • *Resource requirements* • *Risk register* **EEFs** **OPAs**	**Expert judgement** **Analogous estimating** **Parametric estimating** **Three-point estimating** **Bottom-up estimating** **Data analysis** • *Alternatives analysis* • *Reserve analysis* **Decision making** **Meetings**	**Duration estimates** **Basis of estimates** **Project doc. updates** • *Activity attributes* • *Assumption log* • *Lessons learned register*

Key Outputs

DURATION ESTIMATES

Duration estimates define the team's expectation for the number of work periods that will realistically be required for each activity to be completed. The duration estimates are shown in quantitative terms and include a range of possible results. For example, a duration estimate of 3 weeks ± 4 days indicates that the activity will take at least 11 days and no more than 19. Incorporating realistic duration estimates into the network diagram will extend the activities out over time. The resulting schedule will be analyzed against and adjusted to fit within the project's milestones and constraints in the Develop Schedule (6.5) process.

> Duration estimates **do not** include any lags.

BASIS OF ESTIMATES

The **basis of estimates** explains the logic behind each activity estimate, helping the team and stakeholders understand and evaluate the duration estimates. The basis of estimates document records descriptive details related to the following:

- Methods used to develop the estimate
- Assumptions
- Constraints
- Estimate range
- Confidence level
- Risks that could impact the estimate

PROJECT DOCUMENTS UPDATES

The following project documents may be updated to reflect the most current information related to duration estimates and the basis of estimates:

- Activity attributes
- Assumption log
- Lessons learned register

The duration estimates calculated are inserted into the **activity attributes**. Any assumptions made in developing the duration estimates, such as skill levels required or availability, must be documented in the **assumption log**. Any efficient or poor methods of developing estimates are recorded in the **lessons learned register**.

Key Inputs

PROJECT DOCUMENTS

Project documents supply the information related to activities, team skills and resources required, and constraints necessary to create realistic in-depth activity estimates.

- **Activity list and activity attributes**—logical relationships, lead vs. lag, and dependencies
- **Milestone list**—specific key events and deadlines
- **Resource breakdown structure, resource calendars, resource requirements**—resource needs and availability
- **Assumption log, risk register, and lessons learned register**—factors that may positively or negatively impact durations

> Estimating uses documents produced by Planning processes in multiple knowledge areas (Project Integration, Schedule, Resources, Risk).

EEFS AND OPAS

EEFs and OPAs provide more detailed and organizational specific information that is used to accurately estimate activity durations.

- **EEFs**
    - Duration-estimating databases
    - Productivity metrics
    - Team member locations

- **OPAs**
    - Historical duration information
    - Project calendars
    - Estimating policies
    - Lessons learned—methods to estimate effectively

Key Tools and Techniques

Four estimating techniques are commonly used to translate project and activity information into the duration estimates that the next schedule process, Develop Schedule (6.5), requires. Develop Schedule will use the estimates to build out the project schedule and schedule baseline.

- Analogous estimating
- Parametric estimating
- Bottom-up estimating
- Three-point estimating

ANALOGOUS ESTIMATING

Analogous estimating uses historical data from similar projects to produce a gross value estimate for a project's activity duration.

This method is typically used when limited data of a current project is available. To account for this deficiency, specific parameters from previous comparable projects are used. When analogous estimating is used, the size and complexity of the comparable project must be considered. The method is most reliable when the previous activities are similar in fact, not just appearance.

> Analogous estimating is less costly and time consuming than other estimating methods. However, it is also the **least** accurate.

PARAMETRIC ESTIMATING

Parametric estimating uses a statistical or numerical relationship to calculate activity durations.

The algorithms used can be derived from historical data or established industry standards. This method can be applied to an entire project or a section of a project. The quality of the estimate is directly related to the accuracy of the model or algorithm.

Here is a simple example of parametric estimating to calculate the labor hours to lay flooring in a construction project: (100 sq. feet of flooring) × (2 labor hours required per sq. foot) = 200 labor hours.

BOTTOM-UP ESTIMATING

Bottom-up estimating aggregates estimates of individual lower-level activities to create the project duration. As the name implies, starting at the work package level (lowest level), individual activities are estimated and rolled up to each component of the WBS. When work cannot be confidently estimated, the activity is decomposed further. This is the most precise method of estimating; however, it is time-consuming and requires the participation of team members, as well as requiring **expert judgement**.

> Bottom-up estimating requires significant resources and time, but can be **very accurate**.

THREE-POINT ESTIMATING

Three-point estimating uses a mathematical equation—the triangular distribution—to incorporate risk and uncertainty into the estimate. The triangular distribution method is used to calculate the expected activity duration when limited historical data is available.

This calculation method operates under the assumption that you have created three activity duration estimates:

- Most likely (tM)
- Optimistic (tO)—best case
- Pessimistic (tP)—worst case

Notice that there is a variable (tM, tO, or tP) listed next to each estimation. Each of these variables will be used in the three-point cost estimating equations. These variable types and the equation will also be used to calculate cost estimates in the Estimate Costs (7.2) process.

On the exam, you will be given best-case, most-likely, and worst-case estimates and will be asked to calculate the overall schedule estimate (tE) using the triangular distribution:

$$tE = (tO + tM + tP) / 3$$

DATA ANALYSIS

Developing the most realistic activity estimates requires alternatives analysis and reserve analyses.

Alternatives analysis is used to determine the optimal approach to accomplish specific work. This type of analysis involves evaluating resource allocation levels, schedule compression techniques, and make-or-buy decisions.

Reserve analysis is used to calculate the amount of contingency and management reserves that must be allocated to account for potential risks in activities.

- Contingency reserves address known-unknowns (for example, project expects rework, but the exact amount is unknown).
- Management reserves address unknown-unknowns (unforeseen work).

> When creating the schedule baseline in 6.5, contingency reserves **are** included, but management reserves are **not**.

EXERCISE: "ACTIVITY DURATION ESTIMATION"

You are the project manager of a project to develop a new organic energy drink. You are estimating the activity time required for obtaining a new formulation that meets organic standards and is chemically stable. The most likely estimate is 15 days, the most optimistic is 13 days, and the worst case is 23 days.

What is the estimated activity duration (using the three-point estimating method)?

a. 13 days
b. 15.3 days
c. 17 days
d. 19 days

Using the three-point estimating method

- tE = (tO + tM + tP) / 3
- cE = (13 days + 15 days + 23 days) / 3
- **cE = 17 days**

EXERCISE ANSWER: "ACTIVITY DURATION ESTIMATION"

You are the project manager of a project to develop a new organic energy drink. You are estimating the activity time required for obtaining a new formulation that meets organic standards and is chemically stable. The most likely estimate is 15 days, the most optimistic is 13 days, and the worst case is 23 days.

What is the estimated activity duration (using the three-point estimating method)?

a. 13 days
b. 15.3 days
c. 17 days
d. 19 days

DEVELOP SCHEDULE (*PMBOK GUIDE*® 6.5)

Summary

The Develop Schedule process uses the schedule activities, sequences, and estimates created by processes 6.2–6.4 to define a comprehensive final schedule model and schedule baseline.

Creating the model is the final schedule process that completes that task of transforming the scope into a detailed and realistic schedule with clearly defined planned dates for activity and project completion.

Before the schedule can be officially acted upon, it must be formally approved by the sponsor. The approved schedule model becomes the schedule baseline, which is used throughout the project to

- Track and evaluate project progress (6.6 Control Schedule)
- Evaluate the impact of change requests (4.6 Perform Integrated Change Control)

Develop Schedule I.T.T.O.

6.5 Develop Schedule	Inputs	Tools and Techniques	Outputs
	Project management plan • *Schedule mgt. plan* • *Scope baseline* **Project documents** • *Activity attributes* • *Activity list* • *Assumption log* • *Basis of estimates* • *Duration estimates* • *Milestone list* • *Proj. schedule network diagrams* • *Project team assignments* • *Resource calendars* • *Resource requirements* • *Risk register* **Agreements** **EEFs** **OPAs**	**Schedule network analysis** **Critical path method** **Resource optimization** **Data analysis** • *What-if scenario analysis* • *Simulation* **Leads and lags** **Schedule compression** **Proj. mgt. information system** **Agile release planning**	**Schedule baseline** **Project schedule** **Schedule data** **Project calendars** **Change requests** **Proj. mgt. plan updates** • *Schedule mgt. plan* • *Cost baseline* **Project doc. updates** • *Activity attributes* • *Assumption log* • *Duration estimates* • *Lessons learned register* • *Resource requirements* • *Risk register*

Key Outputs

SCHEDULE BASELINE

The **schedule baseline** is the approved version of the schedule model used to evaluate actual vs. planned progress throughout the project.

The baseline defines the project's start and finish dates and must be approved by the project sponsor. Once approved, the schedule baseline can only be changed using the Perform Integrated Change Control process.

The project's schedule variance will be determined in Control Schedule (6.6) by comparing actual progress against the schedule baseline.

> The schedule baseline is one of the project's three baselines: **scope**, **schedule**, and **cost**.

PROJECT SCHEDULE

The **project schedule** is the final schedule model, fully incorporating all activity interactions, resource requirements, and schedule constraints in a clear visual format.

The schedule defines the planned start and finish dates for the project and all activities by

- Linking activities
- Inserting durations
- Defining and incorporating milestones
- Incorporating and adjusting to meet resource requirements

The three most common schedule modeling methods are bar chart, milestone chart, and project schedule network diagram.

Bar charts present the sequence and duration of activities using horizontal bars to represent start and finish dates. The format is known as a Gantt chart and provides for simple evaluation of current project progress. The Gantt chart allows the flexibility to consolidate or break apart activities to show the level of detail desired.

Activity Identifier	Activity Description	Calendar units	Project Schedule Time Frame				
			Period 1	Period 2	Period 3	Period 4	Period 5
1.1	Develop and Deliver New Product Z	120					
1.1.1	Work Package 1: Component 1	67					
1.1.2	Work Package 2: Component 2	53					
1.1.3	Work Package 3: Integrated Components 1 and 2	53					

Milestone charts use the same background structure as bar charts, but only show milestone dates, such as the schedule start and completion of deliverables. Key dates are often identified using diamonds. The simple display focuses attention on key dates without distractions.

Activity Identifier	Activity Description	Calendar units	Project Schedule Time Frame				
			Period 1	Period 2	Period 3	Period 4	Period 5
1.1.MB	Begin New Product Z	0					
1.1.1.M1	Complete Component 1	0					
1.1.2.M1	Complete Component 2	0					
1.1.3.M1	Complete Integration of Components 1 & 2	0					
1.1.3.MF	Finish New Product Z	0					

The **project schedule network diagram** is the most detailed schedule model, using both bars and activity-on-node format to show all activities and critical paths. The diagram provides a visual representation of the relationships between activities, key milestones, and activities on the critical path.

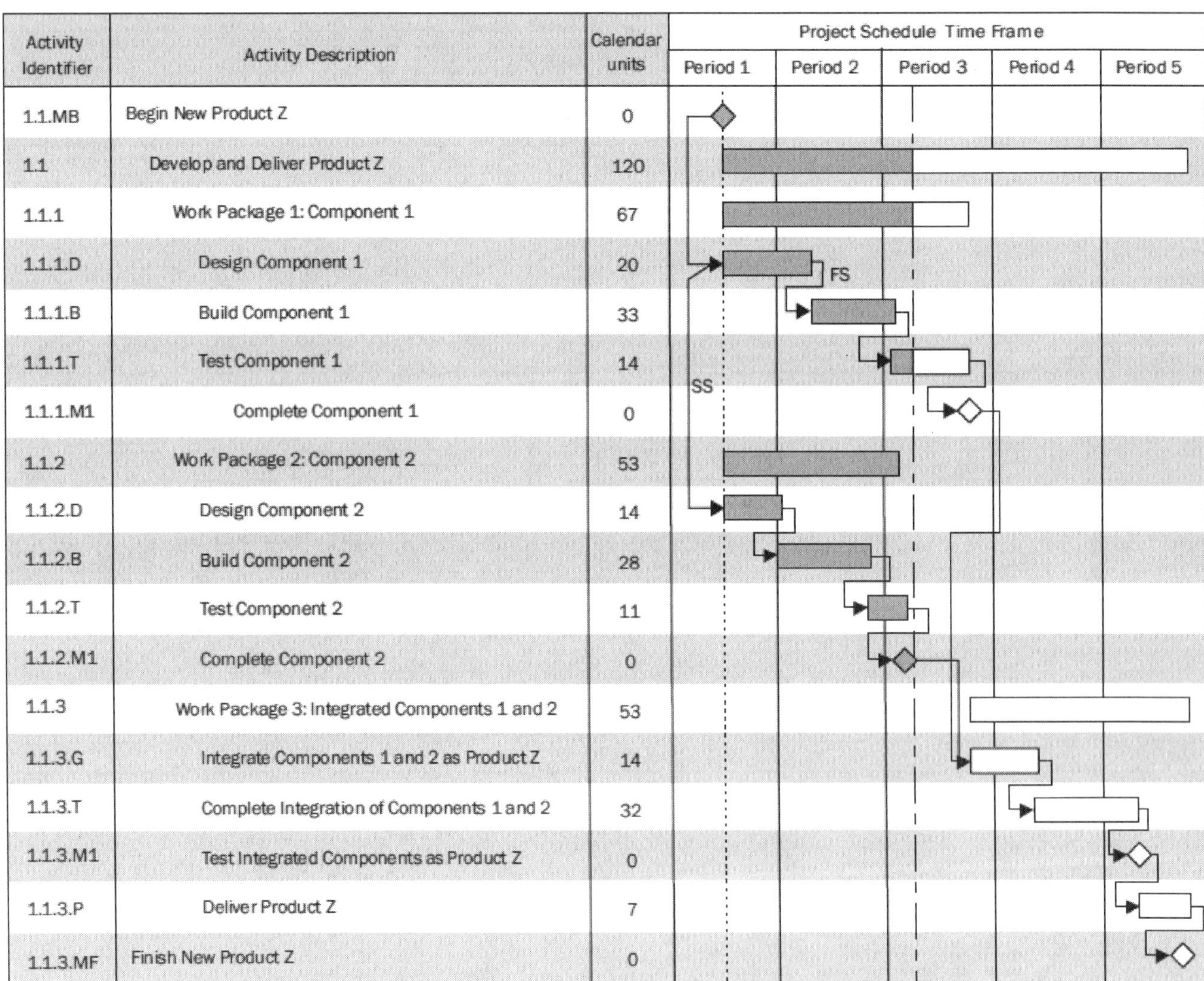

Activity Identifier	Activity Description	Calendar units	Project Schedule Time Frame				
			Period 1	Period 2	Period 3	Period 4	Period 5
1.1.MB	Begin New Product Z	0					
1.1	Develop and Deliver Product Z	120					
1.1.1	Work Package 1: Component 1	67					
1.1.1.D	Design Component 1	20					
1.1.1.B	Build Component 1	33					
1.1.1.T	Test Component 1	14					
1.1.1.M1	Complete Component 1	0					
1.1.2	Work Package 2: Component 2	53					
1.1.2.D	Design Component 2	14					
1.1.2.B	Build Component 2	28					
1.1.2.T	Test Component 2	11					
1.1.2.M1	Complete Component 2	0					
1.1.3	Work Package 3: Integrated Components 1 and 2	53					
1.1.3.G	Integrate Components 1 and 2 as Product Z	14					
1.1.3.T	Complete Integration of Components 1 and 2	32					
1.1.3.M1	Test Integrated Components as Product Z	0					
1.1.3.P	Deliver Product Z	7					
1.1.3.MF	Finish New Product Z	0					

SCHEDULE DATA

Detailed **schedule data** is defined and recorded while creating the project schedule model. It provides detailed and descriptive information into the project's milestones, schedule activities, resource requirements over time, activity attributes, assumptions, and constraints. The schedule data developed is recorded in the appropriate **project documents**.

The graph below is an example of the detailed schedule data produced. The graph is a resource histogram, depicting the weekly resource requirement against the internal capacity available.

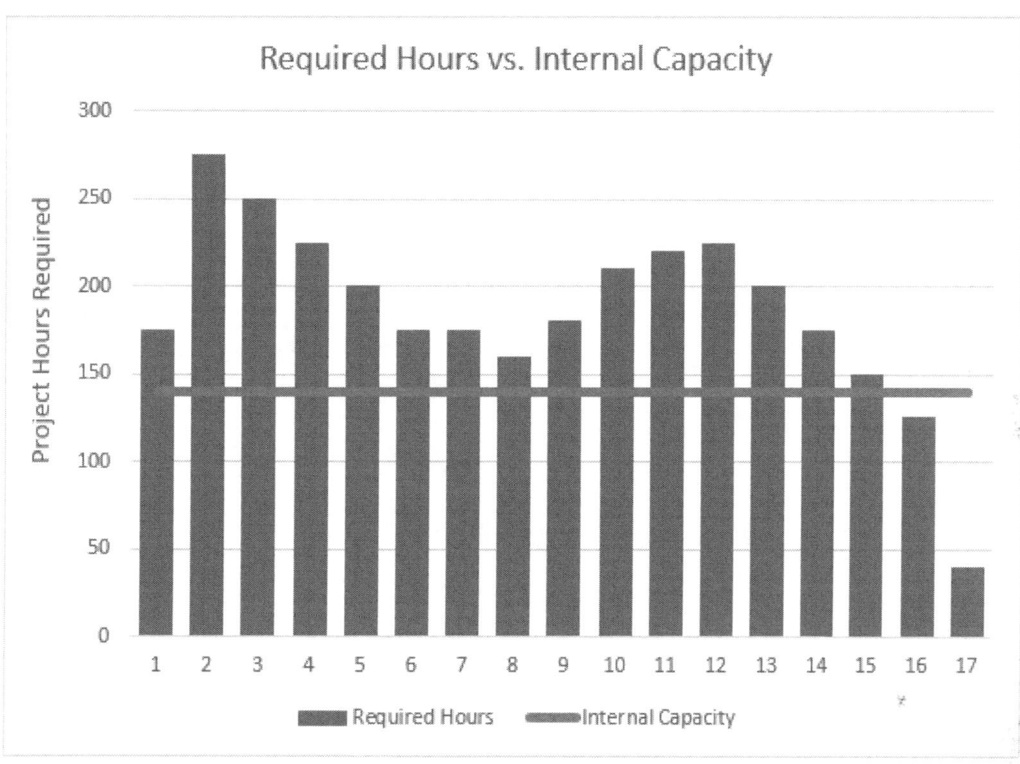

PROJECT CALENDAR

The **project calendar** visually depicts the days and shifts when scheduled activities can be completed (available vs. non-available days). Individual calendars can be established to define work schedules for different activities.

CHANGE REQUESTS

Modifications to the project schedule, during creation, may necessitate changes to the scope or cost baselines. All modifications to an approved baseline must pass through the Perform Integrated Change Control (4.6) process.

Key Inputs

The schedule plan, numerous project documents, agreements, and the scope baseline provide the information needed to build and test the schedule model.

PROJECT MANAGEMENT PLAN

The **schedule management plan** defines the scheduling method and the software to be used.

Remember, the **scope baseline** is made up of the **scope statement**, **WBS**, and **WBS** dictionary. These three documents provide project deliverable details that must be considered when building the schedule model.

PROJECT DOCUMENTS

Sequencing project activities requires a detailed understanding of multiple project aspects. The key information required and the project documents that supplies it are defined below:

- Work periods per activity (duration estimates)
- Predecessor and successor relationships (activity attributes)
- Lead and lags (activity attributes)
- Resource requirements and availability (resource requirements, resource calendars)
- Key milestones (milestone list)
- Key assumptions (assumption log)

AGREEMENTS

The schedule of how and when vendors will perform their work must be incorporated into the schedule model.

> The schedule model incorporates project document outputs from Risk, Schedule, Project Integration, and Resource Mgt. processes.

Key Tools and Techniques

SCHEDULE NETWORK ANALYSIS

Schedule model development is an iterative activity involving progressive testing and refinement to optimize resource utilization and meet milestone dates.

Multiple focused techniques are used to complete a thorough analysis:

- Critical path method
- Resource optimization
- What-if scenarios
- Simulation analysis
- Schedule compression

By conducting multifaceted analysis, the project team can calculate the longest path through the project (critical path) and define opportunities to reduce risk, improve timing, and optimize resource allocations.

CRITICAL PATH METHOD

The **critical path method** provides an understanding of the minimum project duration and the flexibility available in the schedule by analyzing the path of activities needed to complete the project.

The sequence of activities with the longest path through the project is known as the critical path. Identifying it is important because the length of time of the critical path is also the shortest possible project duration. Activities on the critical path have the lowest amount of flexibility in when they can be completed. This flexibility is defined as **float**.

> The critical path is defined as the sequence of activities that represents the **longest path** through the project, which determines the **shortest possible project duration**.

In critical path methodology there are two types of float: free float and total float. Free float measures the amount that an individual activity can be delayed without affecting the early start date of any successor activity. Total float is the amount of time a schedule activity can be delayed from its early start date without delaying the project finish date. The critical path has the least total float, usually zero.

> Free and total float measure the amount of time an activity can be delayed ***DIFFERENTLY***.
> **Free float** = Without delaying the early start of a successor activity
> **Total float** = Without delaying the project finish date

Completing the critical path method of analysis involves a structured approach to building and analyzing a project's network diagram. This analysis determines each activity's

- Early start
- Early finish
- Late start
- Late finish

These values are used to calculate the free float and total float, and identify the critical path. A complete example is provided on the next pages to help you understand the critical path method.

First, you must understand the basic structure that will be used. The critical path method is called activity-on-node (AON) or precedence diagramming method (PDM). This method represents each activity in a project sequence as a node.

The critical path method begins with defining the structure of the information on each node. Each node is structured to display information as shown in the next image.

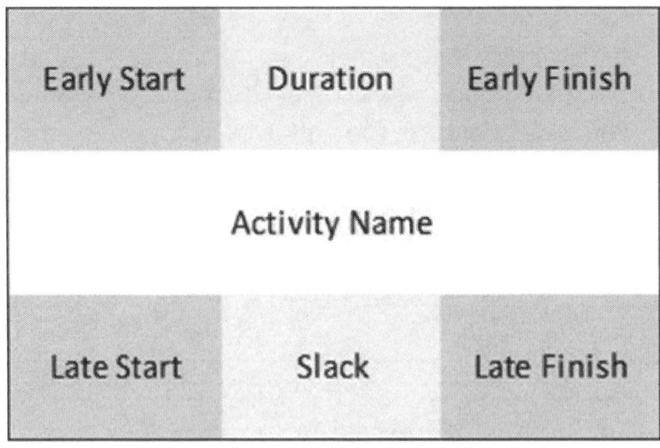

The critical path method follows a structured approach. The key portion of the method is completing the forward pass and the backward pass. The following steps will be explained in detail.

1. Build the network diagram
2. Insert the duration of activities
3. Conduct forward pass
4. Conduct backward pass
5. Calculate float to determine critical path

1. Building a network diagram

The network diagram is the foundation of the critical path method. In terms of PMP® processes, the project sequence network diagram is produced as an output of Sequence Activities (6.3).

On the exam, the network diagram may or may not be provided. If it is not provided, you will be given a chart that lists the activities and details for each. To answer these questions, you must first construct the network diagram.

This example will use data from the table below:

Activity Name	Predecessor Activity	Relationship	Duration	Dependency
A	Start	Finish-Start	1	Mandatory
B	A	Finish-Start	3	Mandatory
E	B	Finish-Start	4	Mandatory
H	E	Finish-Start	4	Mandatory
K	H, I, J	Finish-Start	4	Mandatory
C	A	Finish-Start	2	Mandatory
F	D, C	Finish-Start	4	Mandatory
I	E, F	Finish-Start	2	Mandatory
D	A	Finish-Start	5	Mandatory
G	D	Finish-Start	3	Mandatory
J	G	Finish-Start	7	Discretionary

Based on the information in the previous table, construct the network diagram using the structured relationships defined. Since all the relationships are based on the commonly used start-finish relationship, there is no special notation. Notice that the relationship between G and J is discretionary. You should produce a network diagram that looks like the next image.

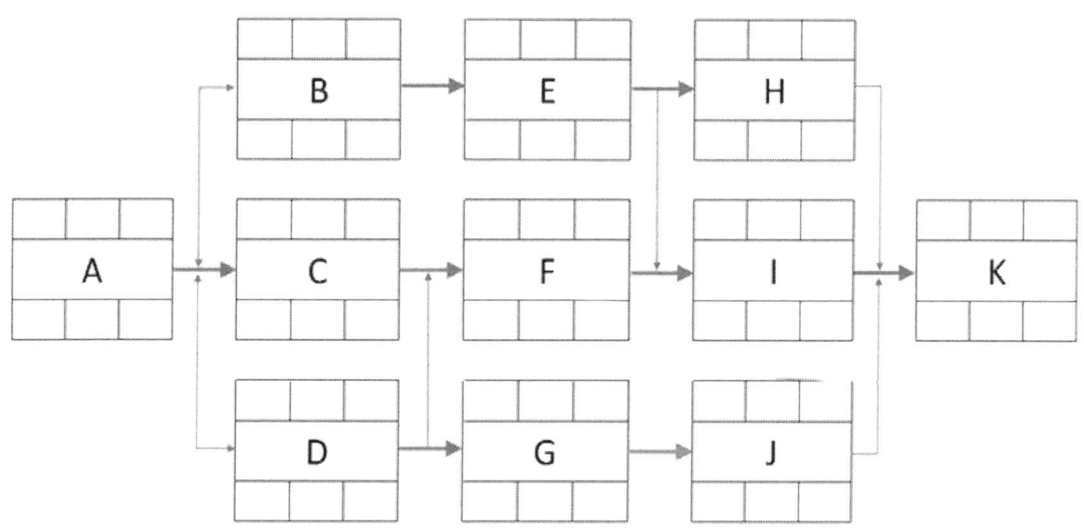

2. Insert the duration of activities

Once the network diagram is created, the next step is to fill in the durations based on the data provided in the table.

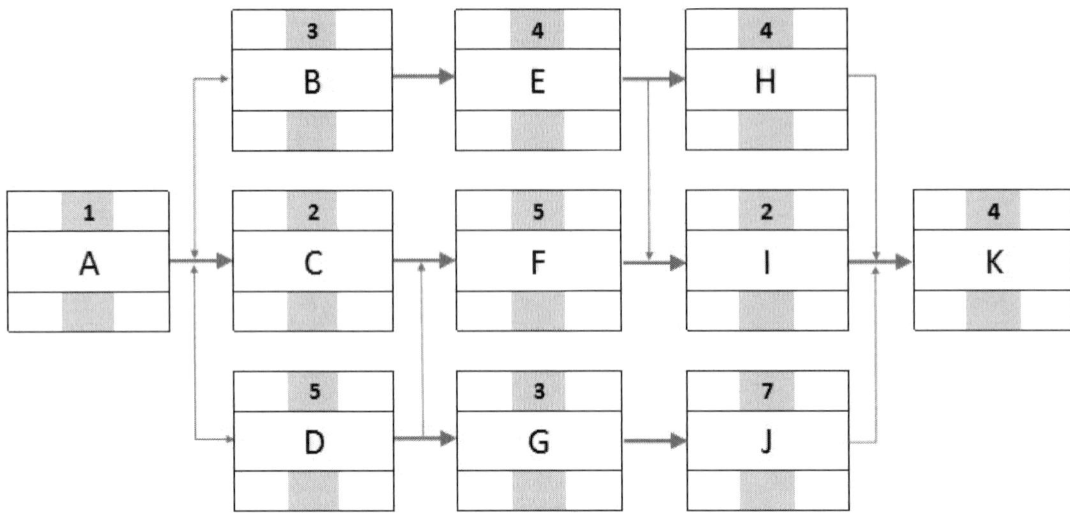

3. Conduct forward pass

The forward pass is used to calculate the early start and finish of each activity. The process for conducting the forward pass is as follows:

- Starting with the first node (activity A)
  - Insert early start
  - First activity early start = 0
- Calculate the early finish for each node
  - Early finish = Early start + Duration
  - Translate the early finish to early start of all successors
  - When two activities flow into one activity (E and F into I), use the later of the early finishes (**11** vs. 8)
- Calculate early start and early finish for all nodes

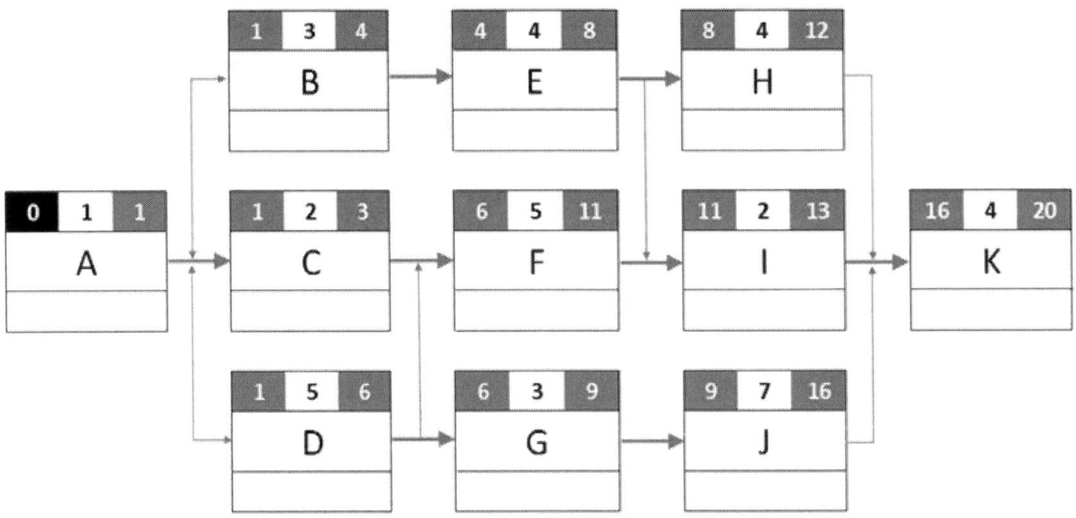

4. Conduct backward pass

The backward pass is used to calculate the amount of freedom a path or activity has before it affects the critical path. The process for conducting the backward pass is as follows:

- Starting with the first node, the far right node (activity K)
  - Copy the early finish into the late finish section
    - Example: Late finish = 20
- Calculate the late start of each node
  - Late start = Late finish - Duration
  - Translate the late start to late finish of predecessor
  - When two activities flow back into one activity (F and G into D), use the later of the early late starts (**6** vs. 9)
- Calculate late finish and late start for all nodes

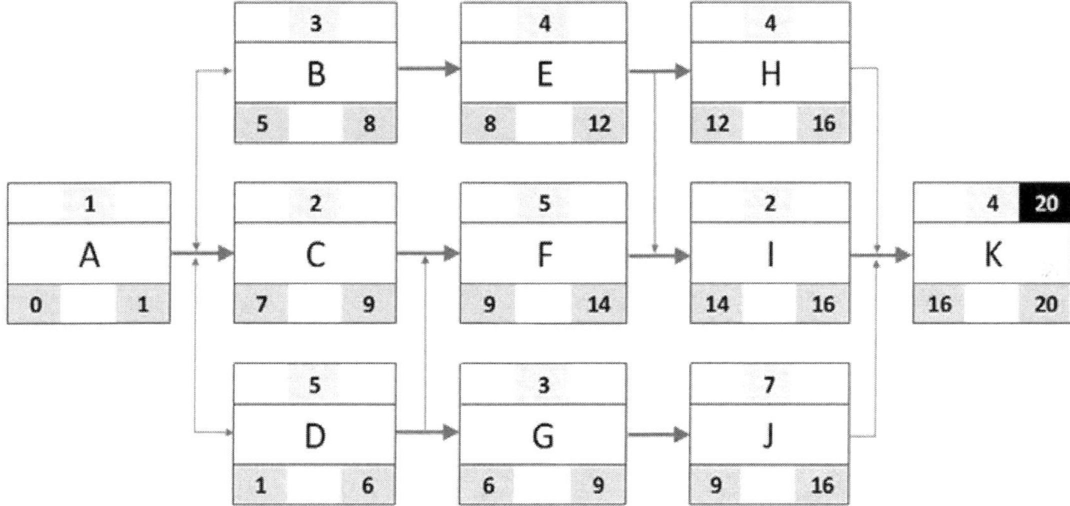

5. Calculate float to determine critical path

Float is calculated by subtracting early start or finish from late start or finish.

- Float = Late start - Early start
- Float = Later finish - Early finish

The **critical path** is the longest path where float is equal to zero.

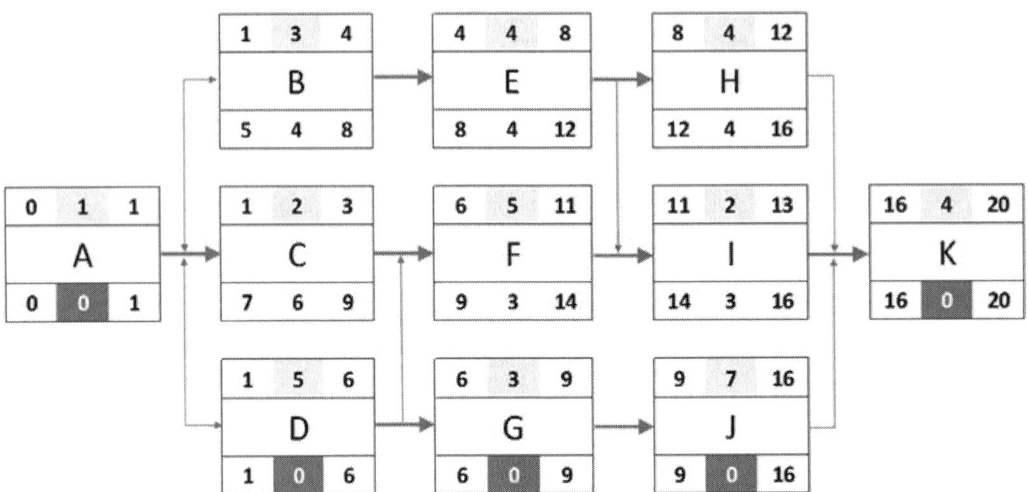

If the project falls behind schedule, the float is negative; if the project is ahead of schedule, the float is positive. The purpose of the critical path method is to focus management efforts on activities that can improve performance.

> **Negative float** = Activity must start before predecessor completes to meet finish date
> **Positive float** = Activity can be delayed and not impact finish date

RESOURCE OPTIMIZATION

Schedules must be tested and adjusted to ensure that each activity can be adequately staffed at the prescribed time defined. Resource leveling and resource smoothing are two techniques used to adjust the schedule model to meet the resource demand and constraints.

Resource leveling is used to balance activities across a finite supply of resources. This technique is used when resources are overallocated or have limited availability. When done, the activities in question are moved within the available float, and this may impact the critical path.

Resource smoothing is used to adjust schedule activities to not exceed resource limits. When used, the activities are only delayed within their float, free or total, so there is no change in the critical path.

> Resource smoothing has NO impact on the critical path.
> Resource leveling may cause the critical path to change.

WHAT-IF SCENARIO ANALYSIS

Project teams challenge the schedule assumptions and design by using what-if scenario analysis to identify opportunities and bolster stability.

What-if scenario analysis involves evaluating diverse scenarios to understand their potential impact on project objectives. The results are used to determine the amount of schedule reserves needed and to define appropriate response plans.

> Project teams aim to understand and correct for project risk by asking: "What would be the impact if this happened?"

SIMULATION ANALYSIS

Monte Carlo simulation analysis integrates the risk data available into a simulation model to calculate the range of potential schedule impacts. The risk data used is developed during the risk planning processes (11.1–11.5). The simulation models provide a statistical distribution of the potential project outcomes.

> Simulation analysis asks: "What is the probability that we finish by this date?"

SCHEDULE COMPRESSION

Crashing and fast tracking are two methods that can be used to shorten the critical path and project duration.

Crashing reduces the time of an individual activity by adding resources. This technique is only used when the activity can benefit from more resources. Some activities do not finish faster with more resources.

Fast tracking reduces the project time by transferring activities done in sequence to be completed in parallel. The time to complete each activity does not change, just when it occurs.

The image below provides examples of crashing and fast tracking. Notice that the length of activity A in the crashing example changes. This indicates that labor was added to expedite activity completion time. In the fast-tracking example, the time required to complete activity B does not change, only its relationship with the predecessor activity.

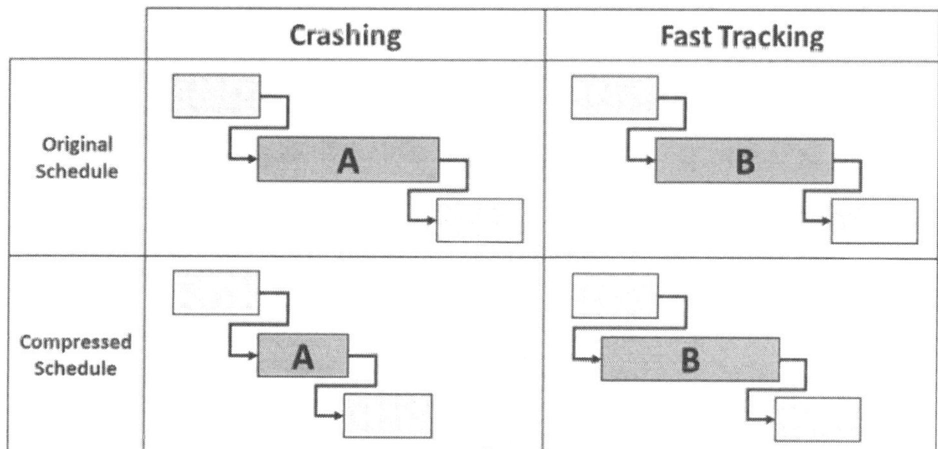

> You can find crashing and fast-tracking opportunities by asking: "Could these activities be done in sequence?" *(Fast-tracking)* "How much faster could this be done if we added resources?" *(Crashing)*

Case Study: "Finding a Way to Meet the Deadline"

John walked to the large project schedule network diagram on the war room wall, drew a bright red vertical line eight weeks to the left of the originally projected finish date, and waited for his core team members to arrive.

The line was the result of a call John received from the VP of Operations early that morning. Getting his call always seemed bittersweet. John loved the access, but every call seemed to bring a new hurdle that inevitably made his job just a little harder. The call this morning was no different.

"John, I've spoken to Sara. She says you're making progress. I don't see it, but I'll trust her."

"Thank you, sir. The team is totally committed to delivering on time and within budget."

"That's good because that's why I'm calling. I need the project to be completed earlier. I know you're just getting started, but other projects are lagging and we need something to make up the difference. I'm calling you because I know you can get it done. Can I count on you?"

John had agreed. He didn't feel that it was really a question, more of a mandated challenge. Staring at the diagram, he wondered if it was possible. The team had built a great schedule, but now he would ask them to compress it. Also, he had just gotten the schedule baseline approved; if they found a way to meet the deadline, he would need to use the Change Control process to update the schedule baseline. This fact brought some degree of comfort. He would follow the rules—no more shortcuts.

As the team arrived, John explained the situation. Surprisingly, the team was eager to meet the request. They immediately began by questioning every activity on the diagram, asking, "Could this activity be done in sequence with its predecessor?" and "If we added resources, how much faster could this be completed?" Little by little, they began to find opportunities. As they made modifications, they updated the diagram on the computer. After four hours, they had accomplished their task.

As the new diagram printed, John reviewed the schedule on the computer. He found two great examples of where they had found ways to compress the schedule. He went to the white board and drew both examples. He would use these to help explain the changes if any questions came from the Change Control process.

CASE STUDY QUESTIONS: "FINDING A WAY TO MEET THE DEADLINE"

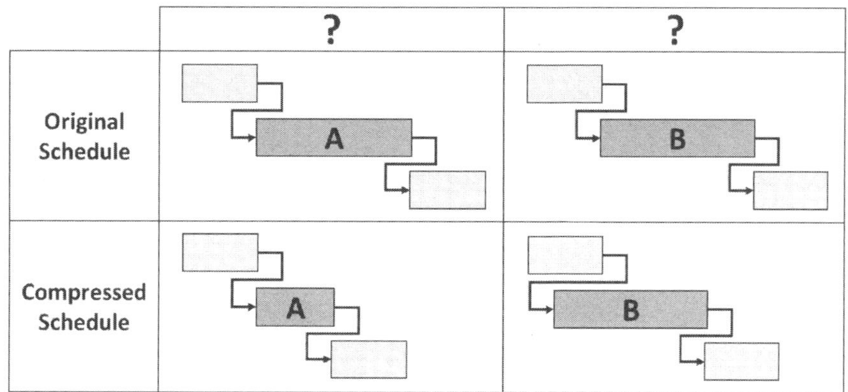

Which schedule compression technique did the team use in example A?

a. Resource smoothing
b. Fast tracking
c. Crashing
d. Resource leveling

Which schedule compression technique did the team use in example B?

a. Resource smoothing
b. Fast tracking
c. Crashing
d. Resource leveling

What is the largest impact of crashing that John must evaluate and account for?

a. Potential impact to product quality
b. Cost impact of adding resources to task A
c. Possible overworking of team members
d. Impact to communication activities

CASE STUDY ANSWERS: "FINDING A WAY TO MEET THE DEADLINE"

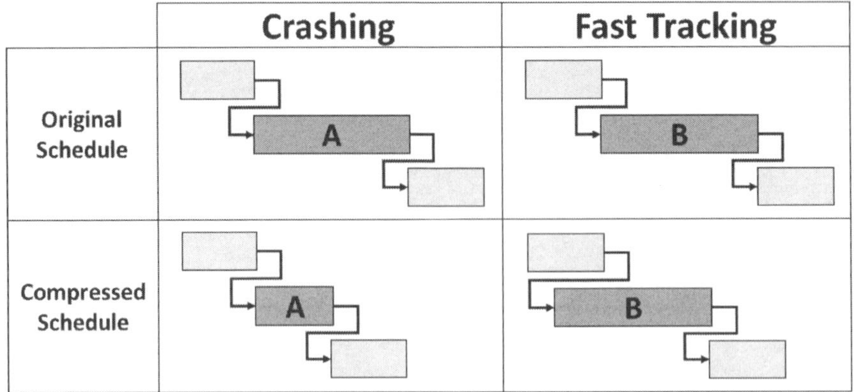

Which schedule compression technique did the team use in example A?

a. Resource smoothing
b. Fast tracking
c. Crashing
d. Resource leveling

Which schedule compression technique did the team use in example B?

a. Resource smoothing
b. Fast tracking
c. Crashing
d. Resource leveling

What is the largest impact of crashing that John must evaluate and account for?

a. Potential impact to product quality
b. Cost impact of adding resources to task A
c. Possible overworking of team members
d. Impact to communication activities

PLAN COST MANAGEMENT (*PMBOK GUIDE*® 7.1)

Summary

The cost management plan is another subsidiary plan of the project management plan. In creating the cost management plan, the project manager defines how costs will be estimated, budgeted, managed, monitored, and controlled.

The nature of the project, whether predictive or agile, should be considered when developing the cost management plan. The most specific difference is in when cost projections and estimates will be created. On predictive projects, detailed cost projections are established for the entire project very early in the project life cycle. In comparison, adaptive or agile projects expect high levels of change and employ just-in-time planning of detailed estimates.

Regardless of the method employed, cost planning should start as early in the project as possible to ensure that an accurate baseline is defined to obtain resources and measure progress.

Plan Cost Management I.T.T.O.

7.1 Plan Cost Mgt.	Inputs	Tools and Techniques	Outputs
	Project charter **Project management plan** • *Schedule mgt. plan* • *Risk mgt. plan* **EEFs** **OPAs**	**Expert judgement** **Data analysis** **Meetings**	**Cost management plan**

Key Outputs

<u>COST MANAGEMENT PLAN</u>

The cost management plan is the only output of the Plan Cost Management process. This plan defines how the project's costs will be planned, structured, and controlled. More specifically, the plan informs the methods that will be taken in the next two cost processes in the Planning process group to estimate the costs of individual activities and aggregate them into the official project cost baseline.

The cost management plan defines the conventions that will help create clarity, consistency, and confidence in the cost estimates and cost baseline.

- Units of measure—clearly defined units that prevent confusion
- Level of precision—how costs will be rounded up or down
- Level of accuracy—the range by which cost must be specified
- Organizational procedure links—how costs will link to the WBS
- Control thresholds—agreed-upon amounts that trigger action
- Rules of performance measurements—methods by which performance will be monitored
- Reporting formats—frequency and format

Key Inputs

The charter, schedule and risk management plans, and relevant EEFs and OPAs provide the information needed to create the cost management plan. The **project charter** defines the preapproved financial resources. The processes and controls defined in the **schedule and risk management plans** impact how costs will be calculated.

Currency exchange rates and other market conditions related to the availability of resources are **EEFs** that will directly influence cost estimates. Financial control procedures established in an organization and the historical cost data examples are **OPAs** that will help inform and guide the cost management plan.

Key Tools and Techniques

Expert judgement and **data analysis** techniques are used to integrate all project-specific factors to create a well-defined cost management plan.

Individuals with experience on similar projects can provide expert judgement on the best methods to perform cost estimating and budgeting and the practice of earned value analysis. **Alternate analysis techniques** can be used to plan the appropriate method of project funding and acquiring resources.

ESTIMATE COSTS (*PMBOK GUIDE*® 7.2)

Summary

The Estimate Costs process is the first of two cost processes in the Planning process group used to create the project's baseline budget.

As the name suggests, this process produces cost estimates as an output. Cost estimates approximate the total amount of monetary resources that the project requires. Additionally, the Estimate Costs process produces the basis of estimates document, which provides the context and rationale used to create the estimates.

Cost estimates are built on the foundation established in the details of the project schedule, resource requirements, and risk register documents. These documents provide the context and depth of information the team needs to estimate the cost of completing the project.

The cost estimates produced will be used in the next process, Determine Budget (7.3), to create the cost baseline. The cost baseline is critical to the project, in that it authorizes the funds for project use and is the standard by which project spending is monitored and evaluated.

> Estimate Costs, Estimate Activity Durations, and Estimate Activity Resources **ALL** have similar types of process outputs:
> **(1)** estimates, **(2)** basis of estimates, and **(3)** project documents updates.

Estimate Costs I.T.T.O.

	Inputs	**Tools and Techniques**	**Outputs**
7.2 Estimate Costs	**Project management plan** • *Cost mgt. plan* • *Quality mgt. plan* • *Scope baseline* **Project documents** • *Lessons learned register* • *Project schedule* • *Resource requirements* • *Risk register* **EEFs** **OPAs**	**Expert judgement** **Analogous estimating** **Parametric estimating** **Bottom-up estimating** **Three-point estimating** **Data analysis** • *Alternatives analysis* • *Reserve analysis* • *Cost of quality* **Proj. mgt. information system** **Decision making** • *Voting*	**Cost estimates** **Basis of estimates** **Project doc. updates** • *Assumption log* • *Lessons learned register* • *Risk register*

Key Outputs

The major outputs of Estimate Costs are **cost estimates** and **basis of estimates**.

COST ESTIMATES

Cost estimates are calculated and recorded for every type of cost that could be experienced when completing the project. This includes both costs associated with labor, material, equipment, services, and facilities and additional costs related to financing and risks.

Once calculated, the costs are organized into three categories: probable costs, contingency amounts, and management reserves. **Probable costs** are the costs related to the completion of the project work defined in the project schedule. **Contingency amounts** are resources allocated to be applied when addressing identified risks. **Management reserves** are resources that are set aside to be used only when funding unplanned work.

The costs are calculated using one of the four estimating techniques (analogous, parametric, bottom-up, three-point) described in the next Tools and Techniques section. The costs are often documented in a format that will allow the estimates to be understood at both a summary and detail level.

Cost estimates should be reviewed and refined throughout the project life cycle. As a rule, the preciseness of the cost estimate will increase as the project progresses. This is reflected in the rough order of magnitude (ROM) of the estimates. Early in the project the ROM may indicate a range of ±25%; however, later the ROM may be ±5%.

> Costs are estimated for ALL the resources that will be charged to a project (labor, facilities, equipment, etc.)

BASIS OF ESTIMATES

Basis of estimates explains the logic behind the cost estimates, allowing the team to understand how the costs were derived. The basis of estimates can provide information to help create clarity when communicating with stakeholders.

Supporting information within the basis of estimates includes

- Description of the basis of estimates
- Assumptions
- Constraints
- Estimate range

PROJECT DOCUMENTS

Project documents are updated when new and improved information is uncovered while estimating costs. New assumptions defined while estimating costs are recorded in the **assumption log**. Additionally, risk responses developed and agreed upon during the Estimate Costs process must be documented in the **risk register**. After completing the estimation, all best practices identified should be recorded in the **lessons learned register**.

> The risk register and lessons learned register can serve as **BOTH** inputs to and outputs of Estimate Costs (7.2).

Key Inputs

Project management plans and **project documents** provide the estimation methods and the detailed description of the work to be completed necessary to create cost estimates. The **EEFs** relevant to the project can significantly impact the actual cost estimates and must be considered and evaluated.

PROJECT MANAGEMENT PLANS

The **cost management plan** defines the method by which cost estimates will be calculated and the level of precision and accuracy demanded.

Project teams use the **WBS** and **WBS dictionary** to identify and understand the work needed to produce each project deliverable listed in the **scope statement**. The WBS and WBS dictionary documents are extremely valuable in that they segment a description of the work needed to produce each WBS component.

Additionally, the **quality management plan** defines the activities and approaches that will be taken to manage project quality. These need to be integrated in the total cost estimates.

PROJECT DOCUMENTS

The **project schedule** and **resource requirements** take cost estimation to the next level. These provide a granular description of exactly what is going to be required to complete each work package. Specifically, they lay out the type, quantity, timing, and total amount of time each physical and team resource is required.

The **risk register** (created in 11.2 Identify Risks) contains a detailed and prioritized list of the project risks identified. The risk responses created must be factored into the cost estimates.

EEFs

Market conditions, exchange rates and inflation, and **published commercial information** on material costs and pay rates for skilled and unskilled labor are used to help create accurate cost estimates.

OPAs

Cost estimating policies and **templates** are OPAs that will be used in the Estimate Costs process.

Key Tools and Techniques

Every PMP® exam will feature a handful of cost estimating questions. Being able to identify the type of cost estimation technique described and to calculate cost estimates using the three-point and beta distributions below will help you get every question right.

ESTIMATING TECHNIQUES

Four estimating techniques are commonly used to determine the cost of resources needed to deliver the project schedule. These techniques were defined and explained in the Estimate Activity Duration (6.4) process in the Schedule Management knowledge area.

Analogous estimating involves using similar activities from previous projects to model the cost estimates. Think of "analogous" as a "project analogy" to help remember how the estimating method works.

Parametric estimating uses numerical rates and relationships to calculate cost estimates. Parametric estimating questions on the exam often reference rates from previous projects and commercial databases. Common examples of rates are cost per square footage in construction and work completion per labor hour.

Bottom-up estimating is a very detailed method of estimating in which every lower-level component of the WBS is estimated. Each component is "rolled-up" to create a higher-level estimate. This is the most accurate but most time intensive method of cost estimating.

Three-point estimating uses a mathematical equation to incorporate risk and uncertainty into the estimate. There are two distinct three-point estimating methods: triangular and beta distribution. The three-point estimating method uses three cost estimate projections:

- Most likely (cM)
- Optimistic (cO)—Best case
- Pessimistic (cP)—Worst case

Notice that there is a variable (cM, cO, cP) listed next to each estimation. These are the same type of variables that were used to calculate the activity estimates in Estimate Activity Durations (6.4). The only difference is that instead of representing the most likely, optimistic, and pessimistic schedule durations, these estimates define cost projections.

On the exam, you will be given estimates for the best case, most likely, and worst case and will be asked to calculate the overall cost estimate (cE) using one of two equations:

- Triangular distribution:

$$cE = (cO + cM + cP) / 3$$

- Beta distribution:

$$cE = (cO + 4cM + cP) / 6$$

Notice that both equations have the same structure, but they put different weight on the most likely cost estimate. Additionally, the beta distribution is divided by 6, not 3 like the triangular distribution.

Calculating cost estimates will be on your PMP® exam. They are easy questions—**if you practice them**. Complete the exercise in the next section!

DATA ANALYSIS

In addition to estimating, three data analysis techniques are used to provide unique lenses to evaluate cost options and calculate the required reserves to account for identified risks and the total cost of quality.

Alternatives analysis evaluates the cost impact of different options.

Reserves analysis calculates the amount of reserves that should be incorporated into the estimate to account for cost uncertainty. Most specifically, contingency reserves are included to account for identified risks. Contingency reserves are included within the cost baseline.

Cost of quality is used to evaluate and plan for the projected costs of conformance and nonconformance. The cost of conformance involves all preventative costs to build a quality product and any appraisal costs to assess the quality of the product. The cost of nonconformance includes the costs related to rework and scrap and all external costs incurred from liabilities, warranty payments, and lost business.

Project management information systems often contain simulation software, which makes creating and evaluating estimations easier and faster.

EXERCISE: "COST ESTIMATION"

A project has begun to refurbish an ocean pier in a southern U.S. state. The area has a history of dramatic and quick changes in weather conditions that could impact the equipment and labor required to complete the project. It has been determined that these fluctuations would cause variations in the total cost of the project. Given the projected weather, the most likely cost estimate is $25 million, the most optimistic is $22 million, and the worst case is $34 million. Calculate the cost estimate using triangular and beta distribution methods.

What is the cost estimate?

- Using the triangular distribution method?

  a. $22 million
  b. $25 million
  c. $26 million
  d. $27 million

- Using the beta distribution method?

  a. $22M
  b. $25M
  c. $26M
  d. $27M

EXERCISE ANSWERS: "COST ESTIMATION"

A project has begun to refurbish an ocean pier in a southern U.S. state. The area has a history of dramatic and quick changes in weather conditions that could impact the equipment and labor required to complete the project. It has been determined that these fluctuations would cause variations in the total cost of the project. Given the projected weather, the most likely cost estimate is $25 million, the most optimistic is $22 million, and the worst case is $34 million. Calculate the cost estimate using triangular and beta distribution methods.

What is the cost estimate?

- Using the triangular distribution method

  a. $22 million
  b. $25 million
  c. $26 million
  d. **$27 million**

  Solution:

  - cE = (cO + cM + cP) / 3
  - cE = ($22M + $25M + $34) / 3
  - **cE = $27M**

- Using the beta distribution method

  a. $22M
  b. $25M
  c. **$26M**
  d. $27M

  Solution:

  - cE = (cO + 4cM + cP) / 6
  - cE = ($22M + (4 × $25M) + $34) / 6
  - **cE = $26M**

DETERMINE BUDGET (*PMBOK GUIDE*® 7.3)

Summary

Determine Budget builds upon the cost estimates produced in Estimate Costs (7.2) to create the project's official cost baseline and the total project budget. Project cost baseline and budget are different! The cost baseline is the approved version of the budget and is shown over a time-phased scale. The budget adds a management reserve onto the cost baseline. The management reserve is only used when unforeseen work that is within the project scope is identified.

Establishing the cost baseline is essential to project success, as it is one of the three project baselines. The cost baseline will be used as the cost standard by which the project will be monitored and evaluated. This baseline includes the costs estimated for the work defined in the schedule and a contingency reserve to assign funds to costs related to identified risks.

To be official, the cost baseline must be approved by the sponsor before the funds are authorized to be used. Once the cost baseline is approved, all future changes can only be made using the Perform Integrated Change (4.6) process.

> The cost baseline is one of three project baselines:
> **(1) cost**, **(2) schedule**, and **(3) scope**.

Determine Budget I.T.T.O.

	Inputs	Tools and Techniques	Outputs
7.3 Determine Budget	**Project management plan** • *Cost mgt. plan* • *Resource mgt. plan* • *Scope baseline* **Project documents** • *Basis of estimates* • *Cost estimates* • *Project schedule* • *Risk register* **Business documents** • *Business case* • *Benefits management plan* **Agreements** **EEFs** **OPAs**	**Expert judgement** **Cost aggregation** **Data analysis** • *Reserve analysis* **Historical info. review** **Funding limit reconciliation** **Financing**	**Cost baseline** **Project funding requirements** **Project doc. updates** • *Cost estimates* • *Project schedule* • *Risk register*

Key Outputs

COST BASELINE AND PROJECT FUNDING REQUIREMENTS

The **cost baseline** and **project funding requirements**, produced as outputs of Determine Budget (7.3), inform the amount of resources allocated and when they will be available. Additionally, they are used to evaluate the project's actual vs. planned performance. A visual representation of the interaction between the cost baseline and funding requirements is shown in the next diagram.

The cost baseline (the dark black sloping line) shows the expected project costs over time. The fact that each of the cost baseline's individual components is directly linked to schedule activities allows the baseline to be depicted on a graph over time.

Notice the step-wise pattern of the funding requirements, in contrast with the smooth cost baseline line. Funds are often released gradually over the course of the project, coinciding with the project schedule. The amount of funding releases may not be uniform in timing or quantity.

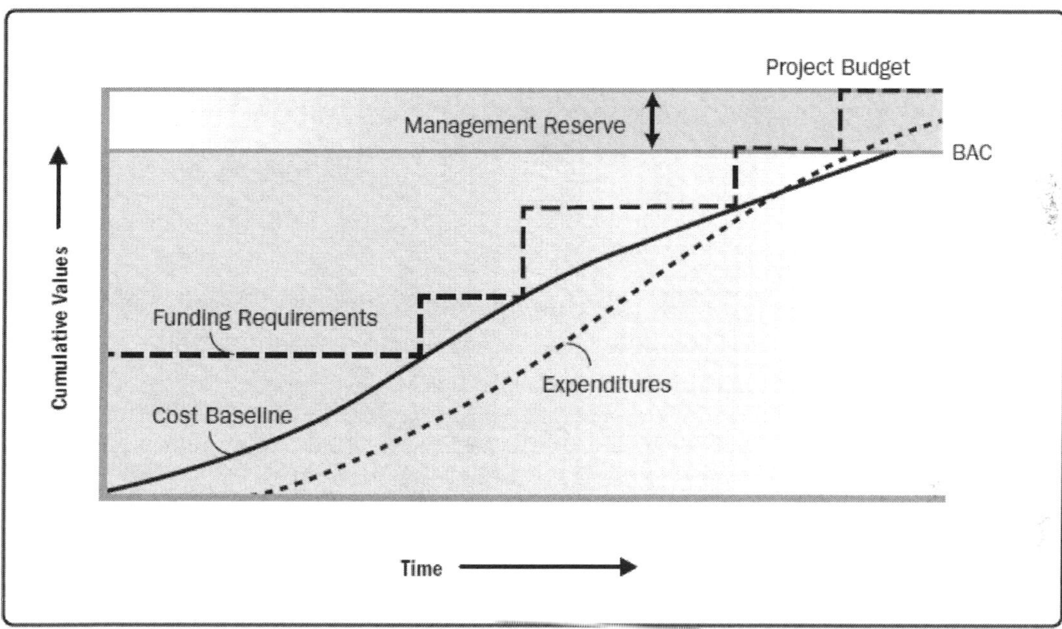

The cost baseline is created by aggregating cost estimates and calculating a contingency reserve. This process is done twice: first at the individual activity level and then at the work package level. The diagram below shows the method of accumulation. The work package cost estimates and contingency reserve are rolled up by control account to form the cost baseline. A management reserve is added to the cost baseline to make up the total project budget.

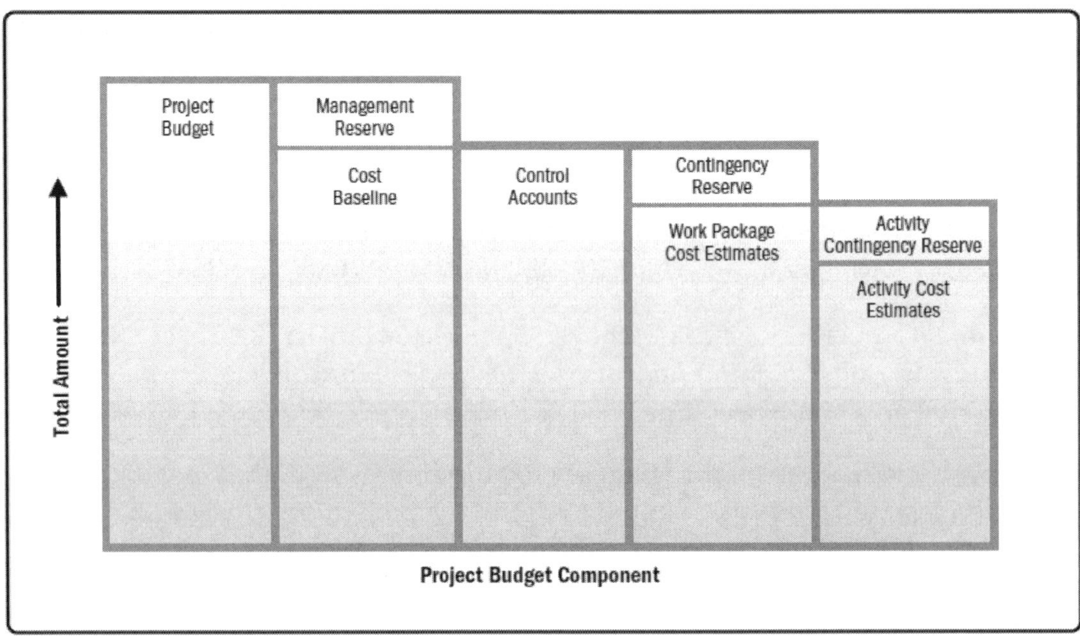

The project budget and cost baseline are different!
The budget **includes** the management reserve; the cost baseline **does not**.

Key Inputs

As with many processes, Determine Budget does not operate in isolation. The information needed to create the cost baseline is driven from the detailed analysis and investigation that has gone into the creation of the project schedule, cost estimates, and risk register.

Additionally, the cost and resource management plans and the scope baseline are key inputs, as they provide the structure on which estimated costs are aggregated.

PROJECT DOCUMENTS

Project documents provide the detailed information used to fully build out and finalize the baseline and project budget. The **cost estimates** provide granular detail of activity-level costs within each work package. The **basis of estimates** provides context to how the estimates were calculated and any assumptions that were made.

The **project schedule** links each activity to a defined start and finish time. This perspective is critical to defining the time-based funding requirements and evaluating the funding availability. Combining the totality of the information provided by these three previous documents and the information in the **risk register** helps the team calculate the appropriate contingency reserves.

BUSINESS DOCUMENTS

The business case and benefits management plan were both created prior to the project charter being approved. These documents are valuable inputs to this process, in that they inform what the initial projects and expectations were of the project's benefits.

The **business case** defines the financial success factors for the project. The **benefit management plan** includes the initial target benefit amount and schedule. The projected benefit can be defined in terms of the net present value of the project returns, the realization timeframe, and the total amount of benefits to be delivered.

PROJECT MANAGEMENT PLANS

The **cost management plan** defines how to structure costs within the baseline and budget. The **scope baseline** defines the WBS structure that will be used to aggregate cost estimates.

The **resource management plan** provides additional depth of information on common rates and other foreseen costs that will be used to build out the full project budget.

AGREEMENTS

Many projects use **agreements** with vendors to obtain strategic resources, products, services, or labor. The terms, schedules, and costs defined in these agreements must be incorporated in the cost baseline. The agreements may also provide insight into risks that could impact the quantities of contingency reserves allocated.

Key Tools and Techniques

The cost estimates and limitations of funding constraints must be analyzed and balanced to create a cost baseline. The foundation of the baseline is built through **cost aggregation**. It is through this process that cost estimates created in Estimate Costs (7.2) are first grouped by work packages, then control accounts, and finally at the entire project level, in accordance with the WBS.

Data analysis helps to define the appropriate levels of contingency and management reserves. In mapping out the costs by schedule, the time-based funding requirements must be reconciled with the reality of funding availability. Limitations in the amount of funding available over time may require adjustments in the project schedule. This type of analysis is known as **funding limit reconciliation**.

> The contingency reserve accounts for identified risks.
> The management reserve accounts for unplanned work.

Case Study: "Understanding the Costs"

John paced around the table waiting for the finance analyst to deliver the verdict. As he waited, John laughed and mumbled to himself, "Cost, quality, and schedule. Pick two."

The team had rallied to satisfy the recent request to compress the schedule. Now they were dealing with the actual impact to the project. The challenge was to deliver on time while mitigating the negative impacts. The analyst was now revising the cost estimation and finalizing the budget to incorporate the new schedule.

Fifteen minutes later the analyst broke the silence: "The changes definitely had an impact, but it's not as bad as we thought. And before you ask, I do think we can still make the spending cap they put on us." In addition to the schedule compression, the VP had also dictated the maximum amount that could be spent on the project. John had learned to expect frantic early morning calls from the VP, dictating changes to some characteristic of the project.

John high-fived the analyst, causing him to pause before he continued his explanation. "John, I'm really glad we chose to estimate like we did. Breaking things down to the smallest component of work and rolling the costs up made the process of evaluating the changes a lot easier."

A clear picture of the future began to materialize in John's head as the analyst continued, "The reality of the schedule compression is that the actual work didn't change much, just when and how we are going to get it done. The impact of the changes is obvious when you look at the cost baseline curve over time." He pointed to the graph on his computer screen. "See how it ramps up quicker than the last version?" Turning toward John, the analyst got serious. "This change does bring along more risk. We all know that we will need to do a good amount of redesign. We just don't know how much."

"Yes, it's our biggest unknown cost." Sara had told John to look for these types of costs in their last meeting and, just like most things, what she mentioned somehow seemed to appear.

"Exactly. If the amount of redesign isn't too bad, then we might only have to pay a little overtime and still not have much of a cost increase. However, if it turns out there is more redesign work than we thought, then we are going to have to hire outside consultants to help do the work."

John sheepishly asked, "And they cost more?"

"A good amount more."

"If you're right, I don't see any way around this. If we know we might have to spend some amount extra on consultants, how do we incorporate that into the budget?"

"That unknown cost is factored into this reserve." The analyst pointed to the screen showing John where the potential cost of the consultants was incorporated.

John nodded and put his hand on his chin, trying to act the role of a calm and calculating project manager. "OK, I understand. Great work. Let's get the cost baseline and the funding schedule packaged up. I want to get them to Sara as soon as possible."

Case Study Questions: "Understanding the Costs"

What method of estimating did the team use to estimate the cost?

a. Bottom-up estimating
b. Analogous estimating
c. Parametric estimating
d. Projected estimating

Which type of reserve did the team use to factor in the increased risk of needing to use higher-cost consultants?

a. Management reserve
b. Contingency reserve
c. Safety reserve
d. Scope modification reserve

Which type of reserve would be included to account for the occurrences when the team identifies future work that is not in the schedule but is within the project scope?

a. Management reserve
b. Contingency reserve
c. Safety reserve
d. Scope modification reserve

Case Study Answers: "Understanding the Costs"

What method of estimating did the team use to estimate the cost?

a. **Bottom-up estimating**
b. Analogous estimating
c. Parametric estimating
d. Projected estimating

Which type of reserve did the team use to factor in the increased risk of needing to use higher-cost consultants?

a. Management reserve
b. **Contingency reserve**
c. Safety reserve
d. Scope modification reserve

Which type of reserve would be included to account for the occurrences when the team identifies future work that is not in the schedule but is within the project scope?

a. **Management reserve**
b. Contingency reserve
c. Safety reserve
d. Scope modification reserve

PLAN QUALITY MANAGEMENT (*PMBOK GUIDE*® 8.1)

Summary

In planning quality, the project manager's primary concern is to gather the necessary benchmarking information and customer requirements so that they can be incorporated along with adequate quality metrics into a plan that can be followed.

The standards, requirements, metrics, and actions defined in the quality management plan will provide guidance and direction in the Manage Quality Control and Control Quality processes. This plan and the ability of the project team to adhere to it will have a direct influence on the resulting total cost of quality (COQ) for the product.

> The cost of preventing mistakes is LESS than the cost of correcting mistakes found by inspection or use.

The nature of the project (predictive vs. adaptive or agile) should be considered when drafting the quality plan. Adaptive or agile projects will use frequent quality review steps and retrospectives throughout the project, rather than broader milestone checkpoints used with a predictive approach.

Plan Quality Management I.T.T.O.

8.1 Plan Quality Mgt.	Inputs	Tools and Techniques	Outputs
	Project charter **Project management plan** • *Requirements mgt. plan* • *Risk mgt. plan* • *Stakeholder engmt. plan* • *Scope baseline* **Project documents** • *Assumption log* • *Req. documentation* • *Req. traceability matrix* • *Risk register* • *Stakeholder register* **EEFs** **OPAs**	**Expert judgement** **Data gathering** • *Benchmarking* • *Brainstorming* • *Interviews* **Data analysis** • *Cost-benefit analysis* • *Cost of quality* **Decision making** • *Multicriteria decision analysis* **Data representation** • *Flowcharts* • *Logical data model* • *Matrix diagrams* • *Mind mapping* **Test and inspection planning** **Meetings**	**Quality management plan** **Quality metrics** **Project mgt. plan updates** • *Risk mgt. plan* • *Scope baseline* **Project documents updates** • *Lessons learned register* • *Req. traceability matrix* • *Risk register* • *Stakeholder register*

Key Outputs

QUALITY MANAGEMENT PLAN

The quality management plan and the quality metrics incorporated into it are the primary outputs of this process. They describe the activities and resources necessary for the project team to achieve the project's quality objectives.

As a subsidiary plan to the project management plan, the quality management plan defines the following:

- Quality standards
- Quality objectives
- Quality roles and responsibilities
- Deliverables and processes that will be subject to quality reviews
- Quality control measures and management activities to be used to track and adhere to them
- Quality tools to be used

> The quality management plan also defines procedures for dealing with nonconformance, corrective actions, and continuous improvement.

QUALITY METRICS

Quality metrics refer to the descriptions and attributes of the product and how they can be quantified and measured so that the Control Quality process can verify compliance to them. Performance to these specifications will be used to provide status updates during communications to stakeholders and sponsors throughout the project. The following are some examples of project-specific quality metrics:

- Percentage of tasks completed on time
- Number of defects identified per day
- Total downtime per month
- Customer satisfaction scores

PROJECT MANAGEMENT PLAN UPDATES

Creation and improvements to the quality management plan may require specific project plan updates such as updates to the **risk management plan** and **scope baseline**. Changes to elements like the scope baseline will need to go through the Integrated Change Control process via a change request when specific quality management activities warrant such changes.

PROJECT DOCUMENTS UPDATES

When recording quality requirements, updates to the **requirements traceability matrix** will be needed along with updates to the **risk register** when new risks related to quality are uncovered. Other documents that may be updated include the lessons learned register and stakeholder register.

Key Inputs

When creating the quality management plan, the project manager uses information from the **project charter** and **scope baseline**. Additional inputs come from the **requirements management plan** and **risk management plan**.

Project documents also serve as points of referral in the Plan Quality Management process. **Requirements documentation** can be a good reference, as it describes how individual items meet the business need for the project. Also, the **requirements traceability matrix** helps link specific requirements from their origin to the deliverables that satisfy them.

EEFs AND OPAs

There may be unique factors and assets related to the project that will weigh heavily on the way the quality management plan and metrics are designed. Enterprise environmental factors related to government regulations, industry rules, and standards as well as marketplace conditions may be big influencers. The organization may also have quality management systems in place that can be either restrictive or advantageous.

Key Tools and Techniques

The actions and methods used in the Plan Quality Management process seem similar to the tools and techniques used in other processes, but in many instances, they can go much deeper and flesh out very specific information. Data gathering through **benchmarking** can shed light on factors and requirements that had not been previously uncovered. Data analysis in this process deals with **cost-of-quality** assessments that can be extremely revealing and cause substantial changes to internal processes and procedures if managed wisely. The cost of poor quality can be magnitudes higher if discovered by the customer than if poor quality is addressed at the source.

Cost of Conformance	Cost of Nonconformance
Prevention costs (build a quality product) • *Training* • *Document processes* • *Equipment* • *Time to do it right* **Appraisal costs** (assess the quality) • *Testing* • *Destructive testing loss* • *Inspections*	**Internal failure costs** (found by the project team) • *Rework* • *Scrap* **External failure costs** (found by the customer) • *Liabilities* • *Warranty* • *Lost business*
Money spent during the project to avoid failures	Money spent during and after the project because of failures

Cost of quality (COQ) includes **ALL** quality-related costs over the entire life of the project.

DATA REPRESENTATION

Data representation techniques present processes and data visually. They are used to understand relationships, develop ideas, and support informed decision making. Some of the representations that are useful in planning quality management are

- Flow charts
- Logical data model
- Matrix diagrams

DECISION MAKING

Upon use and interpretation of data through the analysis and representation techniques already discussed, **multicriteria decision analysis** can be performed to systematically analyze and rank variables and alternatives. If inconclusive or further ongoing assessments are deemed necessary, project teams may turn to **test and inspection planning** to keep close ties on project quality.

CASE STUDY: "PLANNING QUALITY MANAGEMENT"

"This one line sums up our major challenge: 'the designs must conform to all existing and new regulations'."

John was reading to the team the acceptance criteria defined in the product scope statement. With the cost, schedule, and scope baselines all finalized and approved, John was now focusing the team's attention on fleshing out the quality management plan. Having worked his entire career in the Quality department, John had seen firsthand the impact one simple line in the acceptance criteria could have on quality costs and therefore project costs.

"We need to define how we are going to manage and validate quality throughout the project, and document it in the quality management plan." The processes of developing the schedule and cost management plans and reacting to the multiple VP-directed changes had both created and highlighted multiple risks. The cost of quality (COQ) or, more specifically, the cost of poor quality, was among the highest.

"The give and take of what we are doing is trading an investment in the cost of conformance for a reduction in the total cost of nonconformance." John held his hands out on either side of his body, acting as though he were an uneven scale. The manufacturing engineer on the team added detail to the difference between internal and external nonconformance failure costs. "Once we start manufacturing, the cost of fixing problems goes up. If a problem gets to the customer, the cost goes way up. It is better that we find and fix the issues now."

As the team brainstormed their approach, they agreed on the fact that they wanted to try to build quality and conformance into the process from the beginning. While this made sense, they grappled with the reality that the projected number of redesigns would make it impossible to spend the time or money to fully inspect every redesign.

Leaning on approaches taken by similar projects, drawn from the project management hub, the team devised both a statistical sampling and an audit plan. As the audit plan began to take shape, the team identified the need to create an audit checklist. The audit checklist would be used by both the engineers performing the redesign and the quality auditors. The corollary benefit of the checklist is that it would make training the quality inspectors simpler and would provide a quality metric to track during the project.

In further building out the quality audit plan, the team defined the process by which the auditors would inspect the drawing redesign process. The results would be used as a quality metric. Before completing the quality management plan, they confirmed with the financial analyst that in fact the upfront cost of conformance was projected to significantly reduce future nonconformance costs. John thanked the team for their work. The team was coming together nicely. Good things were definitely in their future, he hoped.

Case Study Questions: "Planning Quality Management"

John's use of best practices from similar projects to help define the statistical sampling and audit plan was an example of what data gathering technique?

a. Interview
b. Brainstorming
c. Benchmarking
d. Cost-benefit analysis

The new government regulations are defined as what type of input for the Planning Quality Management process?

a. Organizational process asset (OPA)
b. Enterprise environmental factor (EEF)
c. Agreement
d. Project document

The team used what type of analysis to evaluate the cost effectiveness of an increased investment in cost of conformance?

a. Risk analysis
b. Cost-benefit analysis
c. Cost forecasting
d. Earned value analysis

CASE STUDY ANSWERS: "PLANNING QUALITY MANAGEMENT"

John's use of best practices from similar projects to help define the statistical sampling and audit plan was an example of what data gathering technique?

a. Interview
b. Brainstorming
c. Benchmarking
d. Cost-benefit analysis

The new government regulations are defined as what type of input for the Planning Quality Management process?

a. Organizational process asset (OPA)
b. Enterprise environmental factor (EEF)
c. Agreement
d. Project document

The team used what type of analysis to evaluate the cost effectiveness of an increased investment in cost of conformance?

a. Risk analysis
b. Cost-benefit analysis
c. Cost forecasting
d. Earned value analysis

PLAN RESOURCE MANAGEMENT (*PMBOK GUIDE*® 9.1)

Summary

Resource planning is focused on defining the approach and methods that will ensure that the correct resources are available at the right place and at the right time. The Plan Resource Management process creates the resource management plan that defines how physical and team resources will be estimated, acquired, managed, and used throughout the project.

The methods defined in the resource management plan can impact the cost, schedule, risk, and quality. In addition to the work to be done, the plan must consider the project's unique aspects such as

- Team environment
- Geographical locations and dispersion
- Cultural issues
- Internal politics

> Resource planning is concerned with BOTH physical and human resources.
> Physical = Equipment, materials, facilities, and infrastructure
> Human = Team members (full, part-time, and contract)

Plan Resource Management I.T.T.O.

	Inputs	Tools and Techniques	Outputs
9.1 Plan Resource Mgt.	**Project charter** **Project management plan** • *Quality mgt. plan* • *Scope baseline* **Project documents** • *Project schedule* • *Requirements doc.* • *Risk register* • *Stakeholder register* **EEFs** **OPA**	**Expert judgement** **Data representation** • *Hierarchical charts* • *Responsibility assignment matrix* • *Text oriented formats* **Organizational theory** **Meetings**	**Resource mgt. plan** **Team charter** **Project doc. updates** • *Assumption log* • *Risk register*

Key Outputs

RESOURCE MANAGEMENT PLAN

The resource management plan is the primary output of this process, and it describes the methods and tools that will be used to categorize, allocate, manage, and release project resources. It is a subsidiary plan of the project management plan.

This process establishes resource plans that will work directly with the processes used to develop the schedule and budget. In particular, the Plan Resource Management process provides guidance for

1. **Physical resources**
    a. Identifying and quantifying needs
    b. Acquiring resources
    c. Controlling resources
    d. Releasing resources
2. **Human resources** (project team)
    a. Roles and responsibilities definition
    b. Acquisition of team members
    c. Graphically displaying the organization chart
    d. Project team management
    e. Team training and recognition
    f. Releasing team members

TEAM CHARTER

The team charter aligns every team member to an agreed-upon set of core values and expectations by which the team is expected to operate. It establishes clear guidelines regarding

- Acceptable behavior
- Codes of conduct
- Communication methods
- Decision making

Leveraging team input in developing and refining the team charter helps create a more productive team environment where each member can share opinions, gain perspective, and feel valued.

> Team charter is **different** than project charter!
> **Project charter** = Formal authorization of the project
> **Team charter** = Team's agreed-upon operating guidelines

Key Inputs

PROJECT CHARTER

The project charter provides insight into high-level requirements and capital availability that can be used as guidelines in determining potential resource levels and possible capacity constraints that may be imposed by insufficient capital availability.

SCOPE BASELINE

The scope baseline, which is the approved version of the scope statement, WBS, and its associated WBS dictionary can be useful to determine the expected resources need to produce defined deliverables.

PROJECT DOCUMENTS

For project documents, **requirements documentation** dictates the type and amount of resources needed, while the **project schedule** defines when these resources are needed. The **risk register** highlights resource-related issues, and the **stakeholder register** can identify the people who control some of the resources that will be called upon.

EEFs AND OPAs

Cultural, geographic, and company policy factors must be analyzed and incorporated into the approach used in the resource management plan. Consider the following factors and assets and how they may influence the plan:

- **Enterprise environmental factors (EEFs)**
    - Organizational culture and structure
    - Geographic distribution of facilities and team resources
    - Skills set and availability of resources
    - Competition in the marketplace
- **Organizational process assets (OPAs)**
    - Company's HR and physical resource policies
    - Safety and security policies

Key Tools and Techniques

Data representation techniques provide clear visuals of team structures and roles. Three common data representation techniques are used to document and communicate team member roles and responsibilities:

- **Hierarchical chart**
    - Traditional top-down visual
    - Used for WBS and team structure
- **Assignment matrix**
    - Aligns resources to each work package
- **Text-oriented format**
    - Detailed descriptions of resource requirements

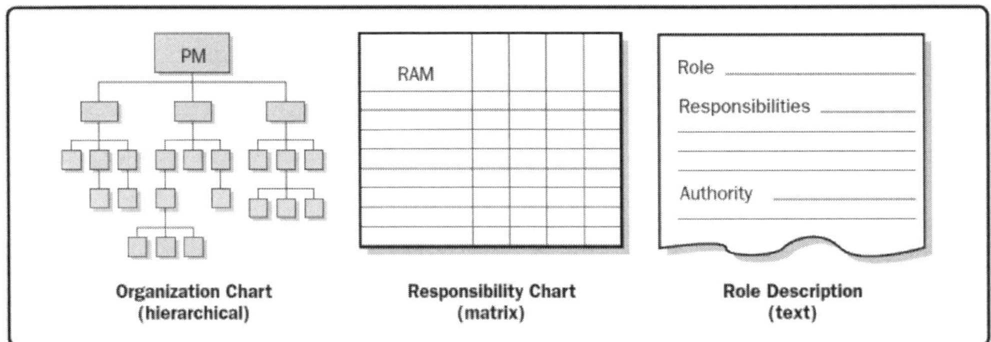

Organizational theory informs the best method to manage and develop a team, explains how teams behave, and recommends approaches to best manage them.

ESTIMATE ACTIVITY RESOURCES (*PMBOK GUIDE*® 9.2)

Summary

Working directly with the Estimate Costs (7.2) process, Estimate Activity Resources (9.2) approximates the total physical and human resource needs of the project. It identifies the type, quantity, and characteristics of the resources required to complete project deliverables.

The resource requirements defined in Estimate Costs (7.2) will be used to define

- Team and resource assignments and calendars (9.3 Acquire Resources)
- Cost baseline (7.3 Determine Budget)

> Est. Costs (7.2), Est. Activity Durations (6.4), and Est. Activity Resources (9.2)
> ALL have similar output structures:
> **(1)** estimates, **(2)** basis of estimates, and **(3)** document updates.

Estimate Activity Resources I.T.T.O.

9.2 Estimate Activity Resources	Inputs	Tools and Techniques	Outputs
	Project mgt. plan • *Resource mgt. plan* • *Scope baseline* **Project documents** • *Activity attributes* • *Activity list* • *Assumption log* • *Cost estimates* • *Resource calendars* • *Risk register* **EEFs** **OPAs**	**Expert judgement** **Bottom-up estimating** **Analogous estimating** **Parametric estimating** **Data analysis** • *Alternatives analysis* **Project mgt. info. system** **Meetings**	**Resource requirements** **Basis of estimates** **Resource breakdown structure** **Project doc. updates** • *Activity attributes* • *Assumption log* • *Lessons learned register*

Key Outputs

RESOURCE REQUIREMENTS

Resource requirements are the primary output of Estimate Activity Resources. The focus of this process is on defining what is needed to complete every work package and activity defined in the WBS. Resource details are used in Acquire Resources (9.3) to build team assignments and resource calendars including such things as type of resource, quantity, and any comments, assumptions, and valid information.

Resource Requirements			
Project Name:		Date:	
ID #	**Resource Group**	**Quantity**	**Comments/Assumptions**

BASIS OF ESTIMATES

The basis of estimates explains the logic behind each resource requirement, allowing the team to understand how the estimates were derived. It includes supporting information such as:

- Description of the basis of estimates
- Assumptions
- Constraints
- Estimate range

The basis of estimates can also provide information to help build out the schedule and budget and to communicate with stakeholders.

Basis of Estimates					
	Project Name:			Date:	
Description	**Method Used**	**Assumptions/Constraints**	**Risks**	**Estimate Range**	**Confidence Level**

Key Inputs

PROJECT MANAGEMENT PLAN

Within the project management plan are subsidiary plans such as the **resource management plan** and **scope baseline** that will provide salient information in estimating activity resources.

PROJECT DOCUMENTS

Project documents provide the detailed descriptions that the team members use to investigate and identify the resources needed to do the work. These documents provide additional perspectives that often influence the nature and number of human and physical resources needed; costs and risks must be balanced. Some important documents include the following:

- Activity list and activity attributes—a primary data source used to estimate resource needs:
  - Resource requirements
  - Activity locations
  - Assumptions and constraints
- Assumption log
- Cost estimates
- Risk register

The **EEFs and OPAs** relevant to the project must also be evaluated and planned for. They often impact resource availability and scheduling factors. EEFs such as resource locations and availability, and team skills and capability are critical factors. OPAs such as policies regarding staffing, supplies, and equipment need to be considered when estimating activity resources.

Key Tools and Techniques

Similarly to Estimate Activity Duration and Estimate Cost, Estimate Activity Resources uses the following common methods to determine resource needs.

- **Analogous estimating**
  - Similar activities from previous projects are used to estimate resource needs.
- **Parametric estimating**
  - Parameters are used to calculate an estimate.
    - Example: An activity requires 4,000 hours of coding and needs to finish in a year. There are only 2,000 work hours in a year, so two coders are needed!
- **Bottom-up estimating**
  - Estimates of lower-level components are "rolled up" to create an estimate of the higher-level activities.

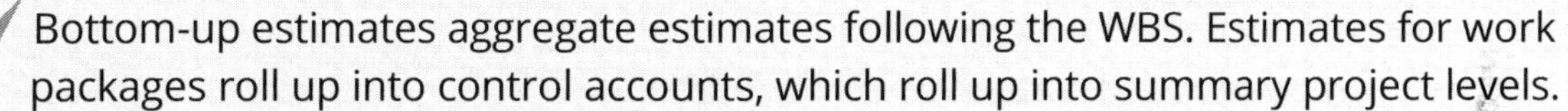

Bottom-up estimates aggregate estimates following the WBS. Estimates for work packages roll up into control accounts, which roll up into summary project levels.

<u>DATA ANALYSIS</u>

Throughout the Estimate Activity Resources process, various options must be evaluated to determine the optimal resource solution given the project's constraints.

Alternatives analysis is most commonly used to evaluate the impact of using various

- Skill levels of team members
- Full-time vs. part-time employees
- Contract vs. company employees
- Sizes and types of machines
- Tools (manual vs. automated)
- Make-or-buy decisions

PLAN COMMUNICATIONS MANAGEMENT (*PMBOK GUIDE®* 10.1)

Summary

Communications planning is focused on creating the ideal approach to effectively and efficiently deliver information to the sponsor and each stakeholder. There are two critical factors for successful project communications:

- Developing the appropriate communication strategies (plans)
- Executing the strategies

Plan Communications Management is the process of developing the strategies for successful communication. Once the plan is created, the project manager is responsible for executing it in a thorough and consistent manner. The information communicated and the mediums of message exchange will depend on the importance and purpose of the information communicated. Considering these aspects is important for managing a successful project.

> Communications planning should be performed early in the project and reviewed regularly.

Plan Communications Management I.T.T.O.

10.1 Plan Communications Mgt.	Inputs	Tools and Techniques	Outputs
	Project charter **Project mgt. plan** • *Resource mgt. plan* • *Stakeholder engmt. plan* **Project documents** • *Req. documentation* • *Stakeholder register* **EEFs** **OPAs**	**Expert judgement** **Communication req. analysis** **Communication technology** **Communication models** **Communication methods** **Interpersonal and team skills** • *Communication styles assessment* • *Political awareness* • *Cultural awareness* **Data representation** • *Stakeholder engagement assessment matrix* **Meetings**	**Communications mgt. plan** **Project mgt. plan updates** • *Stakeholder engmt. plan* **Project doc. updates** • *Project schedule* • *Stakeholder register*

Key Outputs

COMMUNICATION MANAGEMENT PLAN

The communications management plan is the primary output of this process. It documents how project communications will be structured, communicated, and monitored for effectiveness. The communications management plan is a subsidiary plan of the overall project management plan, and it defines the specifications related to information communication. It addresses content, methods, formats, frequency, sender, and recipients. Where possible, escalation paths are good additions to a communication plan. The next table is a basic communication plan template.

Communications Management Plan				
Project Name:			Date:	
Message	**Sender**	**Recipients**	**Method**	**Frequency**

> The project schedule and stakeholder register must be updated to reflect planned communication activities.

Key Inputs

PROJECT MANAGEMENT PLAN

An input to Plan Communications Management, the **stakeholder engagement plan** defines the level of information each stakeholder and the overall project will require. This plan, along with project documents such as the **stakeholder register** and **requirements documentation**, with help the project manager develop a sound communication plan.

The stakeholder register classifies each stakeholder's interest and level of influence on the project, which can guide communications planning so that the appropriate messages are delivered to the correct audience.

> Stakeholders' communication needs are uncovered while creating the stakeholder register and requirements documentation. The communications plan creates messaging strategies based on this information.

EEFs AND OPAs

An organization's EEFs can provide the framework, tools, and systems on which communications can occur. The assets of the organization define some of the policies, procedures, and requirements that must be followed.

Key Tools and Techniques

COMMUNICATION TECHNOLOGY

Communication technology, methods, models, and skills must be analyzed to define the ideal approach to satisfying the project's communication requirements. **Expert judgement** is used to analyze communication requirements and determine stakeholders' needs and how to address them.

Communication technology provides methods to exchange information (written, databases, social media, websites, etc.). The following factors can influence the technology selected for communications:

- Urgency of information
- Availability of technology
- Ease of use
- Project environment
- Sensitivity or confidentiality of information

COMMUNICATION METHODS

The three communication methods below allow tailoring the ideal type of communication to each type of audience:

- **Interactive communications**—ideal when back and forth information exchanges are needed
    - Multidirectional communication (two or more)
    - Methods: Meeting, phone call, instant messaging, social media, video-conferencing
- **Push communications**—ideal when communicating directly to specific recipients
    - Sent to specific recipients, but there is no confirmation the information is understood
    - Methods: Letter, memo, email, press release
- **Pull communications**—ideal when communicating with large audiences or transmitting complicated information
    - Allows content access at the user's discretion
    - Methods: Web portal, intranet site, e-learning, lessons learned database

COMMUNICATION MODELS

Understanding communication models helps project managers choose the communication methods that ensure the information distributed is received and understood.

In a basic sender-receiver model, communication occurs between two parties; the information flows from sender to receiver. Encoding occurs when the message is put into text or audio ready for transmission. Transmitting is a message delivery process, and decoding occurs when the message is translated by the receiver into a useable form.

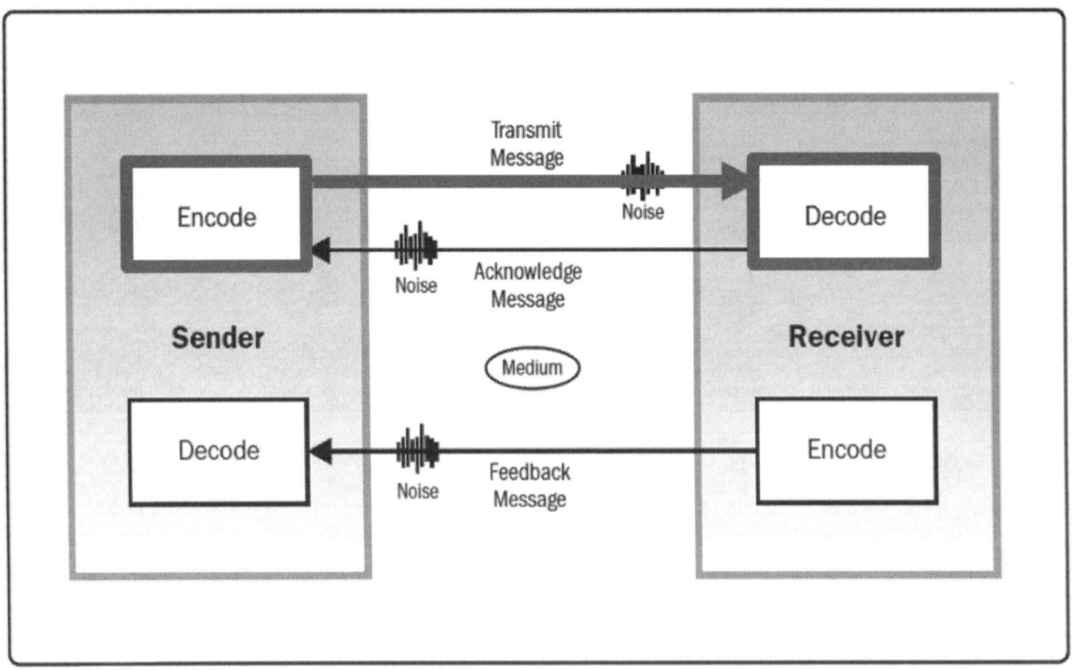

The basic sender-receiver model ensures a message is received, but DOES NOT ensure it is understood.

The interactive communication model builds on the basic model by providing "acknowledge" and "feedback" steps to the communication to ensure that the information was both received and understood. In the interactive model, the additional steps of acknowledgement and feedback are added.

- Acknowledge—The receiver confirms they received the message.
- Feedback
  - The receiver encodes their thoughts on the message.
  - The receiver transmits their thoughts back to the sender.
- Noise is included in the model.
  - Noise is anything compromising the understanding of the message.

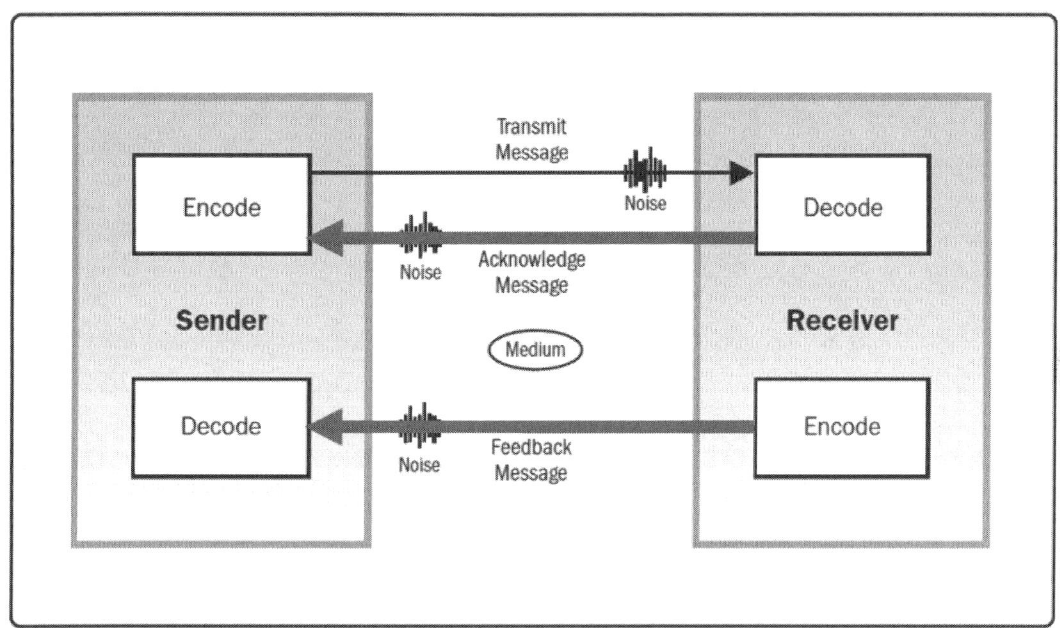

> Noise can be caused by a receiver being distracted or lacking adequate perception, knowledge, or both.

INTERPERSONAL AND TEAM SKILLS

Communication styles, **political awareness**, and **cultural awareness** must be evaluated to ensure the communications plan accommodates the project's unique needs. Style assessments help identify methods and formats for each communication activity. Political awareness emphasizes the power of relationships to help define ways to navigate the environment. Cultural awareness can be leveraged to identify differences between groups, individuals, and organizations.

COMMUNICATION CHANNELS

The number of stakeholders directly affects the total number of potential communication channels that exist for a project. To calculate the number of channels needed based on the number of stakeholders, use this equation:

$$\text{Communication Channels} = [N \times (N - 1)] / 2$$

where N = number of stakeholders

For example, a project with 10 stakeholders has [10 × (10 - 1)] / 2 = 45 potential communication channels. As a result, a key component of planning a project's communications is to determine and limit who will communicate with whom and who will receive what information.

> Communication channels must be recalculated when the number of stakeholders changes.

Case Study: "Planning Communications Management"

"The only thing that seems to be the same in every project is that things will always change."

John had begun to relish his opportunities to learn from Lloyd. Every other Wednesday John spent one hour in Lloyd's office. He shared his progress, good or bad, and tried to ask questions that would help him move the project forward positively. John had come to appreciate the fact that Lloyd never made it easy. Lloyd's method of teaching was not to dictate knowledge. Instead, he asked questions or postulated riddle-like statements. The comment on the only certainty being change was no different. Being an apt student, John took every opportunity to give Lloyd a hard time in his response. "If things always change, why even bother? Maybe the best answer is to give up." John winked, showing Lloyd that he was joking.

"Close, yet so far away. Instead of giving up, why not prepare for it and embrace it? In fact, what helps you reduce change's negative effects?"

John took time to think. He knew this wasn't an empty question. He wanted to find an answer. After a few minutes, he did.

"I see that change is coming, at some time and in some way. What I'm starting to realize is that what matters most is how well I react to it and communicate the status."

Lloyd nodded and posed another question: "If communication is important, shouldn't there be a plan to manage it?" The question was rhetorical. Such was the way with their conversations. John now knew what he was missing. Up to this point he had ideas on how he would distribute information, focused mostly on sending emails to large stakeholders, but now he knew he had to be more calculated and precise.

Over the next two days, he and the team worked through the communication management plan, heavily leveraging the work completed up to this point. They methodically went through the list of stakeholders on the register, evaluating where they fell on the power vs. interest grid and analyzing his understanding of each individual's preferred style of communication.

The result of this analysis and planning was a multipronged communication approach, the cornerstone of the plan being his posting of regular updates on the project management hub. The hub was professional and interactive, allowing stakeholders to check the progress, evaluate all documents, post comments, ask questions, and express concerns. Additionally, he planned to supplement this communication with focused emails when changes occurred, and one-on-one meetings with key stakeholders when urgency and relevancy demanded.

John calculated that the mixture of pull-, interactive-, and push-type communication may lessen the number of requests for updates he would receive from interested stakeholders.

Case Study Questions: "Planning Communications Management"

By posting project updates at regular scheduled intervals on the project management hub that are accessible to all stakeholders, the team is using which method of communication?

a. Interactive communication
b. Push communication
c. Pull communication
d. Focused communication

The plan to send focused emails to key stakeholders when urgency and relevancy demanded is an example of what method of communication?

a. Interactive communication
b. Push communication
c. Pull communication
d. Focused communication

The plan to use one-on-one meetings strategically is an example of what method of communication?

a. Interactive communication
b. Push communication
c. Pull communication
d. Focused communication

Case Study Answers: "Planning Communications Management"

By posting project updates at regularly scheduled intervals on the project management hub that is accessible to all stakeholders, the team is using which method of communication?

a. Interactive communication
b. Push communication
c. Pull communication
d. Focused communication

The plan to send focused emails to key stakeholders when urgency and relevancy demanded is an example of what method of communication?

a. Interactive communication
b. Push communication
c. Pull communication
d. Focused communication

The plan to use one-on-one meetings strategically is an example of what method of communication?

a. Interactive communication
b. Push communication
c. Pull communication
d. Focused communication

PLAN RISK MANAGEMENT (*PMBOK GUIDE*® 11.1)

Summary

The Plan Risk Management process is focused on defining how risks will be identified and managed to increase the chance of the project being successful. Risk planning should start early in the project and be revisited throughout its life cycle. Planning for risk management defines the activities that will

- Identify risks
- Analyze risks
- Develop and implement risk responses
- Exploit or enhance positive opportunities

> Two levels of risk exist in every project:
> **Individual risk** = An uncertain event or condition
> **Overall risk** = The total resulting effect of all risks on a project

Plan Risk Management I.T.T.O.

11.1 Plan Risk Mgt.	Inputs	Tools and Techniques	Outputs
	Project charter **Project mgt. plan** • *All components* **Project documents** • *Stakeholder register* **EEFs** **OPAs**	**Expert judgement** **Data analysis** • *Stakeholder analysis* **Meetings**	**Risk management plan**

Key Outputs

RISK MANAGEMENT PLAN

The sole output of this process is the risk management plan, a subsidiary plan to the project management plan. It describes the structure and process by which risks will be identified, categorized, analyzed, planned, and mitigated or exploited. The risk management plan includes the following key aspects:

- Risk strategy and methodology—general and specific approaches to managing risk
- Roles and responsibilities—who will conduct risk management activities
- Risk funding protocols—rules for accessing contingency or management reserves
- Risk categories—risk categories to be used as group risks (risk breakdown structure common)
- Risk probability and impact
- Definition of levels—predefined levels for grouping risk by severity
- Probability and impact matrix—predefined rules for prioritizing risks by the product of probability multiplied by risk
- Stakeholder risk appetite—the acceptable amount of risk relative to each objective

Key Inputs

Devising the risk management plan begins with analysis of the risk factors already defined in the **project charter**, which outlines known high-level risks. Then, any approved subsidiary plans of the project management plan should have references to the level and type of known risks at the time those plans were created.

Also, standing project documents such as the **stakeholder register** may have information pertaining to each stakeholder's attitudes or tolerances for risks. This provides good supporting information for the risk management plan.

> OPAs can provide existing templates for recording and organizing risks (risk register and risk breakdown structure).

Key Tools and Techniques

Expert judgement from individuals with specialized expertise or experience with similar projects helps to analyze stakeholders' appetite for risks. This allows tailoring a risk management strategy that meets the organization's and project's needs.

Data analysis techniques such as stakeholder analysis can be used in conjunction with the input from subject matter experts as the risk management plan is built.

IDENTIFY RISKS (*PMBOK GUIDE®* 11.2)

Summary

The Identify Risks process is the first step in understanding and managing a project's risks. This process aims to uncover and record individual and overall project risks. All risks must be recorded on the risk register; however, this process is iterative, so new risks identified throughout the project must also find their way onto the register.

Identified risks will be assessed in later processes, within which the following will be defined:

- Impact of each risk (positive or negative)
- Probability of the risk occurring
- Project's overall risk
- Approach to be used to mitigate or exploit each risk

> Identify Risks leverages the entire team and stakeholders to identify and record risks on the risk register.

Identify Risks I.T.T.O.

	Inputs	Tools and Techniques	Outputs
11.2 Identify Risks	**Project management plan** • *Requirements mgt. plan* • *Schedule mgt. plan* • *Cost mgt. plan* • *Quality mgt. plan* • *Resource mgt. plan* • *Risk mgt. plan* • *Scope baseline* • *Schedule baseline* • *Cost baseline* **Project documents** • *Assumption log* • *Cost estimates* • *Duration estimates* • *Issue log* • *Lessons learned register* • *Req. documentation* • *Resource requirements* • *Stakeholder register* **Agreements** **Procurement doc.** **EEFs** **OPAs**	**Expert judgement** **Data gathering** • *Brainstorming* • *Checklists* • *Interviews* **Data analysis** • *Root cause analysis* • *Assumption and constraint analysis* • *SWOT analysis* • *Document analysis* **Interpersonal and team skills** **Facilitation** **Prompt lists** **Meetings**	**Risk register** **Risk report** **Project doc. updates** • *Assumption log* • *Issue log* • *Lessons learned register*

Key Outputs

RISK REGISTER

The **risk register** is the key output of this process. It records specific details on every individual project risk identified by the team and stakeholders. Each individual risk is itemized and characterized by a description, impact, occurrence probability, owner, response, and status.

Risk Register							
Project Name:						Date:	
ID #	**Description**	**Impact**	**Probability**	**Owner**	**Response**	**Status**	**Results**

Each risk listed on the risk register is often linked to the individual WBS activities it affects.

RISK REPORT

The **risk report** is another important output of the Identify Risks process. The risk report provides a comprehensive summary of the total risk from both individual and overall project risks. It indicates risk sources and significant drivers of risk exposure, as well as summarizing the number of threats vs. opportunities and any quantifiable metrics or trends.

The risk report descriptions are continually deepened as the project progresses.

Key Inputs

Project management plans, baselines, and documents present opportunities for both negative and positive risks to occur that affect project success. **All project management plans** should be evaluated for potential risks. In addition, project baselines can pose any number of risks and opportunities and should be analyzed:

- Scope baseline—should be reviewed for deliverable risk exposure
- Schedule baseline—milestone and schedules should be assessed for risk possibilities
- Cost baseline—expense and funding requirement must be evaluated for possible risks

Project documents are also great sources for identifying risks. An **issue log** can call out issues that if not addressed could pose substantial risks to the project. Other good sources for identifying risks are

- Assumption log
- Cost estimates
- Requirements documentation

Important sources of risk identification are **agreements**, contracts and **procurement documents**.

Key Tools and Techniques

EEFs AND OPAs

Enterprise environmental factors highlight examples that can help identify risks, and **organizational process assets** provide the structure by which to record and track risks. EEFs such as published commercial risk databases, benchmarking results, and any industry studies of similar projects can be useful in identifying potential risks.

DATA GATHERING AND DATA ANALYSIS

Data gathering through **brainstorming** and **interviews** can lead to risk identification if conducted in concert with the **expert judgement** of specialists and the use of **prompt lists**. Data analysis by way of **assumption and constraint analysis** and **SWOT analysis** are great methods of identifying risks.

> A skilled facilitator often uses prompt lists to assist experts in drawing out risks related to the project.

PERFORM QUALITATIVE RISK ANALYSIS (*PMBOK GUIDE®* 11.3)

Summary

Perform Qualitative Risk Analysis evaluates each risk on the risk register based on the perception of its probability of occurrence and impact. This process focuses on the items with the highest perceived risks by defining each risk's probability and impact and ranking risks based on their relative priority.

Evaluating risks based on perception introduces the possibility of bias. This must be identified and corrected if found to be present. The prioritized list of risks is then analyzed quantitatively (using data) in the next process, Perform Quantitative Risk Analysis.

> Qualitative risk ratings are subjective, based on perceptions of risk, not numerical data.

PERFORM QUALITATIVE RISK ANALYSIS I.T.T.O.

11.3 Perform Qualitative Risk Analysis	Inputs	Tools and Techniques	Outputs
	Project mgt. plan • *Risk mgt. plan* **Project documents** • *Assumption log* • *Risk register* • *Stakeholder register* **EEFs** **OPAs**	**Expert judgement** **Data gathering** • *Interviews* **Data analysis** • *Risk data quality assessment* • *Risk probability and impact assessment* • *Assessment of other risk parameters* **Interpersonal and team skills** • *Facilitation* **Risk categorization** **Data representation** • *Probability and impact matrix* • *Hierarchical charts* **Meetings**	**Project doc. updates** • *Assumption log* • *Issue log* • *Risk register* • *Risk report*

Key Outputs

PROJECT DOCUMENTS UPDATES

The **risk register** includes occurrence probabilities, impacts, and ownership of the risk response. The **risk report** includes a prioritized list of risks with an overall summary and conclusion. Both outputs, which are originally produced in Identify Risks (11.2), are updated to reflect the now-deeper understanding of the perceived impact of these risks.

>  The prioritized list of risks will be further analyzed in Perform Quantitative Risk Analysis to determine the aggregate effect of individual risks on project outcomes.

Key Inputs

The **risk management plan** will guide the method of addressing risks that are documented in the **risk register**. EEFs and OPAs can provide examples with information drawn from industry studies or internal sources.

Key Tools and Techniques

Data analysis techniques are used to define the probability and impact of each risk so that the risks can be categorized and prioritized. A **risk probability and impact assessment** considers the likelihood that a specific risk will occur, while a **risk data quality assessment** helps evaluate the degree by which risk data can be relied upon.

> Categorizing risks by their root cause or phase affected helps identify where the project is most exposed to risk.

PROBABILITY-IMPACT MATRIX

The probability-impact matrix is a tool used to map each risk by two factors (probability and impact). The grid uses two axes with weighted values, and at the intersection of these two factors is the product of their weighting.

Probability	Threats					Opportunities					Probability
Very High 0.90	0.05	0.09	0.18	0.36	0.72	0.72	0.36	0.18	0.09	0.05	Very High 0.90
High 0.70	0.04	0.07	0.14	0.28	0.56	0.56	0.28	0.14	0.07	0.04	High 0.70
Medium 0.50	0.03	0.05	0.10	0.20	0.40	0.40	0.20	0.10	0.05	0.03	Medium 0.50
Low 0.30	0.02	0.03	0.06	0.12	0.24	0.24	0.12	0.06	0.03	0.02	Low 0.30
Very Low 0.10	0.01	0.01	0.02	0.04	0.08	0.08	0.04	0.02	0.01	0.01	Very Low 0.10
	Very Low 0.05	Low 0.10	Moderate 0.20	High 0.40	Very High 0.80	Very High 0.80	High 0.40	Moderate 0.20	Low 0.10	Very Low 0.05	
	Negative Impact					Positive Impact					

HIERARCHICAL CHARTS

Hierarchical charts are used when risks are categorized by more than two parameters. A good example of such a chart is a bubble chart, with each risk plotted using three factors: x-axis, y-axis, and bubble size.

PERFORM QUANTITATIVE RISK ANALYSIS (*PMBOK GUIDE*® 11.4)

Summary

Perform Quantitative Risk Analysis uses numerical data to define the combined effect of individual project risks. The process defines the project's total risk exposure and recommended responses to individual risks. Quantitative risk analysis is not necessarily performed on all projects and may be more frequently used on large projects. As with qualitative risk analysis, quantitative risk analysis produces a deeper understanding of risk. The single output of this process is the risk report.

> The recommended risk responses produced by 11.4 are used as inputs in Plan Risk Responses (11.5).

Perform Quantitative Risk Analysis I.T.T.O.

	Inputs	Tools and Techniques	Outputs
11.3 Perform Qualitative Risk Analysis	**Project mgt. plan** • *Risk mgt. plan* • *Scope baseline* • *Schedule baseline* • *Cost baseline* **Project documents** • *Assumption log* • *Basis of estimates* • *Cost estimates* • *Cost forecasts* • *Duration estimates* • *Milestone list* • *Resource requirements* • *Risk register* • *Risk report* • *Schedule forecasts* **EEFs** **OPAs**	**Expert judgement** **Data gathering** • *Interviews* **Interpersonal and team skills** • *Facilitation* **Representations of uncertainty** **Data analysis** • *Simulations* • *Sensitivity analysis* • *Decision tree analysis* • *Influence diagrams*	**Project doc. updates** • *Risk report*

Key Outputs

The critical output of this process, the risk report is updated to reflect a summary of the project's overall risk exposure along with a probabilistic analysis, a prioritized risk list, and a risk response plan. Overall, project risk exposure is reflected by two measures: chance of project success (the probability that the project will achieve key objectives) and range of possible outcomes (variability). A detailed probabilistic analysis will discuss major drivers of overall project risks and the amount of contingency reserve needed to provide the desired level of confidence.

Key Inputs

Project management plans and project documents provide the detailed information of each individual risk that is required to define the project's total risk exposure that will be outlined in the risk report.

The project management plans that will be used include

- Risk management plan
- Scope baseline
- Schedule baseline
- Cost baseline

Some of the key project documents that will be used include

- Risk register
- Risk report
- Assumption log
- Estimates (cost, duration) and basis of estimates
- Forecasts (cost, schedule)
- Duration estimates and milestone list

> Quantitative risk analysis is deeper than qualitative risk analysis, requiring robust data and more resources, time, or both.

Key Tools and Techniques

DATA ANALYSIS

Data analysis will be used heavily in Performing Quantitative Risk Analysis. A few key analysis techniques can provide excellent predictive and quantitative results:

Simulation models determine the combined effects of individual project risks to evaluate their potential impact on achieving project objectives.

One of the most commonly used simulation models is Monte Carlo analysis. Analytical software is used to run thousands of simulations of predicted results based on factors and assumptions input into the model. The results of each iteration are documented, producing a graph showing an S-curve representing a cumulative probability density function.

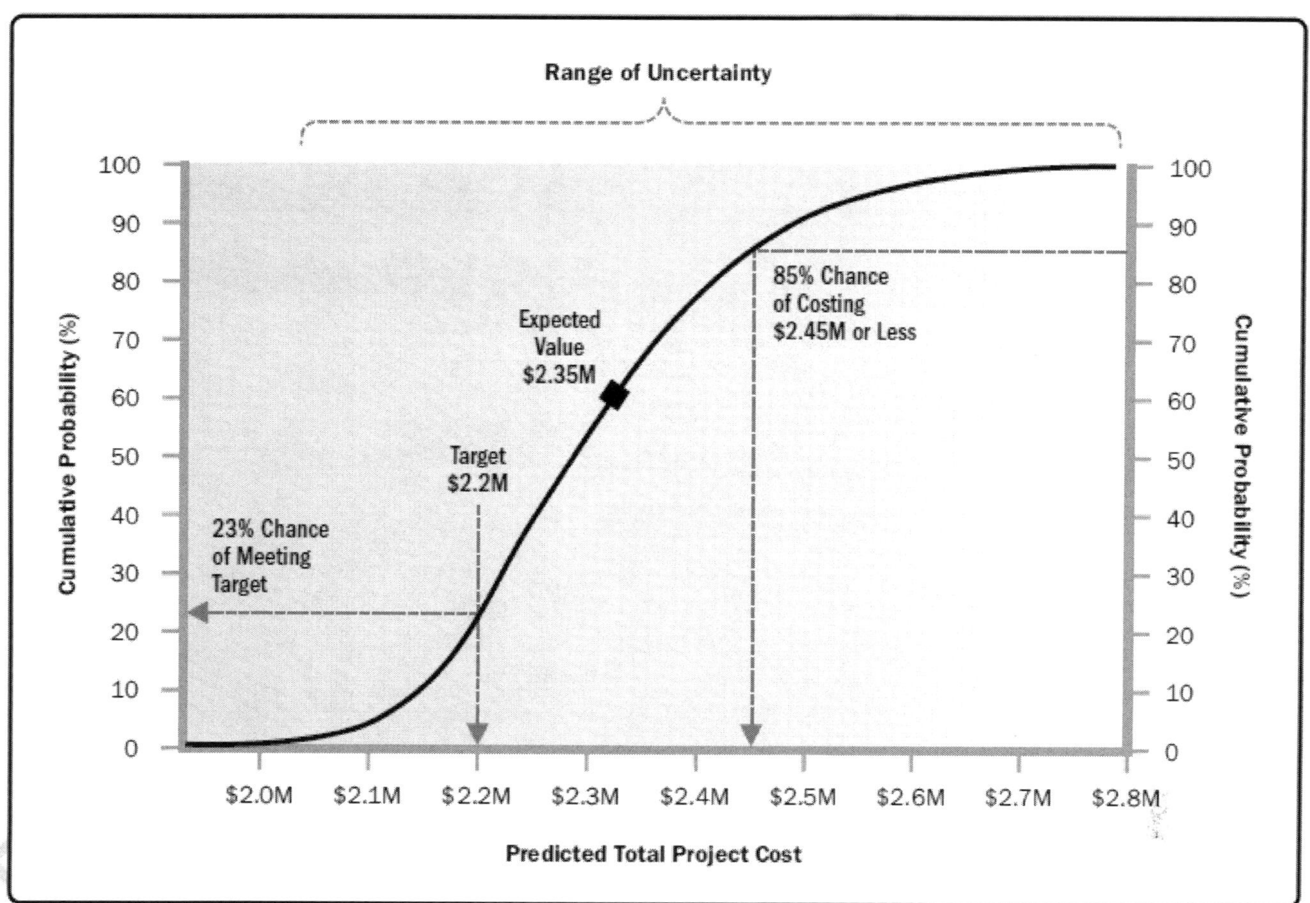

The S-curve from a Monte Carlo risk analysis visually depicts the probability of achieving any outcome.

Sensitivity analysis determines which individual risk has the greatest impact by correlating variations in project outcomes to individual risks. The most common type of sensitivity model is the tornado diagram. It shows the calculated correlation coefficients for each element of risk in the model. The items on the graphic are ordered by descending correlative strength.

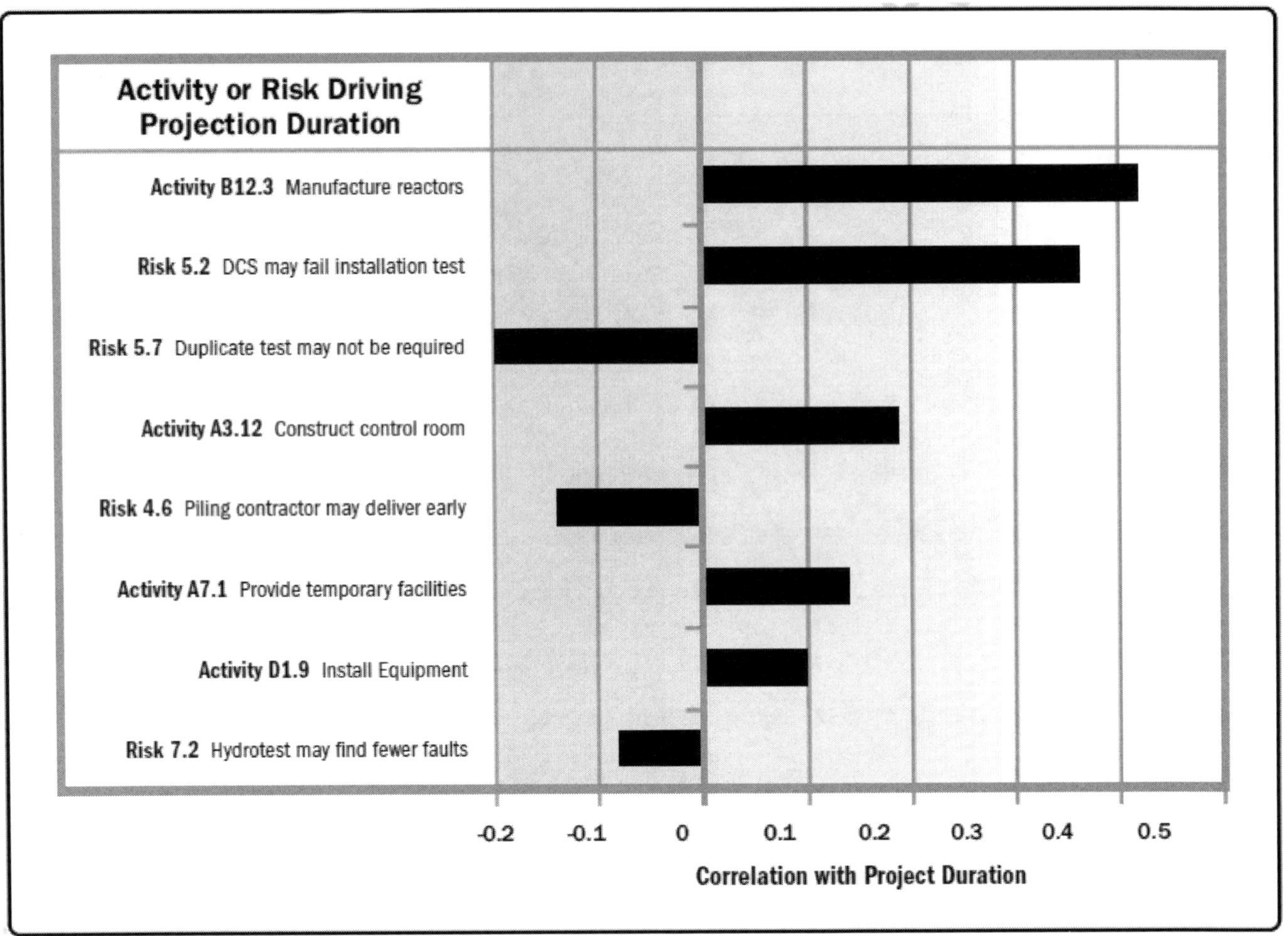

> The tornado diagram shows the amount of impact each risk has on a project output. The higher the coefficient, the greater the impact.

Decision tree analysis is a mathematical method used to select the best of several alternate courses of action. Alternate potential paths of the project are shown using branches, with each representing different decisions or events. Expected monetary values (EMVs) are calculated for each branch, and they are then further augmented with probability and impact estimates. Finally, a net path value is calculated for each branch; the path can be positive or negative.

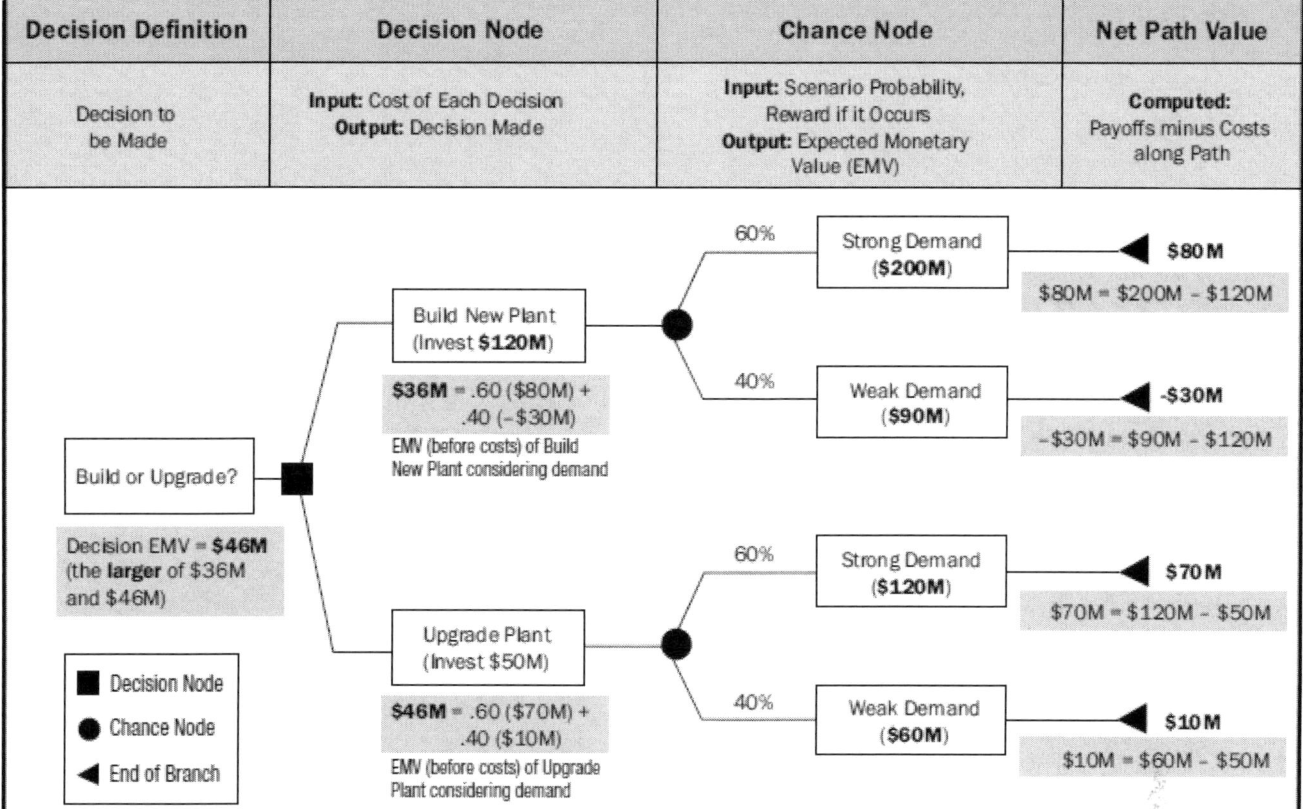

Note 1: The decision tree shows how to make a decision between alternative capital strategies (represented as "decision nodes") when the environment contains uncertain elements (represented as "chance nodes").

Note 2: Here, a decision is being made whether to invest $120M US to build a new plant or to instead invest only $50M US to upgrade the existing plant. For each decision, the demand (which is uncertain, and therefore represents a "chance node") must be accounted for. For example, *strong* demand leads to $200M revenue with the new plant but only $120M US for the upgraded plant, perhaps due to capacity limitations of the upgraded plant. The end of each branch shows the net effect of the payoffs minus costs. For each decision branch, all effects are added (see shaded areas) to determine the overall Expected Monetary Value (EMV) of the decision. Remember to account for the investment costs. From the calculations in the shaded areas, the upgraded plant has a higher EMV of $46M – also the EMV of the overall decision. (This choice also represents the lowest risk, avoiding the worst case possible outcome of a loss of $30M).

PLAN RISK RESPONSES (*PMBOK GUIDE*® 11.5)

Summary

Plan Risk Responses develops the strategies that will be used to address the risks with the project's highest impact overall as well as other individual risks. The project risks identified in Identify Risks (11.2) were further defined, categorized, and prioritized in 11.3 and 11.4, where qualitative and quantitative risk analyses were performed. The next step is to expand on how the project team plans to mitigate the negative risks and exploit the positive ones.

Each risk owner should use a structured approach detailing their action plan that will include primary strategies, backup, and contingency plans. Their countermeasures will be implemented and fully executed in Implement Risk Responses (11.6), and monitored and controlled in Monitor Risks (11.7).

> Contingency plans are fallback plans developed for when the selected strategies don't work!

Plan Risk Responses I.T.T.O.

	Inputs	Tools and Techniques	Outputs
11.5 Plan Risk Responses	**Project mgt. plan** • *Resource mgt. plan* • *Risk mgt. plan* • *Cost baseline* **Project documents** • *Lessons learned register* • *Project schedule* • *Project team assignments* • *Resource calendars* • *Risk register* • *Risk report* • *Stakeholder register* **EEFs** **OPAs**	**Expert judgement** **Data gathering** • *Interviews* **Interpersonal and team skills** • *Facilitation* **Strategies for threats** **Strategies for opportunities** **Contingent response strategies** **Strategies for overall project risk** **Data analysis** • *Alternatives analysis* • *Cost-benefit analysis* **Decision making** • *Multicriteria decision analysis*	**Change requests** **Project mgt. plan updates** • *Schedule mgt. plan* • *Cost mgt. plan* • *Quality mgt. plan* • *Resource mgt. plan* • *Procurement mgt. plan* • *Scope baseline* • *Schedule baseline* • *Cost baseline* **Project doc. updates** • *Assumption log* • *Cost forecasts* • *Lessons learned register* • *Project schedule* • *Project team assignments* • *Risk register* • *Risk report*

Key Outputs

The primary and most important outputs of this process already are updates to the project management plan and the project documents. It must be noted that the project management plans and project documetns also serve as inputs to the Plan Risk Responses. In completing this process, these inputs will be updated and greatly expanded upon, in the end yielding detailed response plans with backup and contingency plans to support the primary response countermeasures in the event they are not effective.

The core inputs that will be critical outputs here are the **risk register** and **risk report**. These documents will be updated to reflect the actions believed sufficient to address all the threats and opportunities faced by the project. With these actions, **change requests** may also be necessary, and updates to project management plan components and project documents will be required.

> Planned risk responses often require change requests to adjust project baselines and management plans.

Key Inputs

In addition to the **risk register** and **risk report** (which are both critical inputs to and the primary outputs of this process), Plan Risk Responses uses the **resource management plan** and **risk management plan**, as well as the cost baseline, which defines the existing contingency fund.

> The cost baseline includes a contingency fund that is allocated specifically to responding to risks.

Key Tools and Techniques

Strategies for dealing with risks must be evaluated. Whether the risks are threats, opportunities, or overall project liabilities, the project manager must determine how they will be addressed. To do so, it is wise to understand the potential actions that can be taken relative to each. Below are these potential actions and how they align to the different types of risks encountered throughout a project:

- Escalate—elevating the risk to a higher level when it is outside project's scope or authority
- Avoid—change some aspect to eliminate the risk
- Exploit—seek to ensure the opportunity is realized
- Transfer—shift ownership
- Share—transfer part of the liability to a third party
- Mitigate—take actions to reduce liability
- Enhance—take actions to increase probability of occurrence
- Accept—acknowledge and take no action

Potential Strategies for Dealing with Risk			
Action	**Threats**	**Opportunities**	**Overall Project Risks**
Escalate	X	X	
Avoid	X		X
Exploit		X	X
Transfer	X		X
Share		X	X
Mitigate	X		X
Enhance		X	X
Accept	X	X	x

Alternatives analysis and **cost-benefit analysis** of all risk response strategies help the team select the appropriate response and define its project impact. Alternatives analysis is conducted when comparing characteristics or requirements of alternate risk responses. Conducting cost-benefit analysis helps determine risk impacts vs. cost of response, allowing the project team to make informed decisions on if or how a risk is addressed.

> Contingency response strategies are only executed when specific predefined conditions are violated (e.g., missed milestones).

CASE STUDY: PLAN RISK RESPONSES

"Not only are we better prepared, but I think we now have stronger buy-in and engagement from our stakeholders," John mused as he recounted the progress the team had made in finalizing risk response plans.

After identifying and evaluating every significant project risk both quantitatively and qualitatively, the team had spent the last few weeks completing the Plan Risk Responses process. During this process, John and his core team members pushed to ensure that every significant risk identified was assigned to an individual risk owner and that appropriate risk responses were developed.

To complete this effort, they first spent time with each nominated risk owner helping them develop a variety of potential risk response strategies to address the individual risk they were now responsible for. The goal was to develop risk response options that were appropriate, cost-effective, and realistic. John and team had utilized five unique strategies to develop a wide range of potential risk response options. Each of the five strategies, escalate, avoid, transfer, mitigate, and accept, provided a different method by which to deal with the threat each individual risk brought.

Once a variety of potential options were defined, the team coached risk owners to use two different data analysis techniques to evaluate and select the strategy that best met the goal. Alternatives analysis helped to compare the characteristics of each option, while a cost-benefit analysis the effectiveness in terms of cost.

Each individual risk scenario required a tailored approach to best prepare for and mitigate the negative impact.

Once the optimal risk response was selected, the team was diligent in ensuring that trigger conditions and fallback plans were defined for each selected strategy. These helped to ensure that the risk owner understood exactly when the responses should be used and the what should be done if the primary strategies proved ineffective.

The team was now working to develop options for the last significant risk. Schedule planning had identified that there was a risk that during the course of the project the demand for design revisions may outpace the current inhouse capacity available. Walking through the five strategies the team had determined that there was no way to avoid the risk and it was unacceptable to accept the consequences of the risk without action. Additionally, the risk could not be escalated as the redesign activity was well within the scope of project and the risk was not an insurable so transfer was not an option.

John and team knew the only option was to find a way to mitigate the risk by obtaining access to temporary surge resources. He knew these resources would be expensive and would require the allocation of a contingency reserve. Adding complexity to the situation was the fact that he had no idea how to get a contract set up. Before he could finalize the risk response plan he needed to go talk to Sara.

Case Study Questions: Plan Risk Responses

What are the two data analysis methods that are used to evaluate and select the preferred risk response strategy?

a) Alternative analysis and cost-benefit analysis
b) Alternative analysis and risk optimization analysis
c) Quantitative analysis and qualitative analysis
d) Risk analysis and contingency reserve analysis

Which of the following is not a desired characteristic of a proper risk response plan?

a) Appropriate
b) Cost effective
c) Time sensitive
d) Realistic

What are the five alternative strategies that must be considered when dealing with threats?

a) Escalate, Avoid, Transfer, Mitigate, Accept
b) Escalate, Avoid, Expedite, Mitigate, Accept
c) Escalate, Exploit, Share, Enhance, Accept
d) Escalate, Exploit, Transfer/Share, Mitigate/Enhance, Accept

Case Study Answers: "Plan Risk Responses"

What are the two data analysis methods that are used to evaluate and select the preferred risk response strategy?

a) Alternative analysis and cost-benefit analysis
b) Alternative analysis and risk optimization analysis
c) Quantitative analysis and qualitative analysis
d) Risk analysis and contingency reserve analysis

Which of the following is not a desired characteristic of a proper risk response plan?

a) Appropriate
b) Cost effective
c) Time sensitive
d) Realistic

What are the five alternative strategies that must be considered when dealing with threats?

a) Escalate, Avoid, Transfer, Mitigate, Accept
b) Escalate, Avoid, Expedite, Mitigate, Accept
c) Escalate, Exploit, Share, Enhance, Accept
d) Escalate, Exploit, Transfer/Share, Mitigate/Enhance, Accept

PLAN PROCUREMENT MANAGEMENT (*PMBOK GUIDE®* 12.1)

Summary

Strategic decisions often necessitate purchasing products or services from outside sources. Plan Procurement Management guides these decisions and how and when to acquire the services or resources. Plan Procurement Management focuses on documenting procurement decisions, defining the approach, and identifying potential sellers. Detailed documents generated here will be used in other processes to:

- Obtain seller responses, select sellers, and award contracts (12.2 Conduct Procurements)
- Monitor sellers to ensure they meet their obligations (12.3 Control Procurements)
- Close completed contracts (12.3 Control Procurements)

Procurements present opportunities for significant financial and liability risk. Therefore, the project team must seek the assistance of procurement specialists and legal experts.

> Contracts describe the legal relationships and obligations between buyers and sellers. The PMP® test assumes the project team is the buyer of services from a seller.

Plan Procurement Management I.T.T.O.

	Inputs	Tools and Techniques	Outputs
12.1 Plan Procurement Management	**Project charter** **Business documents** • *Business case* • *Benefits mgt. plan* **Project management plan** • *Scope mgt. plan* • *Quality mgt. plan* • *Resource mgt. plan* • *Scope baseline* **Project documents** • *Milestone list* • *Project team assignments* • *Req. documentation* • *Req. traceability matrix* • *Resource requirements* • *Risk register* • *Stakeholder register* **EEFs** **OPAs**	**Expert judgement** **Data gathering** • *Market research* **Data analysis** • *Make-or-buy analysis* **Source selection analysis** **Meetings**	**Procurement mgt. plan** **Procurement strategy** **Bid documents** **Procurement SOW** **Source selection criteria** **Make-or-buy decisions** **Independent cost estimates** **Change requests** **Project doc. updates** • *Lessons learned register* • *Milestone list* • *Req. documentation* • *Req. traceability matrix* • *Risk register* • *Stakeholder register* **OPA updates**

Key Outputs

PROCUREMENT MANAGEMENT PLAN

The procurement management plan documents the requirements and constraints related to the procurement and the specific activities that will be undertaken. It defines both how procurements will be completed and integrated with project work. The specifications that impact procurement are:

- Contract type
- Funding sources and availability
- Roles and responsibilities
- Authorization to sign legal agreements
- Timing requirements
- Procurement metrics
- Constraints and assumptions
- Prequalified sellers

Procurement Management Plan			
Project Name:		Date:	
Roles		**Official Procurement Documents**	
Manager:			
Procurement Department:			
Contract Type		**Coverage Requirements**	
Limitations and Expectations:			

Make-or-buy decisions define the work or services that must be purchased. Developing a **procurement strategy** helps the project team establish the details by which procurement will occur. In addition, the procurement strategy determines contract phases, key milestones, and delivery methods—which may differ based on project type (professional vs. construction projects etc.).

The procurement strategy can also aid in determining the most appropriate contract payment types that should be sought through procurement. Different payment types have different impacts on contract performance and seller engagement. Some payment type examples listed below should always be coordinated with the organization's finance department:

- Lump sum
- Firm fixed price
- Cost plus award or incentive
- Time and materials, etc.

> Legal and procurement expertise is often leveraged to help develop and record the procurement strategy.

BID DOCUMENTS

Bid documents are used to solicit bids from sellers by defining the **procurement statement of work** and the desired form of responses. Bids are provided to prospective sellers in the Conduct Procurements process with the goal of facilitating consistent and appropriate proposals in response to bid requests. Bid documents have specific purposes and are used tactically to obtain information from sellers in a defined manner. Examples include the following:

- **Request for information (RFI)**—used to obtain descriptive information on goods and services from a seller; typically followed by an RFQ or RFP
- **Request for quotation (RFQ)**—method and cost by which sellers would satisfy requirements
- **Request for proposal (RFP)**—most common bid document; plans for solutions not easy to determine

PROCUREMENT STATEMENT OF WORK

The procurement statement of work defines the project needs in a manner sufficient to allow sellers to assess if they can provide the work. Prospective sellers generate bids in the Conduct Procurements process to demonstrate their ability to satisfy the procurement SOW.

Procurement Statement of Work					
Project Name:				Date:	
Description	**Region**	**Duration**	**Deliverables**	**Requirements**	**Comments**

> The procurement statement of work must be clear, complete, and concise.

SOUCE SELECTION CRITERIA

Source selection criteria provide an objective means for evaluating each proposal to select the seller offering the greatest overall value. These criteria are defined and weighted based on importance. Examples of criteria that can be factors for evaluation are

- Capability
- Cost
- Schedule
- Experience
- Financial stability of the bidder, etc.

Source Selection Criteria							
Project Name:						Date:	
Criteria	**Weight**	**Bidder1 Rating**	**Bidder1 Value**	**Bidder2 Rating**	**Bidder2 Value**	**Bidder3 Rating**	**Bidder3 Value**
Cost	8	3	24	7	56	5	40
Schedule	7	7	49	7	49	3	21
Experience	5	5	25	5	25	3	15
Totals:			**98**		**130**		**76**

INDEPENDENT COST ESTIMATES

Independent cost estimates provide a frame of reference for evaluating bids submitted during Conduct Procurements. They are prepared either internally or by an external professional estimator. Any significant difference between the estimate and received bids can indicate procurement SOW issues:

- Ambiguous
- Seller(s) failed to understand
- Seller(s) failed to respond to entire SOW

> Developing procurement plans and documents often uncovers issues that require change requests.

Key Inputs

The project management plan, **business documents**, and project documents are all vital references that will frame the deliverables, requirements, and details necessary to determine what should be procured.

Business documents

- Business case
- Benefits management plan

Project management plan

- Scope management plan
- Quality management plan
- Resource management plan
- Scope baseline

Project documents

- Milestone list
- Project team assignments
- Requirement documentation
- Requirements traceability matrix
- Resource requirements
- Risk register
- Stakeholder register

ORGANIZATIONAL PROCESS ASSETS

OPAs define the structure on which contracts can be established, which will reduce financial risks and increase the likelihood of project success. Inherent in some organizations will be preapproved seller lists or sellers who have standing master service agreements with the organization. This can help streamline seller selection.

Formal procurement policies, procedures, and guidelines are also common for most organizations, and dedicated procurement professionals or procurement departments are likely to exist. Procurement experts will also help determine the best contract types (fixed-price, cost-reimbursable, time and materials etc.) to meet the needs of a project.

Fixed Price Contracts

Fixed-price contract types are used in situations where requirements are well defined and no significant changes are expected. **Firm fixed price** (FFP) contracts are used when prices are set and not subject to change. **Fixed price incentive fee** (FPIF) contracts have a fixed base price, with incentives built in to achieve predefined goals. **Fixed price with economic price adjustment** (FPEA) contracts are contracts with acceptable adjustments for fluctuations in things such as commodity prices.

> In situations where costs could grow, firm fixed price (FFP) contracts put significant financial risk on the seller.

Cost-reimbursable Contracts

Cost-reimbursable contract types are used when the scope of work is expected to change significantly during the project. In these situations, the seller is reimbursed for all allowable additional costs (per contract). If **cost plus fixed fee** (CPFF) contracts are used, the seller receives a fixed-fee payment calculated as a percentage of the initial estimated costs. If **cost plus incentive fee** (CPIF) contracts are used, the seller receives predefined incentives for achieving specific performance levels. If costs exceed predefined levels, the buyer and seller share the costs based on agreed percentages (for example, 80/20). If **cost plus award fee** (CPAF) contracts are used, a majority of the fee is tied to subjective performance criteria.

> In situations where costs could grow, cost plus fixed fee (CPFF) contracts put significant financial risk on the buyer.

Time and Material Contracts

Time and material contracts are hybrids of cost-reimbursable and fixed-price contracts allowing flexibility in the seller capability. These contracts are characterized by hourly rates ($/hr) and are typically used when a precise statement of work cannot be achieved. Common uses are staff augmentation and acquisition of experts.

Key Tools and Techniques

Plan Procurement Management requires **expert judgement** from procurement professionals, cost estimators, and many other subject matter experts. Data gathering and data analysis are essential to prepare for successful third-party engagements that are initiated by procurement agreements. From **market research** to the collaboration of team members in conducting **source selection analysis**, Plan Procurement Management is ripe with information and decision making.

Case Study: "Solving the Procurement Question"

Operating in a balanced matrix structure puts limits on John's actual power. When it came to procurements, Sara made it clear that he didn't have authority to initiate or sign agreements. "If you need a contract, go see Legal" were her instructions. While this limitation initially felt constraining, sitting in the lawyer's office, he was now relieved that he had a specialist he could lean on for help.

Trying to break the ice, John joked, "I googled 'firm-fixed, source selection criteria, and request for quote' and I'm just as confused as when I started. I need help."

Not wasting time, the lawyer began listing off what he knew. "Sara tells me you need to set up a contract for staff augmentation on your project. She says you need consultants who are specialists and you're going to need them in approximately four months. Do you know how many hours of consultant time you need?"

"I know approximately when I will need them, but I don't know exactly how many hours I will need." As John answered, the lawyer pulled out a yellow legal pad and began jotting down notes. As John waited, he asked nervously, "Is not knowing the exact number of hours I need a problem?"

Without looking up, the lawyer responded: "Not a problem at all. We are going to use a type of contract that gives you both the stability and flexibility you need. Basically, a consultant company will assure us a rate per hour, but we will have the flexibility to decide how many hours we use. We will also put a cap on the total number of hours they could charge. That will protect us from the costs shooting to the moon."

John appreciated the efficiency and directness of the lawyer's approach. He attempted to follow in kind by asking what else he needed to provide to help get an agreement signed quickly. The lawyer informed John that he would need his expertise to define the exact details of what was needed—he called this the "procurement statement of work." The lawyer emphasized that the information in the statement of work needed to be clear, complete, and concise.

Additionally, John would need to clarify the criteria that would be used to decide which consultant company to choose. John nodded his understanding of the process. Jumping directly into the task at hand, the lawyer began asking questions to draw out the details he required to create the procurement documents. Within 20 minutes, he had what he needed.

"I will finalize the statement of work and get a request for proposal ready to go out to the engineering consultant companies. I can have the documents drafted in two days. If you can define the criteria, we will have all the procurement documents ready to roll by Friday."

Case Study Questions: "Solving the Procurement Question"

The lawyer recommended a contract type that would assure the contracted firm a defined rate per hour while allowing John flexibility in the total consultant hours used. What type of contract does this describe?

a. Firm fixed price (FFP)
b. Fixed price with economic price adjustment (FPEPA)
c. Cost plus incentive fee (CPIF)
d. Time and material (T&M)

What is the term to describe the criteria that will be used to select which consulting company to establish a contract with?

a. Source selection criteria
b. Procurement evaluation criteria
c. Terms of reference
d. Procurement statement of work

CASE STUDY ANSWERS: "SOLVING THE PROCUREMENT QUESTION"

The lawyer recommended a contract type that would assure the contracted firm a defined rate per hour while allowing John flexibility in the total consultant hours used. What type of contract does this describe?

a. Firm fixed price (FFP)
b. Fixed price with economic price adjustment (FPEPA)
c. Cost plus incentive fee (CPIF)
d. Time and material (T&M)

What is the term to describe the criteria that will be used to select which consulting company to establish a contract with?

a. Source selection criteria
b. Procurement evaluation criteria
c. Terms of reference
d. Procurement statement of work

PLAN STAKEHOLDER ENGAGEMENT (*PMBOK GUIDE*® 13.2)

Summary

Planning Stakeholder Engagement is a matter of developing customized approaches to how each stakeholder will be engaged based on their unique needs, expectations, interest, and influence. This process incorporates detailed information into a document referred to as the stakeholder engagement plan. For each stakeholder, the plan defines the following:

- Influence
- Current and desired engagement
- Strategy or actions to be taken to achieve effective engagement

Having a solid stakeholder engagement plan will be important during the project while managing stakeholder engagement in the Executing process group and measuring performance in the Monitoring and Controlling process group. But its significance does not stop there; it will be a key input in the Plan, Manage, and Monitor Communications processes (10.1, 10.2, 10.3); and it will be revisited as things change, issues arise, and agreements are executed.

> The stakeholder engagement plan is a key input to all Communications processes (Plan, Manage, Monitor).

Plan Stakeholder Engagement I.T.T.O.

13.2 Plan Stakeholder Engmt.	Inputs	Tools and Techniques	Outputs
	Project charter **Project management plan** • *Resource mgt. plan* • *Communications mgt. plan* • *Risk mgt. plan* **Project documents** • *Assumption log* • *Change log* • *Issue log* • *Project schedule* • *Risk register* • *Stakeholder register* **Agreements** **EEFs** **OPAs**	**Expert judgement** **Data gathering** • *Benchmarking* **Data analysis** • *Assumption and constraint analysis* • *Root cause analysis* **Decision making** • *Prioritization and ranking* **Data representation** • *Mind mapping* • *Stakeholder engagement assessment matrix* **Meetings**	**Stakeholder engmt. plan**

Key Outputs

STAKEHOLDER ENGAGEMENT PLAN

The only output of the Plan Stakeholder Engagement process is the stakeholder engagement plan. An example of a template is shown below. Any of the information in the template can—and should—be changed based on a project's specific needs. Nonetheless, the idea is to understand the *who, where, what*, and *how*: Who are the stakeholders? Where do they currently stand relative to engagement? What level of engagement do you need or desire? How will you approach getting them to the engagement level required?

Stakeholder Engagement Plan Template

Stakeholder Engagement Plan					
Project:				Date:	
Stakeholder	**Influence**	**Current Engmt.**	**Target Engmt.**	**Strategy / Approach**	**Risks**

Key Inputs

The **stakeholder register**, generated in Identify Stakeholders, is a key input to building the stakeholder engagement plan. In addition, the **project charter** and **project management plan**, which were inputs to the stakeholder register, become inputs to the engagement plan. At this point, however, the project management plan has developed into a big plan, full of all its subcomponents. Useful here will be the **resource management plan**, **communications management plan**, and **risk management plan**. Other inputs will be derived from project documents such as

- Assumption log
- Change log
- Issue log
- Project schedule
- Risk register

Key Tools and Techniques

Plan Stakeholder Engagement takes input from not only source documents and plans, but also **expert judgement** from people who know the organization and culture. Obtaining this information through data gathering techniques can be accomplished with **benchmarking** or other methods. What the project manager does with the information gathered is considered data analysis. Performing **assumption and constraint analysis** allows processing information into organized and summarized intelligence, which can be displayed through data representation on a **stakeholder engagement assessment matrix** (shown next).

Stakeholder Engagement Matrix

Stakeholder	Unaware	Resistant	Neutral	Supportive	Leading
Stakeholder 1	C			D	
Stakeholder 2			C	D	
Stakeholder 3				C, D	

***C** = Current, **D** = Desired*

> The relative importance of a stakeholder influences the amount of effort allocated to ensuring engagement.

CASE STUDY: "DEFINING THE PATH TO ENGAGEMENT"

Sara always seemed to be able to frame the challenge John faced in a way that was both logically simple and mildly daunting.

In their last meeting she had stated, "Understanding each stakeholder's current engagement level is good, defining the desired level is great, but the real challenge is coming up with a way to get them there."

Since the creation of the stakeholder register, John had begun creating plans to tackle the many project knowledge areas (Scope, Cost, Risk, etc.). The world of stakeholder management was no different. The most positive development was that John was not alone in his efforts. As he progressed through each plan, he began bringing in experts from other departments. These individuals complemented the core group he leaned on daily. The team now met in a conference room and contemplated their current challenge.

"When we created the communication management plan we laid out plans for engaging nearly all of the stakeholders, but we have two left to think through. Each brings a different issue." With that John reorganized the Excel table labeled "Stakeholder Engagement Assessment Matrix" to show stakeholders J and E. The team had made sure to code each stakeholder with a letter to conceal identities in the event the document was inadvertently distributed.

Stakeholder	Unaware	Resistant	Neutral	Supportive	Leading
Stakeholder J	C				D
Stakeholder E		C		D	

"Stakeholder J is currently unaware of the project and is in a high power–high interest position; we need her to be 'leading'." The team nodded their confirmation. "Stakeholder E, on the other hand, is also in a high-power position with medium interest, but unfortunately the interest isn't positive right now. We have him down as 'resistant'. It would be great if he became 'supportive' or at worst 'neutral."

With that, John threw the challenge to the team. Within the hour the team had developed approaches to accomplish both goals. Stakeholder J would be engaged early and in a one-on-one setting using the charter, business case, and SOW. The team was confident that once made aware, stakeholder J would become a 'leader' and would remain a leader through regular status updates.

The approach for stakeholder E focused on leveraging his relationship with stakeholder F. Stakeholder F was a very strong supporter who also had a strong relationship with stakeholder E. John scheduled a meeting with stakeholder F where he would attempt to enlist his assistance in engaging and developing stakeholder E's understanding and approval of the project's positive impacts.

Leaving the meeting, John beat the iteration drum again. "Remember this is just our current approach; we need to see if it really works. If we need to adjust the plan, we can do it. This is a living document." He was starting to sound like Lloyd. Hopefully that was a good thing.

CASE STUDY QUESTIONS: "DEFINING THE PATH TO ENGAGEMENT"

Which document, created by the Identify Stakeholder process, is a key input to the Plan Stakeholder Management process, helping to provide detailed information on each stakeholder?

a. Stakeholder management plan
b. Project charter
c. Stakeholder register
d. Risk management plan

Which data representation tool did the team use to evaluate the current vs. desired engagement levels for each stakeholder?

a. Issue log
b. Stakeholder engagement plan
c. Mind mapping
d. Stakeholder engagement matrix

Case Study Answers: "Defining the Path to Engagement"

Which document, created by the Identify Stakeholder process, is a key input to the Plan Stakeholder Management process, helping to provide detailed information on each stakeholder?

a. Stakeholder management plan
b. Project charter
c. Stakeholder register
d. Risk management plan

Which data representation tool did the team use to evaluate the current vs. desired engagement levels for each stakeholder?

a. Issue log
b. Stakeholder engagement plan
c. Mind mapping
d. Stakeholder engagement matrix

EXECUTING PROCESS GROUP

Executing Process Group Summary

Executing is iterative, and its results may lead to project updates and re-baselining. Changes are executed based on variances to the plan and through a defined change control procedure. The Executing process group is the project life cycle stage when deliverables are produced and most of the project's budget is consumed. The actions taken throughout this process group are:

- Completing the work
- Making deliverables
- Assuring quality
- Communicating
- Engaging stakeholders

In addition, most of the team activities (acquire, develop, manage, and cultivate the team) are performed and, during procurement, sellers are selected and contracts are signed.

Objectives

This is the stage of the project intended to conduct the activities necessary to deliver project objectives and implement the project plan. In this process group the focus is on "doing," through:

- Direct and manage the work
- Manage project knowledge
- Manage quality
- Acquire, develop, and manage resources
- Manage communications
- Implement risk responses
- Conduct procurements
- Manage stakeholder engagement

Key Outputs

The Executing process group bears this name because it is all about delivering the project objectives. Therefore, the key outputs are the following:

- Deliverables
- Work performance data
- Change requests
- Performance assessments
- Performance information
- Reporting
- Resource assignments
- Team assignments
- Communications
- Selecting sellers
- Agreements

DIRECT AND MANAGE PROJECT WORK (*PMBOK GUIDE*® 4.3)

Summary

Direct and Manage Project Work is where the "rubber meets the road" as the team begins executing the planned project activities defined in the project plans. This process focuses on managing the team to complete all activities and achieve the project's objectives. The project manager should direct work performance and resource allocation to produce deliverables, change requests, and work performance data.

All the deliverables and work performance data will be used as inputs in the Monitoring and Controlling process group.

 The deliverables produced are evaluated in Control Quality to confirm they meet standards. If so, deliverables become verified deliverables.

Direct and Manage Project Work I.T.T.O.

4.3 Direct and Manage Project Work	Inputs	Tools and Techniques	Outputs
	Project management plan • *Any component* **Project documents** • *Change log* • *Lessons learned register* • *Milestone list* • *Project communications* • *Project schedule* • *Req. traceability matrix* • *Risk register* • *Risk report* **Approved change requests** **EEFs** **OPAs**	**Expert judgement** **Project mgt. info. system** **Meetings**	**Deliverables** **Work performance data** **Issue log** **Change requests** **Project mgt. plan updates** • *Any component* **Project documents updates** • *Activity list* • *Assumption log* • *Lesson learned register* • *Req. documentation* • *Risk register* • *Stakeholder register* **OPA updates**

Key Outputs

As project work is completed, deliverables, change requests, and work performance data are produced. These are the key outputs of the Direct and Manage Project Work process.

<u>DELIVERABLES</u>

Deliverables are the unique verifiable products, results, or capabilities produced as a result of executing the project.

<u>CHANGE REQUESTS</u>

Change requests are generated to formally propose changes to any deliverable or baseline.

ISSUE LOG

Issues experienced during project execution may require corrective or preventative actions or defect repairs.

WORK PERFORMANCE DATA

Work performance data refers to the raw observations and measurements obtained in work completion. Data is passed on to the Monitor and Control processes, where it becomes input for analysis and decision making.

As with most other processes, project management plans and project documents must be updated to reflect the progress of planned work and approved change requests. In addition, the **cost**, **schedule**, and **scope baselines** must be updated.

> Problems are inevitable in any project. The issue log is used to track issues as they are investigated and resolved.

Key Inputs

ALL project work is an input to Direct and Manage Project Work. Therefore, all project management plans and baselines as well as numerous project documents will be used as inputs.

APPROVED CHANGE REQUESTS

Additionally, approved change requests will provide the direction as to which activities will have alterations to their original plans, and therefore should be executed based on the characteristics of their updated status.

> When a change request is approved in Perform Integrated Change Control (4.6), it flows back to Direct and Manage Project Work (4.3) as an input.

Key Tools and Techniques

Expert judgement is used to evaluate data in project management information systems, and in **meetings** to guide project work execution and manage approved change requests.

PROJECT MANAGEMENT INFORMATION SYSTEM (PMIS)

Project management information systems provide a standard set of tools for capturing, storing, and distributing information to stakeholders about project cost, schedule progress, and performance. They also allow the project manager to consolidate reports from several systems and facilitate report distribution to stakeholders.

> The project manager and team must actively manage both planned work AND approved change requests.

CASE STUDY: "DIRECT AND MANAGE PROJECT WORK"

"A plan is only as good as the execution." John had come to this realization over the past few months as he guided his team through the process of performing the work defined in the project management plan.

While he was happy that he had followed Lloyd and Sara's advice on developing a detailed project management plan, the actual execution of work still proved to require a significant amount of effort. The longer he led the project the more he began to feel as though he was a ship's captain at the helm of a vessel in a storm, fighting to navigate the project to a safe and successful completion. Instead of waves, John faced a barrage of different activity types that he had to ensure were completed during the Direct and Manage Project Work process.

His primary focus was always to ensure that his team of experts were properly executing the project work. However, adding complexity to the situation was the fact that the need for new change requests seemed up to pop-up weekly and approved change requests came back from the Integrated Change Control process that needed to be implemented.

John's biggest surprise was the volume of information generated throughout the process of accomplishing the project work. Per Sara's suggestion, John had his team keep meticulous records on activities details, all key performance indicators, and problems and gaps identified. The raw work performance data (activity details and KPIs) were collected and packaged up to be analyzed by the Monitoring and Control processes while the problems and gaps identified where recorded in a log.

The stress of keeping the team moving forward had been difficult, but days like today made the struggle worthwhile. Today the team had completed a deliverable, the third block of redesigns. John smiled as he flipped through printed copy of the drawings the team had printed out for him. The document was still warm from the printer.

The next step was to ensure that the deliverable satisfied all the quality requirements specified through the Control Quality process. When that was completed and the deliverable was considered a verified deliverable John would lead the sponsor through the process of inspecting the deliverable to obtain formal acceptance.

The project sponsor was strict and demanded and the process for validating the scope was difficult, but the team had successfully passed the inspections for the first two design blocks. He hoped for a similar result on this round.

Case Study Questions: "Direct and Manage Project Work"

Which output produced by the Perform Integrated Change Control process is a key input for the Direct and Manage Project Work process, informing specific actions that must be implemented?

a.) Project requirements
b.) Enterprise Environmental Factors (EEF)
c.) Change Requests
d.) Approved Change Requests

Which project document should John use to record problems, gaps, inconsistencies, or conflicts that occur during the Direct and Manage Project Work process?

a) Project management plan
b) Issue log
c) Assumption log
d) Project charter

Which process will be used to evaluate and approve that the project deliverables produced by Direct and Manage Project Work meet the requirements specified by key stakeholders?

a.) Monitor and Control Project Work
b.) Control Scope
c.) Control Quality
d.) Validate Scope

CASE STUDY ANSWERS: "DIRECT AND MANAGE PROJECT WORK"

Which output produced by the Perform Integrated Change Control process is a key input for the Direct and Manage Project Work process, informing specific actions that must be implemented?

a.) Project requirements
b.) Enterprise Environmental Factors (EEF)
c.) Change Requests
d.) Approved Change Requests

Which project document should John use to record problems, gaps, inconsistencies, or conflicts that occur during the Direct and Manage Project Work process?

a) Project management plan
b) Issue log
c) Assumption log
d) Project charter

Which process will be used to evaluate and approve that the project deliverables produced by Direct and Manage Project Work meet the requirements specified by key stakeholders?

a.) Monitor and Control Project Work
b.) Control Scope
c.) Control Quality
d.) Validate Scope

MANAGE PROJECT KNOWLEDGE (*PMBOK GUIDE®* 4.4)

Summary

The process of Manage Project Knowledge requires using past organizational knowledge to improve the project's outcome and record valuable experiences for future use. This process not only uses existing knowledge, but also creates new knowledge. Both explicit and tacit knowledge should be managed.

- **Explicit knowledge** is the kind of knowledge easily codified using words, pictures, and numbers.
- **Tacit knowledge** is more personal and difficult to express (beliefs, insights, experience, "know-how").

Successful knowledge management relies on project manager's ability to create a project environment where the team is comfortable sharing knowledge, providing tools that allow easy access to information, and helping others codify their tacit knowledge.

> Knowledge management is more than lessons learned.
> It focuses on using or developing explicit and tacit knowledge.

Manage Project Knowledge I.T.T.O.

	Inputs	Tools and Techniques	Outputs
4.4 Manage Project Knowledge	**Project management plan** • *Any component* **Project documents** • *Lessons learned register* • *Project team assignments* • *Resource breakdown structure* • *Source selection criteria* • *Stakeholder register* **Deliverables** **EEFs** **OPAs**	**Expert judgement** **Knowledge management** **Information management** **Interpersonal and team skills** • *Active listening* • *Facilitation* • *Leadership* • *Networking* • *Political awareness*	**Lessons learned register** **Project mgt. plan updates** • *Any component* **OPA updates**

Key Outputs

Throughout the entire project, both best practices and problems must be codified and recorded on the **lessons learned register**. This document will be a key output of Manage Project Knowledge. The lessons learned register is an OPA that is used as an input for many current project processes, as well as being an asset for future projects.

Lessons Learned Register					
Project Name:				Date:	
ID #	Group	Description	What worked well?	What didn't work well?	Opportunities

> At project closing, the lessons learned are transferred to the lessons learned repository for availability to others for use on future projects.

Key Inputs

Managing project knowledge involves more than just documenting information in the lessons learned register. It requires doing so in manner that can be understood and consumed by others. Only codified explicit knowledge can be shared in this way, but this information may lack context and can be open to interpretation. Thus, tacit knowledge needs to become codified so that it can be documented and retained by the organization. To manage project knowledge well, the project manager must rely heavily on organizational knowledge experts, which are an **enterprise environmental factor** and an essential input.

PROJECT DOCUMENTS

Project documents such as the **lessons learned register** are an obvious important input to generating an updated register that will include the new explicit and tacit knowledge. Other documents used for this process will likely be:

- Project team assignments
- Resource breakdown structure
- Source selection criteria
- Stakeholder register

Key Tools and Techniques

Successful project managers use information management tools and interpersonal skills to create an environment where knowledge is effectively shared.

Information management tools provide the forum where information can be both shared and accessed. Examples include the lessons learned register, PMIS, and libraries.

The project manager's interpersonal and team skills will be paramount in tapping into the **expert judgement** of others to successfully codify knowledge and document it. The project manager will need to take the necessary steps to help improve communication sharing and decision making with skills such as:

- Active listening
- Facilitation
- Leadership
- Networking
- Political awareness

> Expert judgement is the gold in knowledge management. The challenge is how to access, communicate, and record it!

MANAGE QUALITY (*PMBOK GUIDE*® 8.2)

Summary

The Manage Quality process translates the quality management plan (created in 8.1 Plan Quality Management) into executable activities that integrate quality policies into the project. The principal objective of this process is quality assurance, with test and evaluation documents and quality reports being the key tangible outputs.

Quality assurance measures the effectiveness of a project's processes. It is achieved by implementing a set of planned and systematic acts that are designed to do the following:

- Design an optimal and mature product
- Ensure that requirements are met (via audits and failure analysis)
- Improve the efficiency and effectiveness of processes and activities

> Managing project quality is considered everyone's responsibility.
> This should include project managers, teams, sponsors, and management.

Manage Quality I.T.T.O.

8.2 Manage Quality	Inputs	Tools and Techniques	Outputs
	Project management plan • *Quality mgt. plan* **Project documents** • *Lessons learned register* • *Quality control measures* • *Quality metrics* • *Risk report* **OPAs**	**Data gathering** • *Checklists* **Data analysis** • *Alternatives analysis* • *Document analysis* • *Process analysis* • *Root cause analysis* **Decision making** • *Multicriteria decision analysis* **Data representation** • *Affinity diagrams* • *Cause and effect diagrams* • *Flow charts* • *Histograms* • *Matrix diagrams* • *Scatter diagrams* **Audits** **Design for X** **Problem solving** **Quality improvement methods**	**Quality reports** **Test and evaluation doc.** **Change requests** **Project mgt. plan updates** • *Quality mgt. plan* • *Scope baseline* • *Schedule baseline* • *Cost baseline* **Project doc. updates** • *Issue log* • *Lessons learned register* • *Risk register*

Key Outputs

TEST AND EVALUATION DOCUMENTS

Test and evaluation documents along with quality reports create the method by which project quality is assessed and monitored. They will be used to evaluate the achievement of quality and adherence to declared standards and specifications outlined in the quality management plan. Examples of this type of documents are:

- Checklists
- Requirements traceability matrix
- Quality audit reports
- Performance scorecards

QUALITY REPORTS

Quality reports are designed to organize and present the quality status of metrics and quality requirements identified in the quality management plan. These reports can be graphical, numerical, or qualitative, and the information they contain will be shared through various mediums. The types and formats of this information may be:

- Quality issues escalated from team
- Process improvement and corrective action recommendations
- Performance expressed in histograms, bar charts, scatter and matrix diagrams

Feedback from Manage Quality may require updating the issue log, lessons learned register, and risk register.

Key Inputs

The **quality management plan** and specific quality-related project documents will provide the foundation on which test and evaluation documents and quality reports are created. The quality management plan defines the acceptable level of quality for the product or project and outlines methods to be followed to ensure that quality is delivered. As a result, this plan will direct the activities during the Manage Quality process.

The key project documents for managing quality include **quality control measurements** and **quality metrics**. Metrics will be used as a basis for developing test scenarios and determining if quality expectations are within boundaries, and if not, initiating the need to identify improvements and possible change requests. Other documents used in Manage Quality are the lessons learned register and risk reports.

Key Tools and Techniques

Various data gathering, analysis, and representation techniques will be used in the effort to manage quality. The project manager will also direct or complete **audits** intended to help manage quality assurance. Upon completion of data collection and data analysis activities such as **root cause analysis**, representing such work can be effective using matrix diagrams and, more specifically, **cause-and-effect diagrams**.

CAUSE-AND-EFFECT DIAGRAMS

The cause-and-effect diagram is a simple but valuable approach to brainstorming and representing the input of experts who collaborate in a facilitated meeting focused on linking potential causes to a specific effect. A cause-and-effect diagram template is shown next.

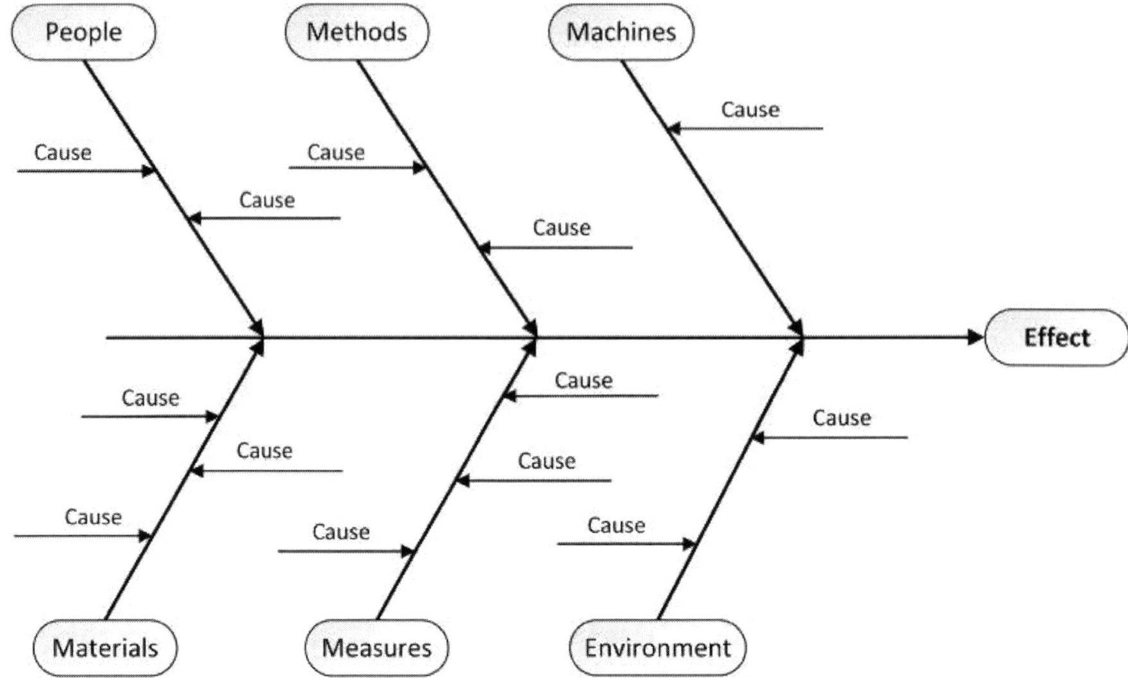

AUDITS

An audit is a set of structured observation techniques used to determine if project activities comply with policies, processes, and procedures. It can be executed with a simple checklist to confirm if metrics or qualitative items are at specification. The value of an audit is the consistent and random use of it rather than declared and planned audit events.

> The results and conclusions from Manage Quality may warrant the initiation of change requests.

ACQUIRE RESOURCES (*PMBOK GUIDE*® 9.3)

Summary

The process of Acquire Resources uses the approved cost baseline and project schedule to obtain the resources required to complete the actual project work. This process delivers resource assignments and calendars that will be used to develop and manage the team.

Depending on the structure of the project environment, the project manager may have direct or indirect control of the team members. Acquire Resources is the first of three Resource Management processes in the Executing process group. It ensures adequate resources are available when needed.

Acquire Resources I.T.T.O.

9.3 Acquire Resources	Inputs	Tools and Techniques	Outputs
	Project mgt. plan • *Resource mgt. plan* • *Procurement mgt. plan* • *Cost baseline* **Project documents** • *Project schedule* • *Resource calendars* • *Resource requirements* • *Stakeholder register* **EEFs** **OPAs**	**Decision making** • *Multicriteria decision analysis* **Interpersonal and team skills** • *Negotiation* **Pre-assignment** **Virtual teams**	**Physical resource assignments** **Project team assignments** **Resource calendars** **Change requests** **Project mgt. plan updates** • *Resource mgt. plan* • *Cost baseline* **Project doc. updates** • *Lessons learned register* • *Project schedule* • *Resource breakdown structure* • *Resource requirements* • *Risk register* • *Stakeholder register* **EEF updates** **OPA updates**

Key Outputs

RESOURCE ASSIGNMENTS

Success here includes both obtaining the resources and detailing the exact time periods when they are needed and available. **Project team assignments** and **physical resource assignments** are documented in the resource management plan. The following descriptive details are recorded:

- Team details
  - Team directory
  - Roles and responsibilities
  - Organizational chart, etc.
- Physical details
  - Names
  - Descriptions
  - Locations
  - Capabilities, etc

RESOURCE CALENDAR

The resource calendar defines the exact time frames when each resource is available. The calendar may be organized by working days, weeks, or shifts across the project schedule.

> Internal resources are acquired from functional managers.
> External resources are obtained using the procurement process.

CHANGE REQUESTS

Change requests, which are evaluated using the Perform Integrated Change Control process, may be outputs of Acquire Resources. Change requests may be due to issues or changes that are derived from shifts in expected resource needs.

PROJECT MANAGEMENT PLAN UPDATES

Project management plan updates to the **resource management plan** or cost baseline can be warranted due to deviations to existing documentation. The **cost baseline** may require updates to reflect approved change requests relative to more or differing resources than anticipated.

PROJECT DOCUMENTS UPDATES

Project documents are necessary when the Acquire Resources process is conducted. Changes or approvals to **resource requirements** will prompt needed updates. **Project schedules** may be impacted by resource availability, while the **resource breakdown structure** identifies the actual resources obtained.

New risks or updates to existing risk status will require updates to the **risk register**, and any new information relevant to the **lessons learned register** should also be recorded.

Key Inputs

PROJECT MANAGEMENT PLAN

Drawn from the project management plan, the **cost baseline** provides limitations to the amount available to spend on resources. Since obtaining internal vs. external resources is done differently, the **resource management plan** instructs on how internal resources are obtained, while the **procurement management plan** instructs on how external resources are obtained.

PROJECT DOCUMENTS

Created during resource planning in Estimate Activity Resources, the **resource requirements** document defines when resources are needed and the maximum available to spend. This document is a key input to the Acquire Resources process. The **project schedule** is used to help determine when resources must be available.

EEFs AND OPAs

A project's unique EEF and OPA conditions must be evaluated and managed to fulfill the resource requirements defined. **Enterprise environmental factors** can have heavy influence on the project's internal resources (skills sets, availability, costs) and impact how they operate based on their environment (for example, organizational structure—matrix or projectized, etc.).

Organizational process assets are also in play when acquiring resources, as OPAs can dictate resource acquisition policies and procedures.

> Weak-matrix organizations offer less access and control of resources; strong-matrix organizations offer more.

Key Tools and Techniques

DECISION MAKING

Multicriteria decision analysis allows the team to evaluate resource options that are available and define the optimal mix of those resources that will best meet the project's needs. Selection criteria are defined by the team to describe and compare resources, and the criteria are weighted to reflect their relative importance. Some selection criteria include:

- Availability
- Location
- Cost
- Experience
- Knowledge or skills

The Acquire Resources process provides various methods of obtaining and structuring team assets to help improve the effectiveness of the project. **Pre-assignment** is practiced when resources—physical or team—are determined in advance. **Virtual teams** are very common and provide flexibility in building a strong project team with resources that are geographically dispersed. Communication becomes extremely important with virtual teams. It is wise to establish expectations and standards to help mitigate risks created by different work schedules and customs.

> To obtain resources, project managers often negotiate with functional managers, other teams, external organizations, and suppliers.

DEVELOP TEAM (*PMBOK GUIDE*® 9.4)

Summary

The Develop Team process is focused on transforming individual team resources into a high-performance collaborative team. The advantages to creating such a team include enhanced project performance and higher employee satisfaction. To successfully develop the team, the project manager should incorporate training, reward, recognition, and assessments into the team development approach. Doing so will improve:

- Individual and team skills
- Team member motivation
- Project performance

The Tuckman ladder defines the five stages of team development: **(1)** forming, **(2)** storming, **(3)** norming, **(4)** performing, and **(5)** adjourning.

Develop Team I.T.T.O.

	Inputs	Tools and Techniques	Outputs
9.4 Develop Team	**Project mgt. plan** • *Resource mgt. plan* **Project documents** • *Lessons learned register* • *Project schedule* • *Project team assignments* • *Resource calendars* • *Team charter* **EEFs** **OPAs**	**Colocation** **Virtual teams** **Communication technology** **Interpersonal and team skills** • *Conflict management* • *Influencing* • *Motivation* • *Negotiation* • *Team building* **Recognition and rewards** **Training** **Indiv. and team assessments** **Meetings**	**Team perf. assessments** **Change requests** **Project mgt. plan updates** • *Resource mgt. plan* **Project doc. updates** • *Lessons learned register* • *Project schedule* • *Project team assignments* • *Resource calendars* • *Team charter* **EEF updates** **OPA updates**

Key Outputs

TEAM PERFORMANCE ASSESSMENTS

Among the key outputs of this process, team performance assessments help track and address team development, status, and needs. The effectiveness of training and team building efforts is evaluated and recorded. Evaluation of a team's overall performance can uncover specific actions needed:

- Training
- Coaching
- Mentoring

CHANGE REQUESTS

Change requests can result from evaluations that identify the need for any additional training and increased resource needs. Any spend to this end affects the project's cost baseline.

PROJECT MANAGEMENT PLANS AND PROJECT DOCUMENTS UPDATES

The project management plan and project documents should be updated when team assessments, actions, or recommendations are made.

Key Inputs

PROJECT MANAGEMENT PLAN

The project management plan and its components set the baseline of project objectives and team expectations on which a highly effective team is built. The project plan establishes the projected methods of training, assessment, and feedback that will be used in managing and developing the team.

PROJECT DOCUMENTS

Project documents such as the **team charte**r define the team's values and operating guidelines. **Team assignments** and the **resource calendar** establish each member's role and define when each member will participate in the project. Lastly, the **project schedule** highlights the phases of the project when training will be needed.

Key Tools and Techniques

One of the challenges of a project manager is to design their team's work environment and communication methods in a way that will foster teamwork, collaboration, and productivity. Work environments where **colocation** is possible can be used to enhance communication and build teamwork. When this is not possible due to geographical differences, the **virtual team** environment can be used; in this case, **communication technology** will become more important than ever.

Meetings allow team-related topics to be communicated and addressed in a collective setting. Starting team meetings with **recognition and rewards** can encourage desired behavior and foster positive performance.

INDIVIDUAL AND TEAM ASSESSMENTS

Individual and team assessments help identify opportunities where training can enhance team members' skills to the level needed. These activities can provide insights into team members' strengths and weaknesses. Common assessment tools include surveys, interviews, and ability tests. Where needed, training can be delivered in multiple formats:

- Formal or informal
- Classroom
- Online or computer-based
- On-the-job training

> Conflict management, influencing, motivation, negotiation, and team building skills are used in team development.

As part of team assessment, it is important to understand the phases teams go through before becoming efficient and productive. Tuckman's ladder describes these phases:

1. **Forming**
    a. Team members meet and learn about the project and their roles.
    b. This phase is characterized by each member acting independently.
2. **Storming**
    a. The team begins to address work, technical decisions, and management approach.
    b. If the team is not collaborative, this environment can be counterproductive.
3. **Norming**
    a. Team members begin to recognize their roles.
    b. Team members begin to work together and learn to trust each other.
4. **Performing**
    a. The team is working well together as a unit.
    b. The team is able to work through issues smoothly and effectively.
5. **Adjourning**
    a. The team completes the work and moves on (typically done in the Close Project process).

CASE STUDY: "DEVELOP TEAM"

It took three attempts for John to get everyone in the team room to notice him. He finally succeeded by whistling loudly and calling out, "Good afternoon!" The team members had been deep in a discussion over a technical issue regarding a drawing. The discussion had been loud and animated, with two parties obviously debating competing proposals, but there was something different in the way they were speaking to each other.

John made note of the slight change in the team member's manner of interaction as he proceeded with his statement. "I wanted to take a moment to recognize the great work Emily and Justine did in leading the Control Quality inspection of design block three. You two did an excellent job in recording and documenting the results of our multiple quality inspections. I am proud to proclaim that design block three meets the quality requirements specified for the deliverable and is now considered a Verified Deliverable!"

With that the room burst into applause. John made eye contact with both Emily and Justine, nodded, and mouthed a silent thank you to each team member. After a few minutes of handshakes and high-fives the team playfully asked, "hey boss, is it ok if we get back to work?" John agreed, but snuck in one last positive note. "The next step is to have the customer validate the scope of design block three and formally accept the deliverable. I would like Emily and Justine to lead the walk through."

With that John acquiesced and the team quickly settled back into their discussion. As he left the room John tried to identify exactly what was different with his team. It was clear that the passion and conviction that each member felt hadn't deteriorated, but now there seemed to be much less finger pointing and arguing. Instead, the discussions were more positive, collaborative, and respectful. This was not always the case. Early in the project the team was a team only in name. In practice, it seemed that everyone was participating in meetings to fight and defend their individual department's needs. Sara had observed this fact and provided John the following advice.

"They don't know each other and they haven't developed the ability to trust yet. It is your job to create the environment to fosters teamwork." John had lost sleep over finding the perfect way to create the environment Sara referenced. He evaluated a variety of options. "Maybe throwing a team party would help, or we could all walk on hot coals, or maybe he would have Action Jackson come down and mandate they work together." In the end he chose a simple, but powerful solution. He had obtained approval for all core team members to shift their work stations to a large shared work room. He posted a banner on the wall proclaiming the space the "Project Command Center" and plastered the walls with the project schedule, charter, and key drawings.

Bringing the individuals together forced interaction. John had guided this interaction by leading the team in morning kick-off and end of day progress status meetings. He had also spent significant time in the first few weeks helping team members negotiate compromises on contentious issues. It was obvious now that the time and effort spent had translated into more positive and productive working environment. In his head John could see his team climbing the Tuckman ladder that Sara had also mentioned. He believed they had now stepped to the next rung. John knew that it was not time to rest on his accomplishments, the new challenge was how to support the team as they continued to move up the ladder.

Case Study Questions: "Develop Team"

The correct order of the five stages of the Tuckman ladder that a team may proceed through are?

a.) Storming, norming, performing, forming, adjourning
b.) Forming, storming, norming, performing, adjourning
c.) Forming, storming, performing, norming, adjourning
d.) Performing, Storming, norming, forming, adjourning

John utilized which strategy to improve the communication and performance of the team members located at the home office?

e) Team building activities
f) Virtual teams
g) Shared work spaces
h) Colocation

In terms of the Tuckman ladder, John's team is most likely transitioning from stage ______ to ______?

a.) Forming to storming
b.) Storming to norming
c.) Norming to performing
d.) Performing to adjourning

Acknowledging and thanking Emily and Justine for the positive work they performed while completing the Control Quality process was an example of what type of tool and technique commonly used during the Develop Team process?

a) Training
b) Recognition and rewards
c) Negotiation
d) Conflict management

By analyzing the effectiveness of colocation and the use of team building and negotiation skills what type of assessment did John produce as an output of the Develop Team process?

a) Team success assessment
b) Performance improvement assessment
c) Team work assessment
d) Team performance assessments

Case Study Answers: "Develop Team"

The correct order of the five stages of the Tuckman ladder that a team may proceed through are?

a.) Storming, norming, performing, forming, adjourning
b.) Forming, storming, norming, performing, adjourning
c.) Forming, storming, performing, norming, adjourning
d.) Performing, Storming, norming, forming, adjourning

John utilized which strategy to improve the communication and performance of the team members located at the home office?

a) Team building activities
b) Virtual teams
c) Shared work spaces
d) Colocation

In terms of the Tuckman ladder, John's team is most likely transitioning from stage _____ to _____?

a.) Forming to storming
b.) Storming to norming
c.) Norming to performing
d.) Performing to adjourning

Acknowledging and thanking Emily and Justine for the positive work they performed while completing the Control Quality process was an example of what type of tool and technique commonly used during the Develop Team process?

a) Training
b) Recognition and rewards
c) Negotiation
d) Conflict management

By analyzing the effectiveness of colocation and the use of team building and negotiation skills what type of assessment did John produce as an output of the Develop Team process?

a) Team success assessment
b) Performance improvement assessment
c) Team work assessment

Team performance assessments

MANAGE TEAM (*PMBOK GUIDE®* 9.5)

Summary

In the Manage Team process, the project manager is actively leading the team, helping them evaluate performance, navigate conflicts, and adjust to successfully deliver outputs. The project manager uses management and leadership methods to ensure optimal team performance. This process is performed in conjunction with Monitor and Control Project Work. Work performance reports are critical inputs, providing insight into the effectiveness of team management. Project manager's active engagement and monitoring of project performance will help to identify necessary corrective and preventative actions and change requests.

Any project manager will come to learn that in any project, conflict is unavoidable. The five key techniques used to resolve conflict are:

1. Withdraw or avoid
2. Smooth or accommodate
3. Compromise or reconcile
4. Force or direct
5. Collaborate or problem solve

Manage Team I.T.T.O.

9.5 Manage Team	Inputs	Tools and Techniques	Outputs
	Project mgt. plan • *Resource mgt. plan* **Project documents** • *Issue log* • *Lessons learned register* • *Project team assignments* • *Team charter* **Work performance reports** **Team perf. assessments** **EEFs** **OPAs**	**Interpersonal and team skills** • *Conflict management* • *Decision making* • *Emotional intelligence* • *Influencing* • *Leadership* **Project mgt. information system**	**Change requests** **Project mgt. plan updates** • *Resource mgt. plan* • *Schedule baseline* • *Cost baseline* **Project doc. updates** • *Issue log* • *Lessons learned register* • *Project team assignments* **EEF updates**

Key Outputs

CHANGE REQUESTS

In managing the team, the project manager will develop change requests and implement corrective actions to remedy and improve team performance. Issues affecting team performance may require corrective or preventative actions, and thus **change requests** may come into play if the actions impact project baselines.

PROJECT MANAGEMENT PLANS

If any actions and corrective measures undertaken to improve team performance affect the **resource management plan**, **schedule baseline**, or **cost baseline**, it must be updated.

PROJECT DOCUMENTS

When managing the team, the project manager should record in the **lessons learned register** any actions taken that worked well along with those that did not. **Project team assignments** should be updated with resulting team changes, and the **issue log** should be updated with any outstanding or resolved issues.

Key Inputs

Work performance reports, issue logs, and team performance assessments are used to identify current and future issues that may affect project success.

Work performance reports, produced as an output of Monitor and Control Project Work, provide the status of schedule, cost, quality, and scope. Issues identified from this information may trigger preventative or corrective measures to help manage the project team.

Issue logs have been updated when specific issues were identified throughout project execution, and this information may help identify areas where corrective actions related to managing the team are necessary.

Team performance assessments highlight areas where improvement can occur and best practices can be shared.

Key Tools and Techniques

INTERPERSONAL AND TEAM SKILLS

Conflict management, decision making, and influencing techniques help the project manager navigate issues that inevitably occur in all projects. **Conflict management** is essential to productively addressing and eliminating issues. The ability to understand the conflict's importance and intensity enables the project manager to select the best course of action to resolve the problem. The five common courses of action for addressing issues are the following:

1. **Withdraw or avoid**—retreating from a conflict, postponing it until you're better prepared or it is solved by others. This approach may cause the issue to worsen, or the issue may be rectified later.
2. **Smooth or accommodate**—emphasizing agreement areas while ignoring or conceding differences in hopes of maintaining harmony. The risk is that the issue may not be adequately addressed.
3. **Compromise or reconcile**—searching for a solution that pleases often resolves issues, but only temporarily. This approach can create a lose-lose situation.
4. **Force or direct**—pushing one's viewpoint through power. This approach can create a win-lose situation.
5. **Collaborate or problem solve**—incorporating multiple viewpoints through dialogue. This approach can create a win-win situation or, in some cases, no solution at all.

Decision making weighs heavily in managing a team, and **emotional intelligence** and **leadership** will serve the project manager well when addressing issues and seeking creative solutions to problems.

MANAGE COMMUNICATIONS (*PMBOK GUIDE*® 10.2)

Summary

Manage Communications is where the communications plan is implemented, allowing the correct information to flow between the team and stakeholders. This process is more than merely transferring information; it should be executed by design to ensure that stakeholders receive appropriate information at the right frequency and through the best medium to facilitate strong stakeholder engagement.

During Manage Communications the project manager evaluates the effectiveness of how their messages were formatted, distributed, and received. This is also an opportunity for stakeholders to request further information or clarification.

Flexibility should be maintained in all aspects of communication:

- Technology
- Methods
- Techniques

> Efficient and effective communication is the goal of Manage Communications.

Manage Communications I.T.T.O.

10.2 Manage Communications	Inputs	Tools and Techniques	Outputs
	Project mgt. plan • *Resource mgt. plan* • *Communications mgt. plan* • *Stakeholder engmt. plan* **Project documents** • *Change log* • *Issue log* • *Lessons learned register* • *Quality report* • *Risk report* • *Stakeholder register* **Work performance reports** **EEFs** **OPAs**	**Communication technology** **Communication methods** **Communication skills** • *Communication competence* • *Feedback* • *Nonverbal* • *Presentations* **Project mgt. info. system** **Project reporting** **Interpersonal and team skills** • *Active listening* • *Conflict management* • *Cultural awareness* • *Meeting management* • *Networking* • *Political awareness* **Meetings**	**Project communications** **Project mgt. plan updates** • *Communications mgt. plan* • *Stakeholder engmt. plan* **Project documents updates** • *Issue log* • *Lessons learned register* • *Project schedule* • *Risk register* • *Stakeholder register* **OPA updates**

Key Outputs

PROJECT COMMUNICATIONS

Throughout the project, critical information is organized and distributed to stakeholders in the form of project communications. Each communication triggers project management plan updates, particularly to **communications and stakeholder plans**.

PROJECT DOCUMENTS UPDATES

Any necessary information that flows back from communications or is a critical piece of those communications may warrant other document updates:

- Issue log
- Lessons learned register
- Project schedule
- Risk register
- Stakeholder register

> Information constantly flows! The challenge of a project team is to effectively gather, evaluate, and distribute information.

Key Inputs

WORK PERFORMANCE REPORTS

Project documents and **work performance reports** supply valuable project information that the project manager is expected to share. Project's communications should entail the following:

- The formatted information transmitted to stakeholders
- Performance reports
- Deliverable status
- Schedule, cost, and scope progress
- Presentations

For sharing performance and status information, the project manager relies on documents such as **quality reports**, **risk reports**, and the **change log**.

PROJECT MANAGEMENT PLAN

The project management plan helps determining what information should be distributed along with the *who* and the *how* for those communications.

> Project documents are regularly updated by other processes. Manage Communications ensures stakeholders are aware of the updates.

Key Tools and Techniques

Various skills, methods, and tools are used to transform information into project communications and transmit them to stakeholders. Project managers' communication skills will be exercised routinely as they observe **nonverbal** communication from others. Their active **listening skills** will help them effectively use **feedback**. **Political and cultural awareness** will play a significant role in how nonverbal and other types of feedback are interpreted, as well as in navigating the organization. All these skills and others collectively comprise a project manager's **communication competence**.

> Project reports are different than work performance reports.
> **Project reports** = Ad hoc reports **Work performance reports** = Official status reports

IMPLEMENT RISK RESPONSES (*PMBOK GUIDE®* 11.6)

Summary

Implement Risk Responses is where the risk responses defined and selected in Plan Risk Responses (11.5) are put into action to achieve the risk response result. It is useless to identify risks and develop response strategies without implementing them. The risk response owners must execute their action plans throughout the entire project. These implementations will be monitored for effect in the Monitor Risks process.

> Risk owners must focus on implementing the planned and agreed-upon risk responses.

Implement Risk Responses I.T.T.O.

11.6 Implement Risk Responses	Inputs	Tools and Techniques	Outputs
	Project mgt. plan • *Risk mgt. plan* **Project documents** • *Lessons learned register* • *Risk register* • *Risk report* **OPAs**	**Expert judgement** **Interpersonal and team skills** • *Influencing* **Project mgt. info. system**	**Change requests** **Project doc. updates** • *Issue log* • *Lessons learned register* • *Project team assignments* • *Risk register* • *Risk report*

Key Outputs

PROJECT DOCUMENTS UPDATES

The impacts and results of implementing risk responses must be documented in order to reflect project status changes and evolving conditions relative to risks. The **risk register** and **risk report** are obvious documents ripe for updates with risk response results. The **issue log** is updated by adding or removing any issues. The **lessons learned register** should be enhanced with information about what has worked and what has not relative to implementing risk responses.

CHANGE REQUESTS

In the process of Implement Risk Responses the team will likely encounter situations where changes are desired and necessary. The project manager should facilitate change requests as an output of this process.

> Implementing risk responses may result in change requests to modify project baselines, plans, or both.

Key Inputs

PROJECT MANAGEMENT PLAN

The **risk management** plan is the main input to Implement Risk Responses.

PROJECT DOCUMENTS

The **risk register** and **risk report** are both outputs and inputs to this process, which aims to enhance, update, or bring closure to the items contained in these documents.

Key Tools and Techniques

Expert judgement and **influencing** skills are important in managing the expectation that the project manager and others have of risk owners delivering on their agreed risk response plans. In many cases the project manager does not have direct authority over the risk owners, for example, when operating in a matrix environment. In these cases, interpersonal and team skills are vital in ensuring risk management plans are implemented.

> Similar influencing skills used in Manage Team (9.5) are used to encourage risk owners to act.

CONDUCT PROCUREMENTS (*PMBOK GUIDE*® 12.2)

Summary

Conduct Procurements uses the procurement documents created in Plan Procurement Management to solicit and evaluate seller responses, and establish a contract. The focus is on determining which seller best fits the unique requirements of the project. Obtaining a signed agreement authorizes work to begin and defines what will be completed (statement of work, deliverables). Agreements will also clarify how progress will be evaluated (reporting, inspections, acceptance criteria).

> The terms and conditions of the contractual agreement become inputs to many management processes.

Conduct Procurements I.T.T.O.

12.2 Conduct Procurements	Inputs	Tools and Techniques	Outputs
	Project management plan • *Scope mgt. plan* • *Requirements mgt. plan* • *Communications mgt. plan* • *Risk mgt. plan* • *Procurement mgt. plan* • *Configuration mgt. plan* • *Cost baseline* **Project documents** • *Lessons learned register* • *Project schedule* • *Req. documentation* • *Risk register* • *Stakeholder register* **Procurement doc.** **Seller proposals** **EEFs** **OPAs**	**Expert judgement** **Advertising** **Bidder conferences** **Data analysis** • *Proposal evaluation* **Interpersonal and team skills** • *Negotiation*	**Selected sellers** **Agreements** **Change requests** **Project mgt. plan updates** • *Requirements mgt. plan* • *Quality mgt. plan* • *Communications mgt. plan* • *Risk mgt. plan* • *Procurement mgt. plan* • *Scope baseline* • *Schedule baseline* • *Cost baseline* **Project doc. updates** • *Lessons learned register* • *Req. documentation* • *Req. traceability matrix* • *Resource calendars* • *Risk register* • *Stakeholder register* **OPA updates**

Key Outputs

AGREEMENTS

The essential output of Conduct Procurements is a contractual agreement, or a mutually binding contract between the buyer and seller. The **selected seller** will be one that offers the best value in satisfying the requirements defined in the procurement statement of work. In this process, sellers within a competitive range may be shortlisted and judged based on the source selection criteria defined in Plan Procurement Management.

The person authorized to sign legal agreements is often a purchasing or legal representative, NOT the project manager.

PROJECT MANAGEMENT PLAN UPDATES

Several components of the project management plan will need to be updated based on final agreement terms. Any procurement agreements will have seller deliverables, contract costs, and schedule expectations that are likely to warrant **change requests** and updates to the

- Scope baseline
- Schedule baseline
- Cost baseline

With the introduction of a third party that will perform activities for and on behalf of the project team, there will be requirements to be met, quality levels to achieve, and a new set of recipients for the communications plan. Therefore, the following documents will need to be updated:

- Requirements management plan
- Quality management plan
- Communications management plan
- Procurement management plan

PROJECT DOCUMENTS UPDATES

Project documents must also be updated to reflect the impact of contractually agreed-upon terms and conditions and to document lessons learned. When agreements are established, the following documents need to be updated:

- Lessons learned register
- Requirement documentation
- Requirements traceability matrix
- Risk register
- Resource calendars
- Stakeholder register

Contract terms define the specific processes to follow to address change requests and mitigate disputes.

Key Inputs

PROJECT MANAGEMENT PLAN

As already stated, Conduct Procurements uses the **procurement management plan**, which is a component of the project management plan. The **procurement documents** contained therein (bid documents and procurement SOW) provide sellers with the information required to develop and submit their proposals. Independent cost estimates and the source selection criteria document help facilitate the evaluation of sellers. Using the procurement plan and these key documents enables selecting sellers and agreements.

The **communication management plan** instructs how to engage sellers and execute communications in the bidding and selection process. Other project management plan components are referenced to ensure alignment to project **scope**, **cost**, **configuration management**, and **risks**.

The lists of preferred or pre-registered sellers are an OPA that is used to solicit bids.

Key Tools and Techniques

Bidder conferences and **advertising** help increase the seller pool and provide the information sellers need to make informed and accurate proposals.

Advertising is used to extend seller pools outside of known or preferred sellers. Common forums used to broaden seller interest are notifications in trade publications or on the company website. Government contracts, for example, require public disclosure.

Bidder conferences are used to provide detailed information to sellers, and are conducted prior to proposal deadlines. These meetings allow all sellers the opportunity to ask questions and gain clarification of requirements and constraints. Non-disclosure agreements (NDA) are often required to safeguard sensitive information shared during a bidder conference.

Expert judgement from a variety of disciplines is used to analyze each proposal and select the seller. Data analysis is performed during review of source selection criteria and **proposal evaluation**. Final signed agreements are almost always achieved through **negotiation**.

Case Study: "Finding the Ideal Contractor"

"The contract is signed. You have surge capacity available, when you need it. I'm sending over the signed documents. If you need additional assistance, schedule a meeting."

As John hung up the phone, he made a note to himself: "The lawyer communicates in the same way the procurement SOW was written: clear, complete, and concise. It's not a bad way to be." As he waited for the final contract to arrive in his email, he thought back over the schedule of events that had transpired during the past weeks. He knew he and his team had played a critical role in selecting the contractor, but the lawyer had handled the lion's share of the work.

The lawyer's initial step was to send a request for proposal (RFP) to a list of potential consultant companies for evaluation. The RFP instructed interested consultants to provide both technical and price proposals. These were first used to prune the submitters into a select group based on their ability to meet basic non-negotiable requirements.

Due to the specialized nature of the assistance needed, the consultants were offered the option of attending a summit to evaluate a sample of the technical drawings and ask questions to gain a deeper understanding of the requirements. The open nature of the event ensured that all contractors had equal access to the procurement requirements, and non-disclosure agreements assured the company protection from a loss of proprietary information.

The final evaluation of the proposals was done by John's team and a group of experts, selected for their unique legal, engineering, schedule, or project management expertise. The team used the source selection criteria and an independent estimate of an industry standard rate per hour to evaluate and select the consultant company to offer the contract to.

The challenge was to balance the desire to hire the most technically competent group with the realistic constraints on timing, capacity, and cost. The selection process took its first victim in a nationally recognized firm with decades of experience. The team had salivated over the prospect of awarding them the contract. Unfortunately, the company could not guarantee sufficient capacity during the date range defined, making them too risky. They were quickly eliminated, and the process of examination and evaluation repeated.

After much discussion and debate, the team had found a company that satisfied all technical, schedule, capacity, and cost constraints. The decision was handed to the lawyer to finalize the deal. From that point on, the lawyer successfully negotiated with the selected seller and the purchasing director signed the contract, formally sealing the deal.

As John opened the contract email, he felt better knowing that having a signed agreement helped reduce project risk. This was one more step on the path to success.

CASE STUDY QUESTIONS: "FINDING THE IDEAL CONTRACTOR"

What type of meeting was used to provide prospective contractors the opportunity to gain a deeper understanding of the procurement statement of work?

a. Procurement conference
b. Question and answer session
c. Bidder conference
d. Bidder meeting

In which process and process group were the source selection criteria developed as an output?

a. Plan Procurement Management / Initiating process group
b. Plan Procurement Management / Planning process group
c. Plan Procurement Staffing / Planning process group
d. Develop Project Management Plan / Planning process group

Which document was not provided to the potential contractors?

a. Source selection criteria
b. Request for proposal
c. Procurement statement of work
d. Project charter

CASE STUDY ANSWERS: "FINDING THE IDEAL CONTRACTOR"

What type of meeting was used to provide prospective contractors the opportunity to gain a deeper understanding of the procurement statement of work?

a. Procurement conference
b. Question and answer session
c. Bidder conference
d. Bidder meeting

In which process and process group were the source selection criteria developed as an output?

a. Plan Procurement Management / Initiating process group
b. Plan Procurement Management / Planning process group
c. Plan Procurement Staffing / Planning process group
d. Develop Project Management Plan / Planning process group

Which document was not provided to the potential contractors?

a. Source selection criteria
b. Request for proposal
c. Procurement statement of work
d. Project charter

MANAGE STAKEHOLDER ENGAGEMENT (*PMBOK GUIDE*® 13.3)

Summary

Managing stakeholder engagement began the moment stakeholders were identified. The stakeholder engagement plan solidified how the project manager should interact with stakeholders. Obviously, every interaction with stakeholders should have a purpose and consequence. The Manage Stakeholder Engagement process is used to adjust stakeholder engagement based on previous interactions with them, as well as implement the plans for approaching stakeholders that the team is yet to engage.

Good communication and negation skills are essential for engaging stakeholders. The project manager should be focused on:

- Maintaining alignment on project objectives
- Addressing issues timely and productively
- Achieving the engagement level defined in the stakeholder engagement assessment matrix

Adapting the stakeholder engagement plan should be based on feedback and change requests. Feedback can be verbal and non-verbal, and the project manager should do the following:

- Raise issues where they exist
- Eliminate issues and risks that can be addressed
- Adjust communication methods
- Improve project processes

> A stakeholder's ability to influence a project is greatest early in the project and decreases as the project progresses.

Manage Stakeholder Engagement I.T.T.O.

13.3 Manage Stakeholder Engmt.	Inputs	Tools and Techniques	Outputs
	Project management plan • *Scope mgt. plan* • *Risk mgt. plan* • *Stakeholder engmt. plan* • *Change mgt. plan* **Project documents** • *Change log* • *Issue log* • *Lessons learned register* • *Stakeholder register* **EEFs** **OPAs**	**Expert judgement** **Communication skills** • *Feedback* **Interpersonal and team skills** • *Conflict management* • *Cultural awareness* • *Negotiation* • *Observation and Conversation* • *Political awareness* **Ground rules** **Meetings**	**Change requests** **Project mgt. plan updates** • *Communications mgt. plan* • *Stakeholder engmt. plan* **Project doc. updates** • *Change log* • *Issue log* • *Lessons learned register* • *Stakeholder register*

Key Outputs

The interactions with stakeholders will reveal varying degrees of requests or changes that need to be integrated using the Integrated Change Control process. As a result, **change requests** are a key output of this process. In addition, as new opportunities to improve the stakeholder engagement approach are discovered, they will trigger project management plan updates to the **communications management plan** and **stakeholder engagement plan**. Other project documents updates include:

- Change log
- Issue log
- Lessons learned register
- Stakeholder register

Key Inputs

PROJECT MANAGEMENT PLANS

The **stakeholder engagement**, **risk**, **and communications management plans** will highlight the approaches to be used to connect and interact with each stakeholder.

> Manage Stakeholder Engagement and Manage Communications work in concert; each focuses effort on aligning stakeholders and assisting in better decision making.

Other factors that will compel the project manager to action will be drawn from project documents such as the **change log**, which could spur the need to engage different stakeholders or remove some from the stakeholder engagement plan. The **issue log** will work in similarly by indicating parties responsible for addressing issues or those stakeholders that need to be apprised of current items on the **risk register** or other outstanding issues.

> Project documents are also used by the team to document issues. Addressing issues helps show stakeholders that their involvement matters.

AGREEMENTS

Contracts or agreements are critical elements to adapting and managing stakeholder engagement. Any new or initiated agreements could warrant new stakeholder engagement.

Key Tools and Techniques

Clear and consistent communication, **conflict management**, and **negotiation** skills help to provide vital information, minimize issues, and foster involvement. Each stakeholder should receive communication in the form best suited to them as defined by the communication management plan.

> Clear and consistent communication and conflict and negotiation skills help to provide vital information, minimize issues, and foster involvement.

During the Stakeholder Engagement process, **expert judgement** should be sought and incorporated through data gathering techniques. Data analysis methods used include **assumption and constraints analysis**. The goal is to translate data into decision making information that can be used for **prioritization and ranking**.

Meetings are a common vehicle to bring subject matter experts together to collaborate and make decisions. The project manager can prepare for meetings with data representation such as the **stakeholder engagement assessment matrix**, or use meetings to prompt **mind mapping** sessions that will allow pulling information from the audience.

Case Study: "Managing Stakeholder Engagement"

"Things are moving forward, but it seems as though I'm spending 75% of my time updating, explaining, and negotiating, and 25% doing. I had no idea it would be this way."

While proud that the project was progressing well, John was surprised that the progress was neither easy nor straightforward. On the contrary, it seemed that problems and issues never stopped. Initially embarrassed and worried, John thought that problems were indications of poor planning. However, very quickly he came to the realization that issues, disagreements, and change requests were the sign of a developing project. In a way, they were healthy. What mattered most was how he managed the issues.

Through the management and negotiation of these issues, John began to realize that the time spent early in the project developing relationships and level setting expectations paid dividends in times of conflict. While conflicts and issues were never good things, what stakeholders most disliked was being caught off guard or ignored. To combat this, John made significant effort to share with stakeholders issues and concerns as soon as they surfaced.

While issues seemed often to be unavoidable, their effects could be minimized through proactive and strategic communication and action. Central to this approach was the use of the issue log and change requests. They helped to keep issues upfront and visible and gave a systematic method for resolving each.

As John's recognition of the value of communication and visibility increased, he began to study and refine what type of updates each stakeholder actually needed and responded best to. Stakeholders with busy hectic schedules often liked quick, focused, and clear communication. Those more focused on the details were eager to receive the thorough multi-page weekly project reports. As John began to refine his communication methods to suit each stakeholder, he updated both communication and stakeholder management plans.

Case Study Questions: "Managing Stakeholder Engagement"

In addition to the stakeholder engagement plan, there are three additional subsidiary plans that John would likely leverage in the Managing Stakeholder Engagement process. Which of the following subsidiary project plans is not an appropriate input to this process?

a. Communications management plan
b. Schedule management plan
c. Stakeholder engagement plan
d. Risk management plan

As a project progresses, will John's stakeholder's ability to influence the project increase or decrease?

a. Increase; stakeholders have greater ability to influence at later stages
b. Decrease; stakeholders have greater ability to influence at earlier stages
c. No change; the amount of influence a stakeholder has is directly related to their power in the organization
d. Impossible to determine; stakeholders can exert influence through the project lifecycle

Which project document did John use to record and communicate problems and concerns?

a. Issue log
b. Assumption log
c. Stakeholder register
d. Communication management plan

CASE STUDY ANSWERS: "MANAGING STAKEHOLDER ENGAGEMENT"

In addition to the stakeholder engagement plan, there are three additional subsidiary plans that John would likely leverage in the Managing Stakeholder Engagement process. Which of the following subsidiary project plans is not an appropriate input to this process?

a. Communications management plan
b. Schedule management plan
c. Stakeholder engagement plan
d. Risk management plan

As a project progresses, will John's stakeholder's ability to influence the project increase or decrease?

a. Increase; stakeholders have greater ability to influence at later stages
b. Decrease; stakeholders have greater ability to influence at earlier stages
c. No change; the amount of influence a stakeholder has is directly related to their power in the organization
d. Impossible to determine; stakeholders can exert influence through the project lifecycle

Which project document did John use to record and communicate problems and concerns?

a. Issue log
b. Assumption log
c. Stakeholder register
d. Communication management plan

Monitoring and Controlling Process Group

Monitoring and Controlling Process Group Summary

The Monitoring and Controlling process group seeks to provide feedback or validation of the integration of Planning, Execution, and Control. Activities are measured against the performance baselines, and sources of variance are determined and addressed. Formal acceptance of deliverables is obtained.

As a key aspect of project management, Monitoring and Controlling is the stage where the project manager must identify changes that might occur or have occurred and proactively or reactively attempt to control those changes.

Objectives

In Monitoring and Controlling, the aim is to "return to the baseline" or "perform an approved integrated change to the baseline." The success of the project is always evaluated in relationship to the current version of the baseline.

The processes in this group deal with collecting information, inspecting, compiling, analyzing, and influencing the factors that cause change. Subsequently, the project manager takes control by applying cost and schedule reserves, and following procedures established by the various components of the project management plan.

Key Outputs

The types of outputs that are relevant to the Monitoring and Controlling process group are:

- Work performance information
- Work performance reports
- Change requests
- Approved change requests
- Accepted deliverables
- Schedule forecasts
- Cost forecasts
- Quality control measures
- Verified deliverables
- Closed procurements

MONITOR AND CONTROL PROJECT WORK (*PMBOK GUIDE*® 4.5)

Summary

The Monitor and Control Project Work process aims to provide the project team and stakeholders insight into the health of the project and to spur the appropriate actions. This process is performed throughout a project's entire life cycle and is focused on three distinct areas:

- Understanding the current state
- Evaluating the effectiveness of actions taken
- Forecasting cost and schedule results

Work performance information is the "currency" used to assess the project's status. The tools and techniques within the process are used to analyze and summarize work performance information into work performance reports. The reports are strategically communicated to the project team and stakeholders through the communication management processes to maintain awareness and engagement.

It is common for the analysis of project progress to identify the need for corrective or preventative actions and defect repairs. When identified, these are formatted into change requests as outputs that flow into the Perform Integrated Change Control (4.6) process for evaluation. Additionally, project documents and plans are updated to reflect new issues and risks identified, and any changes to project forecasts.

> Work performance reports are critical tools used to maintain stakeholder engagement and encourage action.

Monitor and Control Project Work I.T.T.O.

4.5 Monitor and Control Project Work	Inputs	Tools and Techniques	Outputs
	Project management plan • *Any component* **Project documents** • *Assumption log* • *Basis of estimates* • *Cost forecasts* • *Issue log* • *Lessons learned register* • *Milestone list* • *Quality reports* • *Risk register* • *Risk report* • *Schedule forecasts* **Work performance info.** **Agreements** **EEFs and OPAs**	**Expert judgement** **Data analysis** • *Alternatives analysis* • *Cost-benefit analysis* • *Earned value analysis* • *Root cause analysis* • *Trend analysis* • *Variance analysis* **Decision making** **Meetings**	**Work performance reports** **Change requests** **Project mgt. plan updates** • *Any component* **Project documents updates** • *Cost forecasts* • *Issue log* • *Lesson learned register* • *Risk register* • *Schedule forecasts*

Key Outputs

WORK PERFORMANCE REPORTS

Work performance reports summarize project performance and forecasts. Various methods are used in the reports to summarize and display the project status so that it can be easily understood:

- Status and progress reports
- Earned value graphs
- Trend lines and forecasts
- Reserve burndown charts
- Defect histograms
- Risk summaries

The goal of creating and distributing work performance reports is to create stakeholder awareness and to help foster informed decision-making and action. These reports are distributed through the Manage Communications process in the appropriate physical or electronic form.

CHANGE REQUESTS

Change requests are produced to address issues, and opportunities are identified through the analysis of work performance information. More specifically, change requests are required when the actions needed will impact project plans, deliverables, or baselines.

The change requests produced as outputs fall into three categories:

- Corrective actions
- Preventative actions
- Defect repairs

Each of the three categories is focused on addressing a unique aspect of project performance. **Corrective actions** are suggested activities that will realign the current project work with the project management plan. **Preventative actions** ensure future project work is aligned with the project management plan. **Defect repairs** modify nonconforming product or project components.

The corrective or preventative actions, or defect repairs proposed should not be implemented until the change request is approved by the Perform Integrated Change Control (4.6) process.

PROJECT MANAGEMENT PLAN AND DOCUMENT UPDATES

The issues, risks, or best practices identified must be recorded in the **issue log**, **risk register**, or **lessons learned register**. Additionally, any changes to **cost** or **schedule forecasts** should be documented.

> Change requests may be submitted to make corrective actions, preventative actions, or defect repairs.

Key Inputs

WORK PERFORMANCE INFORMATION

Project execution produces work performance data, which is the actual record of what is expended, delivered, or accomplished. However, without a reference against which to compare the data, there is no context to help interpret it.

Work performance data is transformed into work performance information by comparing the data against the project management plan to determine how the project is performing. Data is used to evaluate the project performance in terms of scope, schedule, budget, and quality.

This analysis determines the project's current degree of variance from the plan and identifies where preventative or corrective actions are required.

PROJECT PLANS AND DOCUMENTS

Project plans and documents provide the baseline standards and additional performance data needed to assess progress. The **project plans** provide the expected cost, schedule, and scope progress against which the current status is evaluated. **Project documents** provide the context necessary to help evaluate the status.

AGREEMENTS

Agreements define the specifics on what the seller is to perform or provide. This information is used to provide the baseline on which to evaluate a contractor's work.

> Work performance data is transformed into information by comparing actual vs. planned performance.

Key Tools and Techniques

Data analysis and **decision making** are used to assess current performance, forecast results, and define corrective and preventative actions. Each of the six most common analysis methods provides distinct insight into the project:

- Earned value analysis
- Trend analysis
- Variance analysis
- Root cause analysis
- Alternatives analysis
- Cost-benefit analysis

Earned value analysis provides insight into scope, schedule, and cost planned vs. actual performance. **Trend analysis** is used to forecast future performance. **Variance analysis** helps identify significant differences between planned and actual performance. **Root cause analysis** identifies the main reasons for issues or variances and helps develop the appropriate corrective actions. **Alternatives** and **cost-benefit analyses** are used to evaluate and select the best corrective or preventive actions.

PERFORM INTEGRATED CHANGE CONTROL (*PMBOK GUIDE*® 4.6)

Summary

Regardless of how in-depth a project plan is, at some point during a project's life cycle, there will always be pushes to modify, eliminate, or improve aspects of the project. While well intended, these changes often significantly alter the project risk profile and may extend the project past the approved baselines.

Before the baselines are approved, changes are not required to be evaluated and approved by the Perform Integrated Change Control process. However, once the baselines are approved, all proposals must be formatted as change requests, evaluated, and either approved, rejected, or deferred.

The Perform Integrated Change Control process focuses decision making on key changes, ensuring that the impacts to objectives, plans, and risks are considered.

The process defines an official way to

- Accumulate all change requests
- Evaluate the total impact of each change request using objective standards
- Approve, reject, or defer each change request
- Communicate the decisions

Within the Perform Integrated Change Control process, the evaluation and decision making on change requests is done by a responsible individual or a change control board (CCB). All approved change requests are implemented by the Direct and Manage Project Work (4.3) process.

> Once baselines are established, ALL changes impacting baselines must go through the Integrated Change Control process.

Perform Integrated Change Control I.T.T.O.

4.6 Perf. Int. Change Control	Inputs	Tools and Techniques	Outputs
	Project management plan • *Change mgt. plan* • *Configuration mgt. plan* • *Scope baseline* • *Schedule baseline* • *Cost baseline* **Work performance reports** **Change requests** **EEFs** **OPAs**	**Expert judgement** **Change control tools** **Data analysis** • *Alternatives analysis* • *Cost-benefit analysis* **Decision making** • *Voting* • *Autocratic decision making* • *Multicriteria decision analysis* **Meetings**	**Approved change requests** **Project mgt. plan updates** • *Any component* **Project documents updates** • *Change log*

Key Outputs

APPROVED CHANGE REQUESTS

Approved change requests are the key output of the Perform Integrated Change Control process. It is only when a change request has been approved that the actual changes proposed can be implemented by the Direct and Manage Project Work (4.3) process in the Executing process group.

PROJECT MANAGEMENT AND PROJECT DOCUMENTS UPDATES

No matter if a change request was approved or rejected, the **change log** is used to record the results of each change request evaluation and decision. Additionally, the decision rendered by the change control board must always be communicated to the individual or group requesting the change.

Approved change requests may require the team to revise or create new cost estimates, schedules, risk responses, and resource allocations. The appropriate project management plans and documents must be updated to reflect the approved modifications and revisions.

It is important to remember that when baselines are modified, the record of past performance versus the baseline is not adjusted. The new baseline is only used to drive progress from the date approved and evaluate future progress.

> Approved change requests are implemented by the Direct and Manage Project Work process.

Key Inputs

CHANGE REQUESTS

The submission of a **change request** is the input that initiates the Perform Integrated Change Control process. Change requests can be submitted by any party involved in the project and at any time during a project's life cycle, but they all must be recorded in written form in a change management system. Additionally, change requests are produced as outputs from many processes. All change requests flow to this process as an input.

It is most common for change requests to be submitted to propose corrective actions, preventative actions, or defect repairs. Decision making on changes that do not impact the project plans and baselines usually falls within the authority of the project manager. The changes that impact project plans or baselines must be evaluated by the change control board.

PROJECT MANAGEMENT PLANS, PROJECT DOCUMENTS, AND WORK PERFORMANCE INFORMATION

Project management plans, project documents, and work performance information provide the change control board the detailed project status information and context they require to render a decision on change requests.

The three **baselines** (scope, schedule, and cost) are the most critical; they are the gold standard against which the impact of each change request is evaluated. **Work performance reports** provide clear insight into the project's status and past performance. The **basis of estimates**, **requirements traceability matrix**, and **risk report** are project documents commonly used to evaluate the total impact of the adjustment requests.

EEFs AND OPAs

EEFs and OPAs establish the structure and processes by which the Perform Integrated Change Control process operates and under which changes must be evaluated.

Enterprise environmental factors provide constraints that influence the validity, risk, and impact of the change requests submitted:

- Legal restrictions
- Government standards
- Organizational governance framework
- Contracting constraints

Organizational process assets provide processes and procedures that steer how the Perform Integrated Change Control process operates:

- Change control procedures
- Approval or rejection procedures
- Method to update baselines

> Change requests must be recorded in written form and entered into the change management system.

Key Tools and Techniques

The proper organization and evaluation of change requests requires the use of change control tools and **expert judgement** to perform data analysis, and the use of decision-making techniques.

CHANGE CONTROL TOOLS

Due to the volume and importance of change requests, change control tools are used to maintain order in the Perform Integrated Change Control process. Change control tools help organize and align the following activities:

- Identification of changes
- Documentation of changes
- Decision on changes
- Tracking change implementation

The Perform Integrated Change Control process aims to maintain both change control and configuration control throughout the project life cycle. This process focuses on changes to project documents, deliverables, and baselines. Configuration control focuses on the specifications of deliverables and processes. Changes to both must be managed to keep the project organized and up to date.

> Change requests can only be implemented once they are transformed into **approved** change requests.

DATA ANALYSIS AND DECISION MAKING

Data analysis is used by the change control board (CCB) to evaluate the impact of each change, and decision making is used to render a decision. The two main techniques used are **alternative analysis** and **cost-benefit analysis**. Each method provides a unique perspective on the total impact of the changes.

Once analysis is conducted, the responsible individual or change control board must accept, reject, or defer the change request. The design of the Perform Integrated Change Control process and the role of the project manager will determine whether **voting**, **autocratic decision making**, or **multicriteria decision making analysis** methods are used.

Every change request must be **approved**, **deferred**, or **rejected** by the responsible individual or by the change control board.

CASE STUDY: "PERFORMING INTEGRATED CHANGE CONTROL"

John was startled as Frank burst into his office and started to speak. His door was never closed, and the angle afforded John a clear view of the hallway leading to his office, but Frank had caught him off guard.

It was clear that Frank was excited. He could hardly contain himself as he unloaded a rapid-fire of short statements: "We had an issue, but don't worry. I caught it yesterday and I already fixed it. I got an early look at what training was going to deliver. It was pretty much what we asked for, but I didn't think it was what we really need."

He clapped his hands for effect and continued: "Then an idea popped into my head. Instead of having them make small modifications to what they showed me, why not have them build something better? So I did. I made them change the whole training concept. They are off and running now. It's going to be amazing!"

John threw his hand up, causing Frank to pause and pull in what seemed to be his first breath since entering the office: "Frank, slow down and explain. What problem are you talking about and what exactly did you have changed?"

"It was the training document. I know it's a key deliverable and the requirements were clear and simple. However, the draft I saw was flat and uninspiring. It proved to me that a traditional approach isn't good enough. We don't need a manual; we need a world-class online training course!"

"Frank, what did you do?"

"I told the training team to scrap the current requirements and start creating an online training course. It is going to have videos, pictures with voice-over explanations, and quizzes to make sure everyone understands the new designs. All on-demand and accessible from the company intranet. Maybe later we can even make it a mobile app."

John leaned forward as Frank explained the full extent of what he had done. He began calculating his response as Frank finished. "John, why are you turning red? Sure, this will cost a little more and we won't have the paper version of the manuals, but this is going to be better. Trust me."

CASE STUDY QUESTIONS: "PERFORMING INTEGRATED CHANGE CONTROL"

Which should be John's response to Frank's changes?

a. Great work! Proceed ahead. I like your initiative; you did the right thing.
b. Next time talk to me first. I need to be the person that makes the call on big changes. The buck stops with me.
c. Stop the training team. You're proposing changes to a key deliverable. We need to evaluate your idea quickly and decide if we should put in a change request. That's the only way we make big changes.

What portion of the project management plan must be updated if a change request is submitted, approved, and results in additional costs?

a. WBS dictionary
b. Cost baseline
c. Schedule baseline
d. Communication plan

If a change request is not submitted, but the team believes there is a risk that the training manual may not be sufficient, where should this be recorded?

a. Issue log
b. Assumption log
c. Change log
d. Risk management plan

Case Study Answers:
"Performing Integrated Change Control"

Which should be John's response to Frank's changes?

a. Great work! Proceed ahead. I like your initiative; you did the right thing.
b. Next time talk to me first. I need to be the person that makes the call on big changes. The buck stops with me.
c. Stop the training team. You're proposing changes to a key deliverable. We need to evaluate your idea quickly and decide if we should put in a change request. That's the only way we make big changes.

What portion of the project management plan must be updated if a change request is submitted, approved, and results in additional costs?

a. WBS dictionary
b. Cost baseline
c. Schedule baseline
d. Communication plan

If a change request is not submitted, but the team believes there is a risk that the training manual may not be sufficient, where should this be recorded?

a. Issue log
b. Assumption log
c. Change log
d. Risk management plan

VALIDATE SCOPE (*PMBOK GUIDE*® 5.5)

Summary

The Validate Scope process aims to obtain the customer's formal acceptance of completed project deliverables.

The process is directly linked with Control Quality (8.3) in that verified deliverables flow from the Control Quality process into the Validate Scope process as inputs. The verified deliverables are inspected objectively by the customer against the acceptance criteria defined in the scope statement. If the criteria are met, the deliverable is documented as an accepted deliverable and the documentation is sent to the Close Project or Phase (4.7) process.

> **Control Quality** confirms that quality standards were met.
> **Validate Scope** confirms that that the customer accepts the deliverables.

Validate Scope I.T.T.O.

5.5 Validate Scope	Inputs	Tools and Techniques	Outputs
	Project management plan • *Scope mgt. plan* • *Requirements mgt. plan* • *Scope baseline* **Project documents** • *Lessons learned register* • *Quality reports* • *Requirements doc.* • *Req. traceability matrix* **Verified deliverables** **Work performance data**	**Inspection** **Decision making** • *Voting*	**Accepted deliverables** **Work performance information** **Change requests** **Project documents updates** • *Lessons learned register* • *Requirements documentation* • *Requirements traceability matrix*

Key Outputs

ACCEPTED DELIVERABLES

Accepted deliverables are those that have been approved by the customer or sponsor as meeting the acceptance criteria defined in the project scope statement, which is part of the project's scope baseline. Formal documentation is created for every accepted deliverable and provided to the Close Project or Phase (4.7) process. Additionally, the acceptance of the deliverable is updated in the requirements traceability matrix.

> Accepting each deliverable as it is produced increases the probability that the final product will be accepted.

CHANGE REQUESTS

Not every deliverable will be accepted the first time it is evaluated. When a deliverable is not accepted, the reasons are documented and often a change request is generated. All change requests are fed into Perform Integrated Change Control (4.6) as an input and evaluated.

WORK PERFORMANCE INFORMATION

No matter if the deliverable is accepted or not, the process of evaluating each deliverable generates work performance information that must be documented in project documents. This information includes the status of the deliverables, accepted or not, and the reasons why they were accepted or not. This information is often used to communicate deliverable status to stakeholders.

PROJECT DOCUMENTS

The status and results of deliverable evaluation and acceptance must be documented in three project documents. Validation results are recorded in the **requirements documentation** and **requirements traceability matrix**. The requirements traceability matrix is critical, in that it maintains an accurate record of the status of all deliverables. The **lessons learned register** is used to document specific approaches that worked well in validating deliverables.

> Requirements traceability matrix **links** requirements to the deliverables that satisfy them (originally produced in 5.2 Collect Requirements).

Key Inputs

VERIFIED DELIVERABLES

Verified deliverables are the key input to the Validate Scope process. These deliverables are evaluated against the scope baseline.

PROJECT MANAGEMENT PLANS

The methods and standards used to evaluate and accept the verified deliverables are provided by the project management plans. The **requirements management plan** defines how the requirements are to be validated. The **scope management plan** defines how formal acceptance of the deliverables is conducted. The **scope baseline** is the actual standard by which verified deliverables are compared.

PROJECT DOCUMENTS

Quality reports and **work performance information** provide a historical record of the quality history and characteristics of each deliverable. The **requirements traceability matrix** provides detailed descriptions of the requirements, specifically how they should be validated.

Key Tools and Techniques

INSPECTION

Inspection and **decision making** are used to evaluate that verified deliverables meet the acceptance criteria defined in the project scope statement. Inspection is performed by measuring, examining, and validating each deliverable. Detailed objective inspection and comparison helps to confirm if a deliverable meets the requirements or product acceptance criteria.

DECISION MAKING

Voting is often used when formal acceptance is made by a group of people.

CASE STUDY: "VALIDATE SCOPE"

"John, why didn't you bring these two with you when we Validated Scope for design block two? They seem to know my questions before I even think to ask them." Involving Emily and Justine in the Validate Scope walk through was proving to be a tremendously good idea. The fact that the sponsor was a very demanded and meticulous customer made these comments even more amazing.

John had kicked off the Validate Scope inspection walk through by clearly defining his team's intentions, "we aim to walk you through the block three redesigns in sufficient detail that you will approve the deliverable." After that initial statement John stepped back and allowed Emily and Justine to take over.

The two team members proceeded to methodically lead the sponsor through the process of inspecting the verified deliverable. They were focused and calm, providing excellent explanations of how the unique design features met the project requirements and providing details that showed that they were completed properly. Additionally, they had the expertise and insight to answer any question thrown their direction. The previous two validate scope sessions had taken approximately 4 hours each, but the current session was on pace to finish within three hours.

The team had gone back to the foundational documents to prepare for this session. They referenced the scope and the requirements management plans to understand how the project requirements were to be validated and how formal acceptance would be obtained. Additionally, the team had compiled all quality reports and the requirements traceability matrix.

John now carried a printed requirements traceability matrix on a clipboard. His role in the session was to quietly check off the requirements in question as the sponsor gave his approval. As Emily finished answering the last question on the final drawing John quietly handed the clipboard to Justine, signaling her to close the deal. Justine understand the moment and eagerly proceeded, "Mr. Sponsor, as you can see every requirement has been validated and no change requests are needed. If you agree, I would like to call the design block three deliverable fully and formally accepted!"

The sponsor turned to look at John and in his characteristic monotone delivery stated, "I have one condition you must meet before I am willing to confirm that I formally sign off and approve this deliverable."

John paused momentarily, unsure of what the condition could possibly be. Before John could respond, the sponsor smiled, pointed to Emily and Justine, and enthusiastically stated "you have to assure me that these two will be involved in the next two validate scope sessions."

With that he pulled out a pen and ceremonially signed the requirement traceability matrix with his long sweeping signature. "That was fun, good work. Now when can I expect design block four?"

CASE STUDY QUESTIONS: "VALIDATE SCOPE"

Which process are the accepted deliverable produced by Validate Scope forwarded to as an input?

a.) Perform integrated change control
b.) Control scope
c.) Close project or phase
d.) Control quality

Which process produces the verified deliverables that are used as inputs by the Validate Scope process?

a) Control scope
b) Control Quality
c) Direct and manage project work
d) Monitor and control project work

What type of technique did Hunter and Justine lead the Sponsor through to examine and validate that the design block three deliverable met the acceptance criteria?

a) Testing and product evaluation
b) Root cause analysis
c) Trend analysis
d) Inspection

CASE STUDY ANSWERS: "VALIDATE SCOPE"

Which process are the accepted deliverable produced by Validate Scope forwarded to as an input?

a.) Perform integrated change control
b.) Control scope
c.) Close project or phase
d.) Control quality

Which process produces the verified deliverables that are used as inputs by the Validate Scope process?

a) Control scope
b) Control Quality
c) Direct and manage project work
d) Monitor and control project work

What type of technique did Hunter and Justine lead the Sponsor through to examine and validate that the design block three deliverable met the acceptance criteria?

a) Testing and product evaluation
b) Root cause analysis
c) Trend analysis
d) Inspection

CONTROL SCOPE (*PMBOK GUIDE*® 5.6)

Summary

Control Scope has three main goals:

- Identify when actual scope results vary too far from the scope baseline
- Ensure that all preventative and corrective actions impacting the scope baseline are submitted as change requests to Perform Integrated Change Control (4.6)
- Manage the full implementation of approved change requests

A project manager must guard a project's scope baseline with the highest level of vigilance. Countless times throughout any project's life cycle there will be pushes to modify what the project will deliver. Some of the reasons will be valid and strategic, others will be driven by enthusiasm to create a better product, and others will be in reaction to pressures within or outside the organization. Regardless of its origin, any change must be properly evaluated and approved or rejected.

Guarding the project's scope cannot take place only when evaluating deliverables, during the Validate Scope (5.5) process, but throughout the entire project. Control Scope uses variance and trend analysis to constantly evaluate if the project's actual performance has skewed from what was planned.

When significant variations are identified, corrective and preventative actions are proposed. These actions cannot be directly implemented. Instead, they must be packed in the form of a change request and evaluated through the Perform Integrated Change Control process. Change requests are a major output of Control Scope.

In addition to ensuring that all proposed changes to the project scope are formally evaluated, the Control Scope process also focuses on managing the full implementation of changes when they are approved. Maintaining a detailed level of focus helps to reduce the risk of scope creep.

> Any change affecting the scope baseline
> **MUST** be evaluated using a change request.

Control Scope I.T.T.O.

5.6 Control Scope	Inputs	Tools and Techniques	Outputs
	Project management plan • *Scope mgt. plan* • *Requirements mgt. plan* • *Change mgt. plan* • *Configuration mgt. plan* • *Scope baseline* • *Perf. measurement baseline* **Project documents** • *Lessons learned register* • *Req. documentation* • *Req. traceability matrix* **Work performance data** **OPAs**	**Data analysis** • *Variance analysis* • *Trend analysis*	**Work performance information** **Change requests** **Project mgt. plan updates** • *Scope management plan* • *Scope baseline* • *Schedule baseline* • *Cost baseline* • *Perf. measurement baseline* **Project documents updates** • *Lessons learned register* • *Requirements documentation* • *Requirements traceability matrix*

Key Outputs

CHANGE REQUESTS

Control Scope produces **change requests** to address significant variances between a project's actual performance and the scope baseline. The change requests created flow to the Perform Integrated Change Control (4.6) process as inputs. The change requests are the vehicles used to properly manage baseline changes.

WORK PERFORMANCE INFORMATION

Work performance information will be produced through monitoring and analyzing the actual vs. planned scope progress. More specifically, this information provides context to what issues are impacting the scope, how much they impact the baseline, and the forecast of future performance. Work performance information is also maintained on the number of change requests generated and their status. This information is critical to maintaining proper stakeholder awareness and engagement and must also be used to update project plans and documents.

PROJECT MANAGEMENT PLAN UPDATES

The **scope**, **schedule**, and **cost baselines** must be updated to reflect approved change requests. In some situations, the scope, schedule, or cost variances may be so severe that the revised baseline will need to be created. Additionally, baseline revisions must also be translated to the **performance measurement baseline**.

PROJECT DOCUMENTS

Requirements traceability matrix and **requirements documentation** must be updated to reflect additional or changed requirements from approved change requests.

The identification of variances, creation of change requests, and implementation of approved change requests will often produce best practices that must be recorded in the **lessons learned register**.

Key Inputs

Work performance data and project documents provide the information that will be used to help evaluate project performance.

PROJECT MANAGEMENT PLANS

The **scope baseline** and **performance measurement baseline** are the foundations against which actual performance is evaluated.

PROJECT MANAGEMENT PLANS

The **requirements documentation** and **requirements traceability matrix** provide context that assists the project manager in identifying deviations from the scope baseline. If change requests are approved, these documents will need to be updated to reflect the changes.

WORK PERFORMANCE DATA

Work performance data provides the actual performance information that is used to help identify significant variances between performance and baselines. Also, data on the status of change requests (received, approved) and deliverables (verified, validated, completed) provides context for monitoring the scope. This data will be transformed into work performance information through this process.

Key Tools and Techniques

Variance and trend analyses are the techniques used to determine if the actual scope results vary too far from the established baseline and therefore require corrective or preventative action.

Variance analysis compares the actual results against the baselines. If variance between the two exceeds a defined threshold, corrective or preventative actions are recommended.

Trend analysis evaluates project performance over time to determine if results are improving or deteriorating.

Control Scope is conducted **throughout** the life of the project.

CONTROL SCHEDULE (*PMBOK GUIDE*® 6.6)

Summary

Control Schedule involves monitoring and maintaining an accurate schedule baseline throughout the completion of the project.

This process focuses on calculating and tracking the schedule variance (SV) and schedule performance index (SPI) throughout the project's life cycle. Calculating the SV determines if the project's schedule progress is ahead or behind the approved schedule baseline; the SPI defines how efficiently work is being completed.

Work performance information is generated when calculating and documenting schedule status. Additionally, this information is used for schedule forecast, to determine when the project will be completed. Often the analysis of the schedule status and forecast highlights issues and areas in need of improvement. In these situations, change requests are produced and forwarded to the Perform Integrated Change Control (4.6) process.

> Earned value analysis and iteration burndown chart are tools and techniques that help the team and stakeholders visualize schedule progress.

Control Schedule I.T.T.O.

6.6 Control Schedule	Inputs	Tools and Techniques	Outputs
	Project management plan • *Schedule mgt. plan* • *Schedule baseline* • *Scope baseline* • *Perf. measurement baseline* **Project documents** • *Lessons learned register* • *Project calendars* • *Project schedule* • *Resource calendars* • *Schedule data* **EEFs** **OPAs**	**Data analysis** • *Earned value analysis* • *Iteration burndown chart* • *Performance reviews* • *Trend analysis* • *Variance analysis* • *What-if scenario analysis* **Critical path method** **Project mgt. info. system** **Resource optimization** **Leads and lags** **Schedule compression**	**Work performance information** **Schedule forecasts** **Change requests** **Project mgt. plan updates** • *Schedule mgt. plan* • *Schedule baseline* • *Cost baseline* • *Perf. measurement baseline* **Project documents updates** • *Assumption log* • *Basis of estimates* • *Lessons learned register* • *Project schedule* • *Resource calendars* • *Risk register* • *Schedule data*

Key Outputs

Schedule performance analysis generates work performance information and change requests requiring distribution and documentation.

Work performance information specific to this process defines how the project is performing against the schedule baseline. The schedule variance (SV) and schedule performance index (SPI) are the metrics that provide this insight. The schedule related work performance information (SV and SPI) is fed back into Monitor and Control Project Work (4.5) where it helps track, summarize, and report on the overall project performance.

Schedule variance (SV) measures if the project is ahead or behind the schedule baseline.

- Positive SV = Ahead of schedule
- Negative SV = Behind schedule

The following equation is used to calculate SV:

SV = EV - PV

Schedule performance index (SPI) measures how efficient the team is in completing project work.

- SPI above 1 = More work has been completed that planned (project is more efficient)
- SPI below 1 = Less work has been completed than planned (project is less efficient)

The following equation is used to calculate SPI:

SPI = EV / PV

A detailed explanation of the methods used to calculate these metrics will be given when discussing Control Costs (7.4).

Schedule forecasts are updated when conditions change, namely, when activities are completed or change requests are implemented.

Change requests are initiated when corrective or preventative actions are identified that will modify baselines or project plans.

> Schedule related work performance information (SV, SPI) is fed back (as inputs) into Monitor and Control Project Work (4.5).

Key Inputs

Project plans provide direction on when and how to evaluate project progress. Work performance data provides the actual information that is used to evaluate project progress.

Schedule management plan defines the methods for evaluating and displaying schedule progress. This evaluation is used to determine if change is needed through corrective or preventative actions.

Schedule and performance baselines are the approved standards by which progress is evaluated.

Project schedule and work performance data provide the data on the actual progress: activity status (underway, complete), durations (actual vs. remaining), and percentage complete.

Key Tools and Techniques

DATA ANALYSIS

Data analysis techniques are used to monitor, evaluate, and communicate the project schedule status and the need for improvement.

Earned value analysis determines the amount of variation the project has from the original schedule baseline. The metrics schedule variance (SV) and schedule performance index (SPI) are calculated to provide this insight.

The **iteration burndown chart** tracks the work remaining on the iteration backlog. This chart highlights issues with the speed of work completion vs. the projected completion rate.

Performance reviews are focused on comparison and analysis of specific project performance metrics. Common metrics analyzed are percent complete, the remaining duration of the work in progress, and actual vs. planned start and finish dates.

Trend analysis uses graphs of data to examine project performance over time. This approach helps to determine if performance is improving or regressing.

Variance analysis looks at the differences between planned and actual performance, namely, the start and finish dates of activities and the actual duration of activity completion. Critical to this analysis is defining the root causes of issues and determining if corrective or preventative action is required.

What-if scenarios are used when issues occur or changes are needed to improve schedule performance. Often these situations require the selection of one of the different planned risk responses available. Remember, the planned risk responses were created in the Planning process group (11.5 Plan Risk Reponses). What-if scenario analysis is used to evaluate the actual impact of implementation of a risk response in the current project environment.

> The iteration burndown chart visually shows the amount of work completed and what remains over time.

CRITICAL PATH METHOD

The critical path method is used again to evaluate the impact of potential change requests. The impacts determined will have to be planned for and represented in the appropriate project documents and plans.

RESOURCE OPTIMIZATION, LEADS AND LAGS, AND SCHEDULE COMPRESSION

These techniques are used to find ways to bring the project back into alignment with the plan.

PROJECT MANAGEMENT INFORMATION SYSTEM (PMIS)

The PMIS is used to track schedule completion (planned vs. actual dates), track and report schedule variances, and forecast the impacts of changes to the project schedule model.

CONTROL COSTS (*PMBOK GUIDE®* 7.4)

Summary

Control Costs centers on understanding both the total amount spent and the effectiveness of the money spent to complete project activities. The process uses earned value analysis (EVA) to understand actual vs. desired performance and identify opportunities and risks.

Earned value analysis uses several equations to evaluate the health of a project throughout its entire life cycle. Completing the Control Cost process generates work performance information, cost forecasts, and change requests.

Control Costs I.T.T.O.

7.4 Control Costs	Inputs	Tools and Techniques	Outputs
	Project management plan • *Cost mgt. plan* • *Cost baseline* • *Perf. measurement baseline* **Project documents** • *Lessons learned register* **Project funding requirements** **Work performance data** **OPAs**	**Expert judgement** **Data analysis** • *Earned value analysis* • *Variance analysis* • *Trend analysis* • *Reserve analysis* **To-complete perf. index** **Project mgt. info. system**	**Work performance information** **Cost forecasts** **Change requests** **Project mgt. plan updates** • *Cost mgt. plan* • *Cost baseline* • *Perf. measurement baseline* **Project documents updates** • *Assumption log* • *Basis of estimates* • *Cost estimates* • *Lessons learned register* • *Risk register*

Key Outputs

Control Costs produces information that summarizes project performance to date and forecasts future performance.

WORK PERFORMANCE INFORMATION

Work performance information includes metrics that define how the project is performing against the project baselines:

- Cost variance (CV)
- Cost performance index (CPI)
- Estimate at completion (EAC)
- Variance at completion (VAC)
- To-complete performance index (TCPI)

COST FORECASTS

The forecasted total estimated cost at completion is calculated. The measure is known as estimate at completion (EAC).

CHANGE REQUESTS

Calculating the variance and performance index for cost and schedule often highlights the need for improvement. Change requests will be developed when these improvements necessitate corrective or preventative actions.

PROJECT MANAGEMENT PLAN

Change requests generated by the Control Cost process, when approved, will often require that the cost baseline be adjusted.

PROJECT DOCUMENTS UPDATE

Performance results generated and their effects must be recorded in the appropriate project documents. Common documents updated are

- Lessons learned register
- Risk register
- Cost estimates
- Basis of estimates
- Assumption log

> Cost-related work performance information (CV, CPI, etc.) is fed back as an input to Monitor and Control Project Work (4.5), which tracks, summarizes, and reports on overall project performance.

Key Inputs

Project plans provide direction on when and how to evaluate costs. Work performance data provides the actual information to evaluate costs.

PROJECT MANAGEMENT PLANS

The **cost management plan** defines methods for evaluating and displaying cost progress, and evaluates if change is needed through corrective or preventive actions.

The **cost and performance baselines** are the approved standards by which progress is evaluated.

PROJECT FUNDING REQUIREMENTS

The project funding requirements include projected expenditures plus anticipated liabilities.

WORK PERFORMANCE DATA

Work performance data provides the status of costs:

- Authorized
- Incurred
- Invoiced
- Paid

PROJECT DOCUMENTS

The **lessons learned register** provides insight into methods that could be used to control costs.

Key Tools and Techniques

Earned value management (EVM) integrates scope, schedule, and cost to answer the question, "Has the plan been effective in delivering the desired results?" Cost, schedule, and scope performances are evaluated against baselines. Remember, on the PMP exam you will convert the schedule and scope performance into monetary terms in order to complete each question.

Three performance dimensions are monitored:

- Planned value (PV)
- Earned value (EV)
- Actual cost (AC)

Performance is analyzed against:

- Variance
- Trends
- Forecasts
- Reserves

EVM starts by defining and understanding the current, actual, and planned performance at a defined time.

- Budget at completion (BAC)
  - BAC = Total budget amount allocated for the project
- Planned value (PV)
  - PV = Value of the work that **should be** done
  - Creates the standard by which progress will be measured
- Earned value (EV)
  - EV = Value of the work that **is** done
  - Often used to calculate the project's percent complete
- Actual cost (AC)
  - AC = **Actual** amount spent to complete the work

> Work performance is evaluated at the work package and control account levels.

We'll use two examples to illustrate the concepts and show you how to get every earned value management question right on the exam.

The first example walks you methodically through the process of using all EVM metrics to determine a project's health.

The second example explains PM Master Prep's unique technique to getting every EVM question correct. This is the PM Master Prep "special sauce." We'll present a simple template that allows you to organize the equations in a way that guides you to solving any EVM question.

Earned Value Management Practical Example

The following example will show you how each equation provides unique insight into a project's health.

Question: A project has been initiated to paint four walls in a room. The work is to be completed in four days, and the planned cost of completing each wall is $100. After three days, 2.5 walls have been completed. Using all EVM metrics, what is the schedule and cost health of the project?

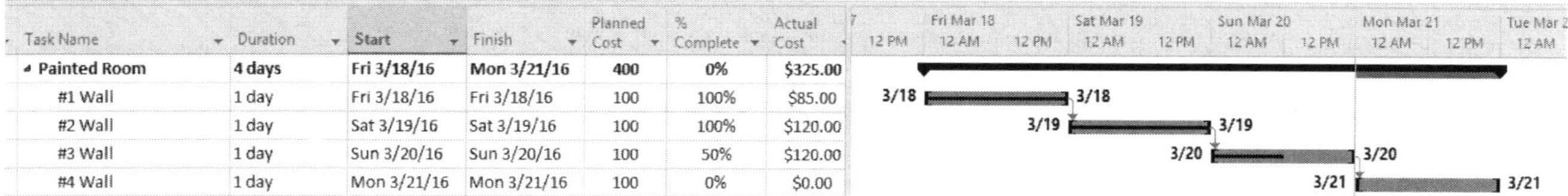

Task Name	Duration	Start	Finish	Planned Cost	% Complete	Actual Cost
Painted Room	**4 days**	**Fri 3/18/16**	**Mon 3/21/16**	**400**	**0%**	**$325.00**
#1 Wall	1 day	Fri 3/18/16	Fri 3/18/16	100	100%	$85.00
#2 Wall	1 day	Sat 3/19/16	Sat 3/19/16	100	100%	$120.00
#3 Wall	1 day	Sun 3/20/16	Sun 3/20/16	100	50%	$120.00
#4 Wall	1 day	Mon 3/21/16	Mon 3/21/16	100	0%	$0.00

Determine the project baseline statistics:

The first task is to define the four basic facts of the project, as they will be used by calculate the cost and schedule metrics.

- BAC = Budget at completion
- PV = Planned value
- EV = Earned value
- AC = Actual cost

Remember that the current status of all baseline statistics must be converted to a monetary value. In the table below you'll find the definition of each metric, its calculated value, and how it was calculated. This same structure will be followed throughout the example.

	Definition	**Calculation**	**Analysis**
BAC	Total budget	**BAC = $400**	The total planned cost for the project is $400
PV	Value of the work that should be done	**PV = $300**	After 3 days, 3 walls were to be completed
EV	Value of the work that is done	**EV = $250**	2.5 walls are completed; each wall is worth $100
AC	Actual spend to complete the work	**AC = $325**	Total spend each day ($85, $120, $120)

Calculate schedule variance (SV) and schedule performance index (SPI):

Schedule analysis determines if the project is ahead or behind the approved schedule baseline and how efficiently work is being completed. The two major schedule related metrics are schedule variance and schedule performance index.

Schedule variance (SV) measures if the project is ahead or behind the schedule baseline.

- Positive SV = Ahead of schedule

- Negative SV = Behind schedule

The equation for SV is SV = EV - PV.

> The SV will be zero at project completion.
> A project is not ahead or behind schedule when the schedule is complete!

Schedule performance index (SPI) measures how efficient the team is in completing project work.

- SPI above 1 = More work has been completed than planned (project is more efficient)
- SPI below 1 = Less work has been completed than planned (project is less efficient)

The equation for SPI is SPI = EV / PV.

> Notice that the SV and SPI equations are nearly identical, but
> SV has a minus sign, and SPI has a division sign between EV and PV.

Calculating SV and SPI

The EV and PV values determined earlier are used to calculate both SV and SPI. The only difference between the two equations is the mathematical operator between EV and PV. The SV equation uses a minus sign between the EV and PV, and the SPI equation uses a division sign.

	Definition	Calculation	Analysis
BAC	Total budget	BAC = $400	The total planned cost for the project is $400
PV	Value of the work that should be done	PV = $300	After 3 days, 3 walls were to be completed
EV	Value of the work that is done	EV = $250	2.5 walls are completed; each wall is worth $100
AC	Actual spend to complete the work	AC = $325	Total spend each day ($85, $120, $120)
SV	Amount that the project is ahead/behind schedule	**SV = EV - PV SV = $250 - $300 SV = -$50**	Negative SV indicates that the project is behind schedule
SPI	How efficient the team is in completing the work	**SPI = EV / PV SPI = $250 / $350 SPI = 0.83**	SPI less than 1 indicates that the team is less efficient in completing the work than projected

Interpreting SV and SPI

The SV was calculated as -$50. The negative value indicates that the project is behind schedule. The SPI was calculated as 0.83. A SPI of less than 1 indicates that the team has been less efficient in completing the work than originally projected.

Calculate cost variance (CV) and cost performance index (CPI):

Cost variance analysis determines if the project is ahead or behind the budget (approved cost baseline) and how efficiently resoruces are spent. The two major cost related metrics follow the same structure as the schedule metrics.

Cost variance (CV) measures the amount of budget deficit or surplus at a given time.

- Positive CV = Under budget

- Negative CV = Over budget

The equation for CV is CV = EV - AC.

As the values in the equation highlight, CV determines if the value of the work that is done is more or less than what was spent to complete the work.

> CV only considers the work that is completed and the resources spent to complete it, not the work that was planned to be completed.

Cost performance index (CPI) measures the cost efficiency of the work completed.

- CPI above 1 = Cost underrun (every dollar spent produced more than one dollar in value)
- CPI below 1 = Cost overrun (every dollar spent produced less than one dollar in value)

The equation for CPI is CPI = EV / AC.

Calculating the CV and CPI

The EV and AC values determined earlier are used to calculate both CV and CPI. As with calculating schedule metrics, the only difference in the equations is what is in between the EV and AC values.

	Definition	Calculation	Analysis
BAC	Total budget	BAC = $400	The total planned cost for the project is $400
PV	Value of the work that should be done	PV = $300	After 3 days, 3 walls were to be completed
EV	Value of the work that is done	EV = $250	2.5 walls are completed; each wall is worth $100
AC	Actual spend to complete the work	AC = $325	Total spend each day ($85, $120, $120)
SV	Amount that the project is ahead/behind schedule	SV = EV - PV SV = $250 - $300 SV = -$50	Negative SV indicates that the project is behind schedule
SPI	How efficient the team is in completing the work	SPI = EV / PV SPI = $250 / $350 SPI = 0.83	SPI less than 1 indicates that the team is less efficient in completing the work than projected
CV	Amount of budget deficit or surplus currently	**CV = EV - AC CV = $250 - $325 CV = -$75**	Negative CV indicates that the project is over budget
CPI	Cost efficiency of the work completed	**CPI = EV / AC CPI = $250 / $325 CPI = 0.77**	CPI less than 1 indicates a cost overrun

Interpreting CV and CPI

The CV was calculated as -$75. The negative value indicates that the project is over budget. The CPI was calculated as 0.77. A CPI less than 1 indicates that the costs exceed the budget at the present time.

Forecasting future project performance:

Forecasting estimates the results at the completion of the project based on the team's performance to date and the future risks defined.

Estimate at completion (EAC) is the expected total cost of all project work. There are three methods used to calculate EAC, each with different assumptions. The assumption most commonly used on the PMP® exam is that the work will continue to be performed at the current CPI (first assumption).

Assumptions:

- Work will continue to be performed at the current CPI:
  - EAC = BAC / CPI
- Work will be performed at the budgeted rate:
  - EAC = AV + (BAC - EV)
- Work will continue to be performed at both the current CPI and SPI:
  - EAC = AC + [(BAC - EV) / (CPI × SPI)]

Forecasting also calculates the expected cost to finish all remaining project work. This is known as the **estimate to complete (ETC)**.

The equation is ETC = EAC – AC.

Calculating EAC and ETC

There are three common methods to calculating a project's EAC. Selecting the correct method is dependent on the conditions that exist and the assumptions that are made. Evaluate the specific question on the exam to determine the appropriate equation to use. The most common approach is to divide the BAC by the CPI.

	Definition	Calculation	Analysis
BAC	Total budget	BAC = $400	The total planned cost for the project is $400
PV	Value of the work that should be done	PV = $300	After 3 days, 3 walls were to be completed
EV	Value of the work that is done	EV = $250	2.5 walls are completed; each wall is worth $100
AC	Actual spend to complete the work	AC = $325	Total spend each day ($85, $120, $120)
SV	Amount that the project is ahead/behind schedule	SV = EV - PV SV = $250 - $300 SV = -$50	Negative SV indicates that the project is behind schedule
SPI	How efficient the team is in completing the work	SPI = EV / PV SPI = $250/$350 SPI = 0.83	SPI less than 1 indicates that the team is less efficient in completing the work than projected
CV	Amount of budget deficit or surplus currently	CV = EV - AC CV = $250 - $325 CV = -$75	Negative CV indicates that the project is over budget
CPI	Cost efficiency of the work completed	CPI = EV / AC CPI = $250 / $325 CPI = 0.77	CPI less than 1 indicates a cost overrun
EAC	Expect total cost at the completion of all project work	**EAC = BAC / CPI** **EAC = $400 / 0.77** **EAC = $520**	If the currect cost efficiency rate is maintained, the toal spend will be $520, exceeding the BAC
ETC	Expected cost to complete all remaining project work	**ETC = EAC - AC** **ETC = $520 - $325** **ETC = $195**	$195 will have to be spent to complete the remaining work

Interpreting EAC and ETC

The EAC value calculated indicates that the final cost of the project will be $520, assuming that the same efficiency will be maintained. Notice that this exceeds the BAC. Corrective or preventative action may be needed to prevent cost overrun. The ETC value of $195 defines the amount of money that will be spent to complete the rest of the project.

Calculating the to-complete performance index (TCPI):

To-complete performance index (TCPI) defines the CPI that must be achieved with the remaining resources to meet a specific management goal. The BAC or EAC could be the management goal. The TCPI results define the "level of difficulty" in achieving the desired business goal. TCPI values greater than 1 are harder to complete; those less than 1 are easier to complete. The specific management goal will dictate which equation is used:

- BAC: The efficiency that must be maintained to complete on plan (BAC)
  - TCPI = (BAC - EV) / (BAC - AC)
- Current EAC: The efficiency that must be maintained to complete the current EAC
  - TCPI = (BAC - EV) / (EAC - AC)

Calculating TCPI

The business goal used to calculate the TCPI was the BAC.

	Definition	Calculation	Analysis
BAC	Total budget	BAC = $400	The total planned cost for the project is $400
PV	Value of the work that should be done	PV = $300	After 3 days, 3 walls were to be completed
EV	Value of the work that is done	EV = $250	2.5 walls are completed; each wall is worth $100
AC	Actual spend to complete the work	AC = $325	Total spend each day ($85, $120, $120)
SV	Amount that the project is ahead/behind schedule	SV = EV-PV SV = $250-$300 SV = -$50	Negative SV indicates that the project is behind schedule
SPI	How efficient the team is in completing the work	SPI = EV / PV SPI = $250/$350 SPI = 0.83	SPI less than 1 indicates that the team is less efficient in completing the work than projected
CV	Amount of budget deficit or surplus currently	CV = EV - AC CV = $250 - $325 CV = -$75	Negative CV indicates that the project is over budget
CPI	Cost efficiency of the work completed	CPI = EV / AC CPI = $250/$325 CPI = 0.77	CPI less than 1 indicates a cost overrun
EAC	Expect total cost at the completion of all project work	EAC = BAC/CPI EAC = $400/0.77 EAC = $520	If the currect cost efficiency rate is maintained, the toal spend will be $520, exceeding the BAC
ETC	Expected cost to complete all remaining project work	ETC = EAC - AC ETC = $520-$325 ETC = $195	$195 will have to be spent to complete the remaining work
TCPI	CPI that must be maintained to complete on plan (BAC)	TCPI= (BAC-EV) / (BAC-AC) TCPI= (400-250) / (400-325) **TCPI = 2.0**	TCPI of 2.0 indicates that the team's cost efficiency must improve from 0.77 to 2.0 to complete on plan. Significant increase unlikely

Interpreting TCPI

The TCPI value of 2.0 indicates that the team's cost efficiency must improve from 0.77 to 2.0 to complete on plan. The sgnificant increase in efficiency required is unlikely.

The "Master Prep" Method to Solving Every EVM Question

Recalling the exact EVM equation to use on a question, during the exam, can be difficult. We have provided you our custom method and template that you will use on the exam to ensure you get every EVM question correct. This section guides you through how to **Understand**, **Remember**, and **Use** the template to solve every EVM question.

Study and practice using the method we provide to remember and use the template. Prior to your exam you should be able to recreate the template from memory. When you start the exam, the FIRST thing you should do is to recreate our EVM template on the blank sheet of paper provided by the testing center.

PM Master Prep **Earned Value Management Template**

BAC		Total budget
PV		Work that should be done
EV		What is done
AC		Actual spend

SV = EV – PV	CV = EV – AC
SPI = EV / PV	**CPI = EV / AC**

EAC = BAC / CPI
Est. to Complete = EAC - AC
Variance at Complete = BAC – EAC

Understanding the EVM Template

The PM Master Prep EVM template is comprised of three sections, each is designed to organize the information and equations you need to solve any EVM question.

1. Project status information
2. Variance and performance index calculations
3. Cost projections

1. Project Status Information

Every EVM question will ask you to assess the a project's current or projected progress in terms of one of the following; scope, schedule, and budget.

While the equation for any EVM problem is relatively simple, the difficulty first arises in obtaining, organizing, and understanding the current state project information. Without this information, you won't be able to solve the problem.

For this reason, start every EVM problem by organizing the current state information in a format that is easy to understand and reference. Utilize the project status information section, shown below, to organize the current state project information. This information will either be defined or deduced from information within the question statement.

Project status information includes:

- Total project **budget**
- Work that **should** be done
- What **is** done
- How much has been **spent**

PM Master Prep	Earned Value Management Template	
BAC		Total budget
PV		Work that should be done
EV		What is done
AC		Actual spend

2. Variance and Performance Index calculations

This section organizes the variance and performance index equations for both Schedule (SV and SPI) and Cost (CV and CPI). Notice that the template seperates schedule and cost equations into two identifcal sections, schedule on the left and cost on the right. Within each side the variance equation is recorded above the performance index equation.

SV = EV – PV	CV = EV – AC
SPI = EV / PV	CPI = EV / AC

3. Cost Projections

The estimate at completion (EAC), estimate to complete (ETC), and variance at completion (VAC) are organized in a way to allow you to easily remember them. We describe this method in the remember section.

EAC = BAC / CPI
ETC = EAC - AC
VAC = BAC – EAC

Remembering the EVM Template

We created the EVM template to provide you with a structured method for solving any EVM question on your exam. Please remember that you will not be able to bring this template into the exam. Instead you will have to recreate it from memory on the blank paper the exam center provides.

Fear not, we have defined a process to help you remember the template and easily recreate it. The method uses memory tricks to help the template stick in your brain. Follow along step by step.

Step 1: Draw the template structure

You will start your exam with a blank sheet of paper. The first you must do is draw the boxes that form the template.

Note that each of the three sections are further divided.

- Top section is broken up into a 4 by 3 grid
- Middle section is broken up into four identical sections
    - Small portion at the top where you will write equations
    - Larger portion below where you will use the equation to calculate answers
- Bottom section is broken up into 3 identical sections

Each section of the template is designed to hold a specific piece of information. However, before you memorize those equations practice drawing the template structure from memory. Once you can recreate the structure move on to step 2.

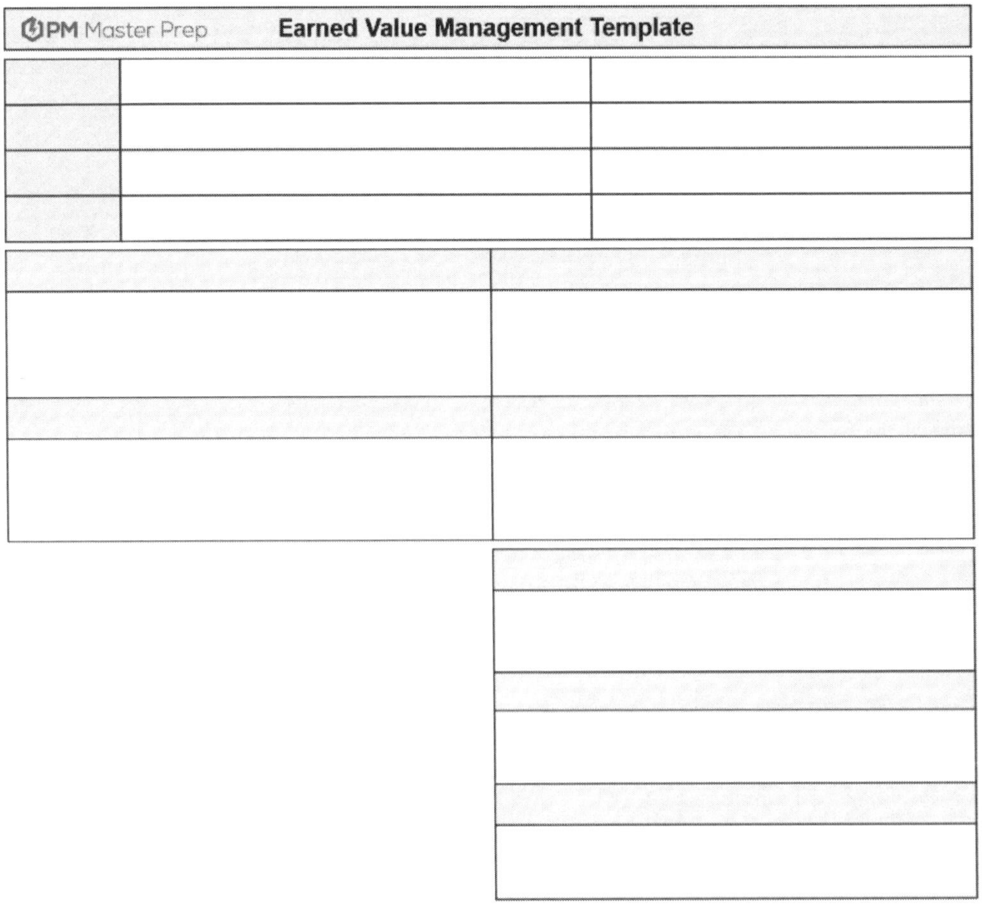

PM Master Prep **Earned Value Management Template**

Step 2: Insert the information into "Project Status Information" section

Say "B Pea, SC"

After you draw the template I want you to say the following two phrases:

- **B Pea, SC**
- **B like the letter, P like the vegetable. SC are the first two letters of the guy's name who made me say this.**

Go ahead and say it again. Burn it into your brain (My name is Scott and I invented this method).

Write the letters of "B Pea, SC" into the top section of the template like I show in the example below. Please notice how the S and the C are written to the left of the template and that there are two lines emanating from the E. These will help you easily create the SV, CV, SPI, and CPI equations later.

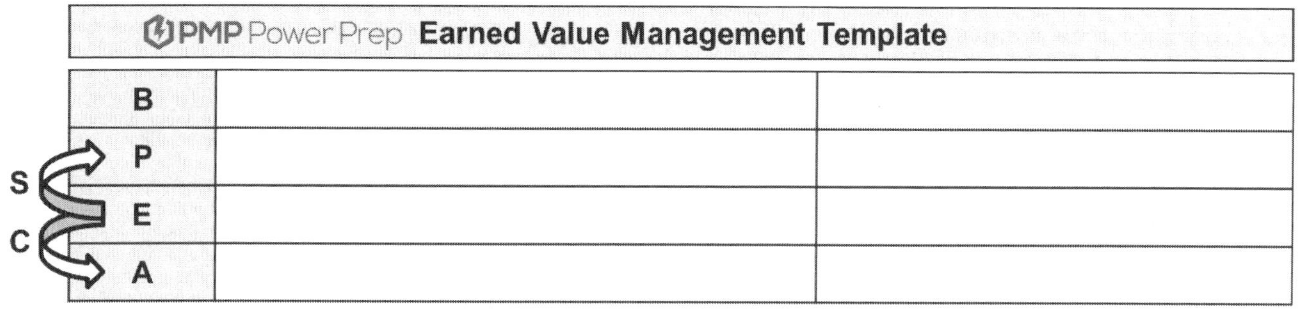

PMP Power Prep **Earned Value Management Template**		
B		
P		
E		
A		

S

C

Complete the top section

The "B Pea, SC" phrase is a memory jogger. It helps you remember the specific EVM variable to write in each box. Each letter that you wrote down is the first letter of a key EVM variable. Having the first letter written down will help you remember the variables needed. Complete filling out each box to incorporate the correct EVM variables.

Note that you will write simple definitions of the four "B Pea" variables to the right. These simple definitions help to provide you a simple and easy to remember reminder of what each variable means. This will help you interpret the information provided in the EVM question to pull out the correct values for each variable.

Just for good measure, go ahead and say the phrase again. Repetition is your friend.

- **B Pea, SC**
- **B like the letter, P like the vegetable. SC are the first two letters of the guy's name who made me say this.**

PM Master Prep	Earned Value Management Template

BAC		Total budget
PV		Work that <u>should</u> be done
EV		What <u>is</u> done
AC		Actual spend

Step 3: Populate the middle section (SV, SPI, CV, CPI)

The middle section contains the four equations that are used to calculate schedule and cost variance and performance index values. The arrows in the top section tell you exactly how to build all four equations.

The left side of the middle section will contain SV and SPI and the right side will contain CV and CPI. Following the arrows in the top section will define every equation needed.

<u>Creating SV and SPI equations</u>

Please note that you wrote the S above the C in the top section. This helps to remind you that the schedule variance and performance index equations will be build first and placed on the left side.

To build the SV equation, start by writing "SV =" in the upper left hand box. Then refer to the top section and follow the "S" arrow from EV to PV. This path defines the order of the equation. Remember that there is a negative between the EV and PV values.

- **SV = EV – PV**

To build the SPI equation, translate the exact variables used in the SV equation down and change the negative sign to a division sign. With that you have created both the SV and SPI equations. Wasn't that easy?

- **SPI = EV / PV**

PM Master Prep	Earned Value Management Template	
BAC		Total budget
•PV		Work that should be done
•EV		What is done
AC		Actual spend

S

SV = **EV – PV**	
SPI = **EV / PV**	

Creating CV and CPI equations

To create the CV and CPI equations you will follow the same process used to create the SV and SPI equations.

Start by writing "CV =" in the upper right hand box, then follow the path of the "C" arrow to define the order of the variables in the CV equation.

- **CV = EV – AC**

Create the CPI equation by translating the exact variables used in the CV equation down and change the negative sign to a division sign. Again, wasn't that easy?

- **CPI = EV / AC**

PM Master Prep	Earned Value Management Template	
BAC		Total budget
•PV		Work that should be done
•EV		What is done
AC		Actual spend

C

SV = EV – PV	CV = **EV - AC**
SPI = EV / PV	CPI = **EV / AC**

Step 4: Populate the bottom section (EAC, ETC, VAC)

The bottom section contains the equations for EAC, ETC, and VAC. As with the previous sections, we have designed the template to help you remember and create the equations for each.

"Last – First – First" to create the EAC equation

EAC is the first equation in the bottom section. To remember how the EAC equation is repeat the phrase:

- **Last – First - First**

The "Last" refers to the last thing you wrote in the middle section. That was EV / AC. While you do not use that exactly, you do use the "EAC" letters that are contained within it.

The "First" refers to the actual first variable you put on the template "BAC".

The next "First" refers to the first variable that you wrote in the last section.

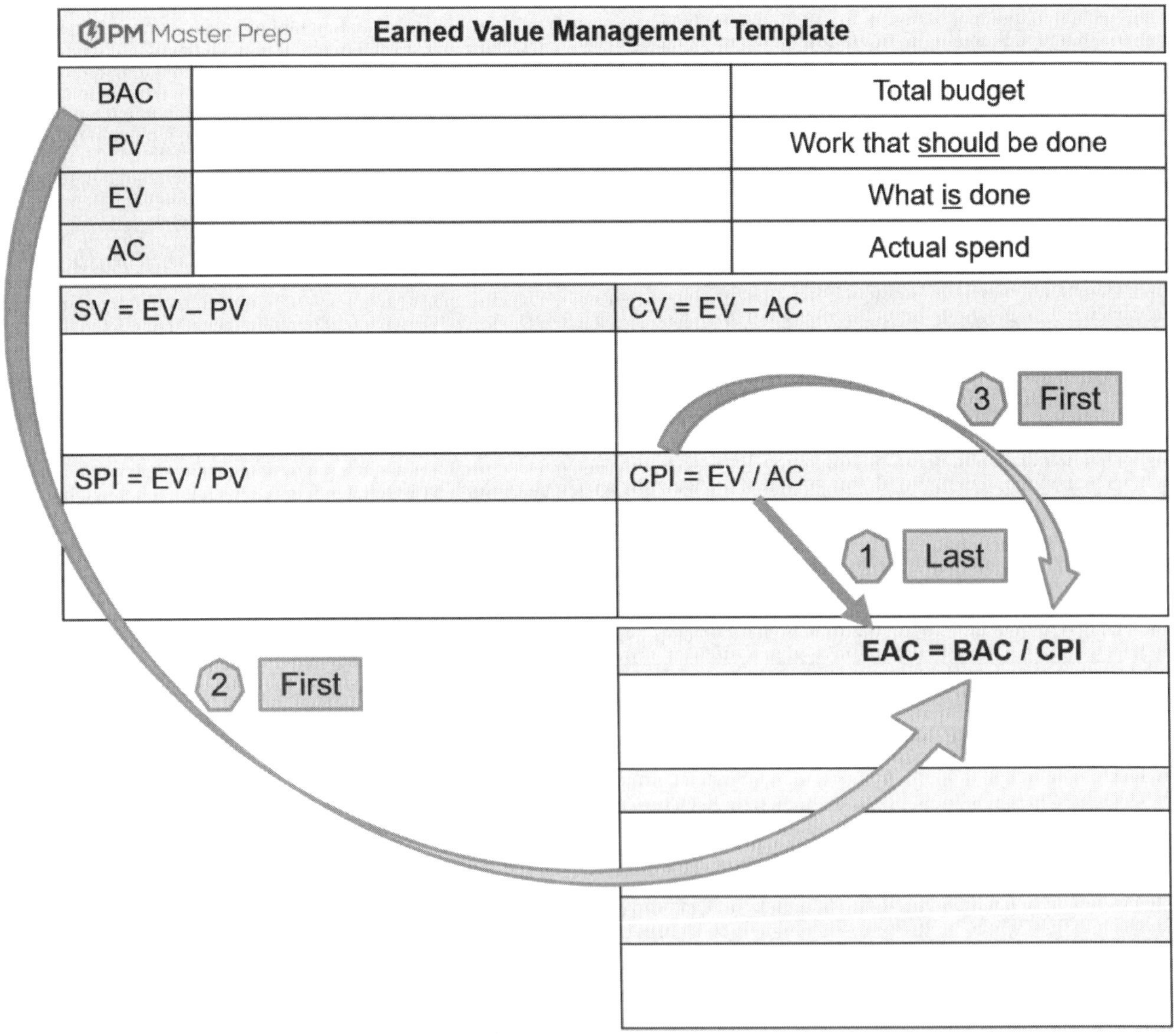

Using a pattern to put EAC in the correct positions

Now that you have created the EAC equation you have to complete the equations for the final two variables (ETC and VAC). Each of these equations uses EAC. Follow the pattern below to put the EAC values in the correct spot of both equations.

- **EAC follows a diagonal line**

PM Master Prep	**Earned Value Management Template**	
BAC		Total budget
PV		Work that should be done
EV		What is done
AC		Actual spend

SV = EV – PV	CV = EV – AC
SPI = EV / PV	CPI = EV / AC

Remember
EAC follows a diagonal

EAC = BAC / CPI
Est. to Complete = EAC - AC
Variance at Complete = BAC - EAC

Allow BAC to drop down to VAC equation

The last memory trick is to allow the BAC value to jump down to the bottom Variance at Completion (VAC) equation. I picture the BAC value hoping over the EAC value to help fill in the last equation.

- **BAC hops down to the bottom equation**

PM Master Prep	Earned Value Management Template	
BAC		Total budget
PV		Work that should be done
EV		What is done
AC		Actual spend

SV = EV – PV	CV = EV – AC
SPI = EV / PV	CPI = EV / AC

EAC = BAC / CPI
Est. to Complete = EAC - AC
Variance at Complete = **BAC** – EAC

Remember
BAC hops down to the bottom equation

Fill in the last three variables (ETC, AC, VAC)

Now that you have gotten to the bottom of the template there are only three variables left to enter. Memorize that these are the last pieces to the puzzle.

- **ETC (Estimate to Complete)**
- **AC (Actual Costs)**
- **VAC (Variance at Completion)**

PM Master Prep — Earned Value Management Template

BAC		Total budget
PV		Work that should be done
EV		What is done
AC		Actual spend

SV = EV – PV	CV = EV – AC
SPI = EV / PV	CPI = EV / AC

EAC = BAC / CPI
ETC = EAC - **AC**
VAC = BAC – EAC

Remember
Last three variables
- **ETC**
- **AC**
- **VAC**

Using the EVM Template

There are two factors to properly using the EVM template to solve every EVM question.

- Creating and recreating the EVM template
- Methodically using the template to solve EVM questions

Creating and recreating the EVM template

Please remember that you will not be able to bring this template into the exam. Instead you will have to recreate it from memory on the blank paper the exam center provides.

> Writing down the EVM template is The FIRST thing you should do.
> Again, the **FIRST** thing you should do when the exam starts!

Additionally, once you create the template on the paper provided by the exam center DO NOT USE that version to solve actual EVM question. Instead keep that version of the template pristine.

> Recreate the template EVERY time you solve an EVM problem.

When you encounter your first EVM question you should copy the template again onto another fresh piece of paper and solve the problem. This may seem like additional work, but it is for a reason.

You will face multiple EVM questions on the exam. You need to work and solve each problem on a separate piece of paper. This will allow you to remain organized and methodical as you solve each problem. Additionally, it helps create a clean record of how you solved each problem that you can use to check your answer.

Methodically using the template to solve EVM questions

Methodically follow the three steps below to solve each problem. The example included below shows how using the three step process will allow you to solve any EVM question.

1. **Identify what the question is asking for**
2. **Identify the given information provided in the question**
3. **Methodically calculate equations from top to bottom to determine the answer**

EVM Example

You are the project manager of a project to widen a 10-mile section of freeway. The approved budget is $50 million, and the approved schedule is 40 weeks. After 22 weeks, your team has completed 6 miles of the freeway, and $32 million has been spent. Calculate the estimate to complete (ETC) using the EVM template.

What is the estimate to complete (ETC)? (Use the EVM template to solve)

a. $20.25 million
b. $21.33 million
c. $23.33 million
d. $53.33 million

1. Identify what the question is asking for..

You are the project manager of a project to widen a 10-mile section of freeway. The approved budget is $50 million, and the approved schedule is 40 weeks. After 22 weeks, your team has completed 6 miles of the freeway, and $32 million have been spent. ***Calculate the estimate to complete (ETC)*** *using the EVM template.*

The question is asking you to calculate the "Estimate to Complete"

2. Identify the given information provided in the question

You are the project manager of a project to widen a ***10-mile*** *section of freeway. The approved budget is* ***$50 million****, and the approved schedule is* ***40 weeks****. After* ***22 weeks****, your team has completed* ***6 miles*** *of the freeway, and* ***$32 million*** *have been spent. Calculate the estimate to complete (ETC) using the EVM template.*

PM Master Prep	**Earned Value Management Template**	
BAC	**$50M**	Total budget
PV	**(22 / 40 weeks((BAC) = $27.5M**	Work that <u>should</u> be done
EV	**(6 / 10 miles) (BAC) = $30M**	What <u>Is</u> done
AC	**$32M**	Actual spend

3. Calculate CV and CPI

SV = EV – PV	CV = EV – AC
	CV = $30M - $32M **CV = -$2M**
SPI = EV / PV	CPI = EV / AC
	CPI = $30M - $32M **CPI = 0.9375**

4. Calculate EAC and ETC

EAC = BAC / CPI
EAC = $50M / 0.9375 **EAC = $53.33M**
ETC = EAC - **AC**
ETC = $53.33M - $32M **ETC = $21.33M**
VAC = BAC – EAC
VAC = $50M - $53.33M **VAC = -$3.33M**

5. Complete solution:

PM Master Prep	**Earned Value Management Template**	
BAC	**$50M**	Total budget
PV	**(22 / 40 weeks((BAC) = $27.5M**	Work that should be done
EV	**(6 / 10 miles) (BAC) = $30M**	What is done
AC	**$32M**	Actual spend

SV = EV – PV	CV = EV – AC
	CV = $30M - $32M **CV = -$2M**
SPI = EV / PV	CPI = EV / AC
	CPI = $30M - $32M **CPI = 0.9375**

EAC = BAC / CPI
EAC = $50M / 0.9375 **EAC = $53.33M**
ETC = EAC - **AC**
ETC = $53.33M - $32M **ETC = $21.33M**
VAC = BAC – EAC
VAC = $50M - $53.33M **VAC = -$3.33M**

The solution to "What is the estimate to complete (ETC)"?

a. $20.25 million
b. $21.33 million
c. $23.33 million
d. $53.33 million

CONTROL QUALITY (*PMBOK GUIDE*® 8.3)

Summary

Control Quality uses the results of all quality management activities to assess performance and ensure the project outputs are complete, correct, and meet the standards and specifications outlined in the quality management plan. In essence, this process determines if the project outputs do what they were intended to do.

Throughout the project, Control Quality compares work results to quality requirements by assessing results at project or product delivery to validate that acceptance criteria have been met.

> Control Quality measures the completeness, compliance, and fitness of the product or service.

Control Quality I.T.T.O.

8.3 Control Quality	Inputs	Tools and Techniques	Outputs
	Project management plan • *Quality mgt. plan* **Project documents** • *Lessons learned register* • *Quality metrics* • *Test and evaluation doc.* **Approved change requests** **Deliverables** **Work performance data** **EEFs** **OPAs**	**Data gathering** • *Checklists* • *Check sheets* • *Statistical sampling* • *Questionnaires and surveys* **Data analysis** • *Performance reviews* • *Root cause analysis* **Inspection** **Testing and product eval.** **Data representation** • *Cause and effect diagrams* • *Control charts* • *Histograms* • *Scatter diagrams* **Meetings**	**Quality control measures** **Verified deliverables** **Work perf. information** **Change requests** **Project mgt. plan updates** • *Quality mgt. plan* **Project documents updates** • *Issue log* • *Lessons learned register* • *Risk register* • *Test and evaluation documents*

Key Outputs

The key outputs of this process are

- Verified deliverables
- Quality control measures
- Work performance information
- Change requests

VERIFIED DELIVERABLES

The key output, verified deliverables, are what confirms that the project outputs do what they were intended to do and meet all quality requirements. Verified deliverables must comply with:

- Specifications
- Standards
- Requirements
- Regulations

> Formal acceptance of the project deliverables obtained later in Validate Scope process CANNOT be completed without verified deliverables produced by Control Quality.

Key Inputs

The inputs the project manager relies upon to achieve the above outputs will define how Quality Control and improvement activities will be performed and evaluated. The quality management plan defines the quality activities and methods to inspect and compare **deliverables** to acceptance criteria. The project manager will also review **approved change requests** and verify their completeness.

DELIVERABLES

Deliverables must be evaluated to ensure they meet the requirements specified by the stakeholders for final acceptance. Using deliverables as the input and conducting inspection will help the project manager obtain verified deliverables.

Key Tools and Techniques

Deliverables are assessed against their performance criteria using data gathering, analysis, and representation as well as inspection and testing. Some data gathering tools useful here are

- Statistical sampling
- Check sheets
- Questionnaires and surveys

The data analysis approach should incorporate **performance reviews** and **root cause analysis**. Additionally, the data representation methods of **cause and effect diagrams, control charts, histograms,** and **scatter diagrams** are used to monitor and evaluate quality throughout the project.

CONTROL RESOURCES (*PMBOK GUIDE*® 9.6)

Summary

Control Resources is the process of ensuring that resources are available as planned and used as effectively as possible. The goal is to ensure the right resource is available at the right place and time, and in the right quantity. This process is performed continuously throughout the project evolution. It is the final process in the Resource Management knowledge area.

Control Resources produces work performance information that does the following:

- Summarizes resource allocation and utilization
- Documents resource expenditures
- Informs stakeholders of status
- Is used to identify and develop corrective actions and change requests

> Control Resources is focused ONLY on the coordination of physical resources, not team members.

Control Resources I.T.T.O.

9.6 Control Resources	Inputs	Tools and Techniques	Outputs
	Project management plan • *Resource mgt. plan* **Project documents** • *Issue log* • *Lessons learned register* • *Physical resource assignments* • *Project schedule* • *Resource breakdown structure* • *Resource requirements* • *Risk register* **Work performance data** **Agreements** **OPAs**	**Data analysis** • *Alternatives analysis* • *Cost-benefit analysis* • *Performance reviews* • *Trend analysis* • *Problem solving* **Interpersonal and team skills** • *Negotiation* • *Influencing* **Project mgt. info. system**	**Work perf. info.** **Change requests** **Project mgt. plan updates** • *Resource mgt. plan* • *Schedule baseline* • *Cost baseline* **Project documents updates** • *Assumption log* • *Issue log* • *Lessons learned register* • *Physical resource assignments* • *Resource breakdown structure* • *Risk register*

Key Outputs

The Control Resources process intends to monitor actual vs. planned resource allocation, and it produces work performance information that can highlight gaps in resource availability.

WORK PERFORMANCE INFORMATION

As a key output, work performance information summarizes if resources are delivered and utilized as planned. It highlights gaps in performance, which can be addressed with corrective or preventative actions through change requests.

CHANGE REQUESTS

Generated to address gaps identified by work performance information, all change requests are evaluated using the Perform Integrated Change Control process. The results of approved change requests must be updated in project documentation.

When changes occur, project management plans must be updated. Those specific to this process are:

- Resource management plan
- Schedule baseline
- Cost baseline

> Resources are released from the project when they are no longer required (as defined in the resource mgt. plan).

In terms of project documents updates, it should be routine by now to record any changes:

- Assumption log
- Issue log
- Lessons learned register
- Physical resource assignments
- Resource breakdown structure
- Risk register

> Project mgt. plans and project documents updates must be done throughout the ENTIRE project life cycle.

Key Inputs

The project management plan and OPAs provide the guidance necessary for managing the complete resource life cycle, including any issues faced. The **resource management plan** defines how resources should be used, controlled, and eventually released.

Organizational process assets include policies for resource assignment and control as well as how resources are re-assigned or released. Escalation procedures for dealing with resource issues may also be included.

> Agreements define the procedures used to remedy issues with externally provided resources.

In controlling resources, **work performance data** is used to evaluate planned vs. actual resource utilization against the baselines established for the project. Work performance data should be provided continuously as actual work is conducted and as an output of Direct and Mange Project Work.

Project documents remain a key input here as well as to numerous other processes. In Control Resources, the **project schedule** and **resource calendar** are key inputs, as they define the *when*, *where*, and *how many* physical resources are used.

Resource requirements and the **resource breakdown structure** provide detailed descriptions regarding resources.

Key Tools and Techniques

DATA ANALYSIS

Data analysis and problem solving are used to evaluate and rectify any resource allocation issues to minimize their effect on project baselines. Data analysis options include the following:

- Alternatives analysis—identifying the best overall option
- Cost-benefit analysis—highlighting the economic impacts of various options
- Performance reviews—measuring, comparing, and analyzing planned vs. actual utilization
- Trend analysis—evaluating if performance is improving or deteriorating
- Problem solving—using structured or methodical approaches to solve problems

> Negotiation and influencing are critical "soft" skills used to obtain additional resources and solve problems.

MONITOR COMMUNICATIONS (*PMBOK GUIDE®* 10.3)

Summary

Monitor Communications provides a lens of reality to evaluate the success of communications and to quickly initiate changes to improve results. This process aims to ensure stakeholder needs are met by:

- Monitoring the actual communications delivered
- Evaluating the effectiveness of communications
- Understanding changes in stakeholder needs
- Triggering changes to the communications plan when warranted

> Monitor Communications creates agility by adjusting methods to best deliver effective communication.

Monitor Communications I.T.T.O.

10.3 Monitor Communications	Inputs	Tools and Techniques	Outputs
	Project management plan • *Resource mgt. plan* • *Communications mgt. plan* • *Stakeholder engmt. plan* **Project documents** • *Issue log* • *Lessons learned register* • *Project communications* **Work performance data** **EEFs** **OPAs**	**Expert judgement** **Project mgt. info. system** **Data analysis** • *Stakeholder engagement assessment matrix* **Interpersonal and team skills** • *Observation and conversation* **Meetings**	**Work perf. info.** **Change requests** **Project mgt. plan updates** • *Communications mgt. plan* • *Stakeholder engmt. plan* **Project doc. updates** • *Issue log* • *Lessons learned register* • *Stakeholder register*

Key Outputs

Work performance information summarizes the effectiveness of communications, and change requests provide recommendations for improvement.

WORK PERFORMANCE INFORMATION

Work performance information helps compare actual vs. planned communications. It also considers feedback on communications through survey results regarding communication effectiveness.

CHANGE REQUESTS

Change requests are generated to adjust communications to improve their effectiveness. All change requests need to be processed via Perform Integrated Change Control. As a result, changes may spur revisions to stakeholder communication requirements including their content requirements, messaging format preferences, or distribution methods.

PROJECT MANAGEMENT PLAN AND PROJECT DOCUMENTS UPDATES

Changes or communication issues along with status of requested changes mandate updating the **communications management plan**, **stakeholder register**, or both. If issues have arisen, the **issue log** should also be updated. Other documents that may need updating include:

- Resource management plan
- Lessons learned register
- Project communications

> Change requests may trigger changes to stakeholders' communication requirements.

Key Inputs

WORK PERFORMANCE DATA

Work performance data and project documents provide information that can be used to evaluate if the project management plan is achieving the desired impacts. Work performance data will contain data on the actual communications that have been distributed, including types and frequency.

PROJECT DOCUMENTS

Project documents such as the **lessons learned register** provide insight into what did and what did not work. Issues that need to be addressed through future communications can be drawn from the **issue log**.

PROJECT MANAGEMENT PLAN

The **communication management plan** and **stakeholder engagement plan** can be referenced to understand existing plans for information dissemination as well as the desired results of communications.

Key Tools and Techniques

Expert judgement and various data representation techniques can be used to gain the perspective necessary to evaluate results and visually depict expected vs. actual engagement levels on the **stakeholder engagement assessment matrix.**

Interpersonal and team skills should be keenly used to engage in **conversations** where this valuable dialog can uncover **observations** necessary in formulating more effective future communications.

> The stakeholder engagement assessment matrix provides the desired engagement level that the communications management plan intended to achieve.

Case Study: "Monitor Communications"

The results from the most recent communications effectiveness survey were in and they indicated that John may have an issue.

The main question on the survey was, "on a scale a scale from 1 to 5, how effective have project communications been in providing the information you need?" The work performance data on the survey was analyzed and indicated while that the average score for the question was 4.1, but there was one stakeholder that registered an answer of 1. Worst of all, it was determined that poor score had come from stakeholder J, the high power-high interest stakeholder for which the team had designed a custom communication strategy.

The strategy was designed to help to transform Stakeholder J from unaware to a leading supporter. The initial results were favorable. However, the results of the current survey indicated otherwise. Prior to reaching out the Stakeholder J, John leveraged a team member to analyze the communication data to determine if there were any obvious issues that may have contributed to Stakeholder J's dissatisfaction.

Through detailed analysis of the actual types and quantities of communication data the team member uncovered that over the past two months only 25% of the scheduled communication emails were sent to stakeholder J and others.

John realized that in his haste to push the team to drive deliverables through the Control Quality and Validate Scope processes he had failed to ensure that the communication management plan was followed. The lapse in disciplined communication was clearly shown in the communication focused work performance data that was tracked. While the updates were continuously posted to the project management hub, the team member tasked in the project plan with sending regular status updates to key stakeholders had missed numerous deadlines.

John vowed to use this realization as an opportunity to improve. The good news what that he now realized what was wrong, now he had to determine what to do about it.

Case Study Questions: "Monitor Communications"

What should John do to mitigate the damage caused by the failure to follow the communication plan and to improve future performance?

a) Meet face the face with the stakeholder to explain the situation, ensure them that the process will be followed in the future, and monitor the work performance data weekly to confirm that the communication plan is being followed.
b) Submit a change request to modify the process by which the progress updates are communicated to the Stakeholder J
c) Remove the team member who was responsible for sending weekly communication updates from the team and inform the remaining team that not following the established communication plan is unacceptable.
d) Send an email to Stakeholder J apologizing for the lapse in communication

Which project document should be updated to document the engagement and communication issue uncovered with Stakeholder J and how it was resolved?

a) Stakeholder engagement matrix
b) Project management plan
c) Change log
d) Issue log

If a change request had been submitted and approved to modify the approach, frequency, or method of communicating information, which document or plan would be least likely to be updated?

a) Communications management plan
b) Stakeholder engagement plan
c) Requirements traceability matrix
d) Lessons learned register

Further analysis of the work performance data uncovered that less than 50% of the stakeholders review the weekly project updates. What should John do to improve the effectiveness of his communication plan?

a) Revise the communications management plan to meet the perceived informational needs of the stakeholders
b) Determine the issue with the current format of weekly project updates (format, method of distribution, etc.) and initiate a change request to alter the communication management plan that better meets the information needs of the stakeholders
c) Create a signature log on all emailed communications to indicate the date and time when each stakeholder opens the project updates
d) Have the project sponsor send an email out to remind all stakeholders of the importance of staying informed as to project progress

CASE STUDY ANSWERS: "MONITOR COMMUNICATIONS"

What should John do to mitigate the damage caused by the failure to follow the communication plan and to improve future performance?

- **a) Meet face the face with the stakeholder to explain the situation, ensure them that the process will be followed in the future, and monitor the work performance data weekly to confirm that the communication plan is being followed**
- b) Submit a change request to modify the process by which the progress updates are communicated to the Stakeholder
- c) Remove the team member who was responsible for sending weekly communication updates from the team and inform the remaining team that not following the established communication plan is unacceptable
- d) Send an email to Stakeholder J apologizing for the lapse in communication

Which project document should be updated to document the engagement and communication issue uncovered with Stakeholder J and how it was resolved?

- a) Stakeholder engagement matrix
- b) Project management plan
- c) Change log
- **d) Issue log**

If a change request had been submitted and approved to modify the approach, frequency, or method of communicating information, which document or plan would be least likely to be updated?

- a) Communications management plan
- b) Stakeholder engagement plan
- **c) Requirements traceability matrix**
- d) Lessons learned register

Further analysis of the work performance data uncovered that less than 50% of the stakeholders review the weekly project updates. What should John do to improve the effectiveness of his communication plan?

- a) Revise the communications management plan to meet the perceived informational needs of the stakeholders
- **b) Determine the issue with the current format of weekly project updates (format, method of distribution, etc.) and initiate a change request to alter the communication management plan that better meets the information needs of the stakeholders**
- c) Create a signature log on all emailed communications to indicate the date and time when each stakeholder opens the project updates
- d) Have the project sponsor send an email out to remind all stakeholders of the importance of staying informed as to project progress

MONITOR RISKS (*PMBOK GUIDE*® 11.7)

Summary

Monitor Risks involves evaluating risk responses, tracking existing risks, and identifying and analyzing new risks. This process tracks the current risk status of all risks identified for the project and assesses the effectiveness of the approach used to achieve the desired risk response outcome. The key outputs of Monitor Risks are work performance information, change requests, and project documents updates.

> The team and stakeholders must be continually updated on the status of risks within the project.

Monitor Risks I.T.T.O.

11.7 Monitor Risks	Inputs	Tools and Techniques	Outputs
	Project mgt. plan • *Risk mgt. plan* **Project documents** • *Issue log* • *Lessons learned register* • *Risk register* • *Risk report* **Work performance data** **Work performance reports**	**Data analysis** • *Technical performance analysis* • *Reserve analysis* **Audits** **Meetings**	**Work perf. information** **Change requests** **Project mgt. plan updates** • *Any component* **Project doc. updates** • *Assumption log* • *Issue log* • *Lessons learned register* • *Risk register* • *Risk report* **OPA updates**

Key Outputs

Implementing risk responses generates work performance information and change requests that must be documented in project management plans and project documents.

WORK PERFORMANCE INFORMATION

Work performance information is drawn from the status, effectiveness, or results of the risk management activities performed by risk owners. The project manager will conduct comparative analysis on actual results vs. expected results and consequently document, disseminate, and communicate these results.

CHANGE REQUESTS

Change requests will be necessary when the results of management activities and the execution of risk response plans yield less than desired results, or other extenuating circumstances require changes.

> Work performance information is fed back as an input into Monitor and Control Project (4.5), which tracks, summarizes, and reports on overall project performance.

Key Inputs

The **risk register** and project management plans such as the **risk management plan** indicate when and how to monitor risks. **Work performance data** and **risk reports** provide information that can be used to evaluate the effectiveness of risk responses and determine if further action or changes are necessary.

Key Tools and Techniques

Data analysis through technical performance analysis allows the project team to perform comparative assessments of the technical accomplishments of risk response activities.

Reserve analysis can be used to compare the actual amount of contingency remaining relative to the amount of risk remaining and decide if the existing reserve is adequate (burndown chart).

Audits must be used to monitor and evaluate the execution and results of risk activity implementations.

> The burndown chart demonstrates if the contingency reserve remaining is sufficient to meet the risk remaining.

Case Study: "Monitor Risks"

Due to the high level of focus and importance placed on the project, John insisted that a Monitor Risk meeting be carried out bi-monthly. The business analyst assigned to run it had segmented the sixty-minute meeting into four equal sections; each designed to address one of the four objectives of the Monitor Risk process.

The analyst always kicked the meeting off by reporting on the status of the agreed-upon risk response plans that were currently being implemented. Once complete, the focus moved to tracking the identified risks, followed by the identification of new risks, and finally an evaluation of how effective the overall risk processes have been.

John watched the meeting progress, speaking for the first time when the analyst paused to transitioned from the first to second section. John took this opportunity to provide his summarize of the status of the tracking of identified risk section by saying, "we were prepared for the worst, but lucky for us that day didn't come!"

John was specifically referring to the risk surrounding the uncertainty in the exact amount of contract labor that would be needed to help complete the drawing redesigns. The two factors that had driven the risk were the uncertainty as to the exact number of revisions that be needed and the speed with which the core team would be able to complete each redesign. John had worried that if a larger than expected number of revisions were needed the total labor cost would expand rapidly. To mitigate the portion of the risk they could impact, the team had developed and implemented process improvements that successfully increased the speed by which they completed revisions.

Even with the improvements, the team still had to utilize expensive contract labor. However, the total cost impact was not currently understood. Over the past week, the financial analyst had worked with the team to perform a technical performance analysis and a reserve analysis related to this risk. A summary of his findings was included in the risk report that sat in front of each team member.

"As you can see, we are 94% complete with the technical drawing redesigns and are 9% ahead of where we expected to be at this time." The group nodded, confirming that they agreed with the summary. "For this reason, I believe that the risk of cost overruns from the use of contract labor has been eliminated."

John pushed the analyst to continue by stating, "tell them the really good news." The analyst proceeded to explain that the combination of lower volume of redesigns and the productivity improvements implemented had resulted in a significant positive impact on the amount of contingency reserve that was used.

Ever the pragmatist, the analyst urged the team not to lose focus, "this is all good news, but we need to remain vigilant and keep communicating. That is the only way we are going to build resilience into our project and it is why the next portion of this meeting is so important! What new risks have you identified?"

CASE STUDY QUESTIONS: "MONITOR RISKS"

Which of the following is not one of the four key objectives of the Monitor Risks process?

a) Monitor the implementation of risk response plans
b) Track identified risks
c) Identify and analyze new risks
d) Assign individuals to implement new corrective actions to eliminate new risks identified

What is the proper frequency at which the Monitor Risks review meetings should be held?

a) Meetings must be held weekly to ensure constant vigilance in monitoring and evaluating project risk
b) Meetings should be held at the completion of each process group
c) Meetings are only required when significant new risks are identified or when current risks can be retired
d) Meeting schedule should be scheduled regularly to align with the based on the project's risk profile and how the project is progressing against its objectives

Which two types of data analysis are used during the Monitor Risk process to compare the schedule vs. actual technical accomplishments and to evaluate the impact of risk on contingency reserves?

a) Qualitative risk analysis and quantitative risk analysis
b) Technical performance analysis and contingency analysis
c) Technical performance analysis and reserve analysis
d) Risk categorization and quantitative risk analysis

Later in the meeting the team identified a new risk, with significant cost and schedule impact, that they believe requires preventative action. What course of action should be followed to address the new issues identified?

a) Inform the entire team of the new risk identified and develop a procedure for mitigating the risk
b) Analyze the risk and submit a change request to the Perform Integrated Change Control process
c) Assign a team member to implement a solution to eliminate the risk
d) Take no action until the actual risk is realized

______________ is the term that describes the approaches and contingencies that project leaders build into their project's risk processes that increase the team's ability to response positively and productivity to emergent unknowable-unknown risks?

a) Project resilience
b) Project risk flexibility
c) Contingency reserves

d) Sensitivity analysis

CASE STUDY ANSWERS: "MONITOR RISKS"

Which of the following is not one of the four key objectives of the Monitor Risks process?

a) Monitor the implementation of risk response plans
b) Track identified risks
c) Identify and analyze new risks
d) Assign individuals to implement new corrective actions to eliminate new risks identified

What is the proper frequency at which the Monitor Risks review meetings should be held?

a) Meetings must be held weekly to ensure constant vigilance in monitoring and evaluating project risk
b) Meetings should be held at the completion of each process group
c) Meetings are only required when significant new risks are identified or when current risks can be retired
d) Meeting schedule should be scheduled regularly to align with the based on the project's risk profile and how the project is progressing against its objectives

Which two types of data analysis are used during the Monitor Risk process to compare the schedule vs. actual technical accomplishments and to evaluate the impact of risk on contingency reserves?

a) Qualitative risk analysis and quantitative risk analysis
b) Technical performance analysis and contingency analysis
c) Technical performance analysis and reserve analysis
d) Risk categorization and quantitative risk analysis

Later in the meeting the team identified a new risk, with significant cost and schedule impact, that they believe requires preventative action. What course of action should be followed to address the new issues identified?

a) Inform the entire team of the new risk identified and develop a procedure for mitigating the risk
b) Analyze the risk and submit a change request to the Perform Integrated Change Control process
c) Assign a team member to implement a solution to eliminate the risk
d) Take no action until the actual risk is realized

____________ is the term that describes the approaches and contingencies that project leaders build into their project's risk processes that increase the team's ability to respond positively and productivity to emergent unknowable-unknown risks?

a) Project resilience

b) Project risk flexibility
c) Contingency reserves
d) Sensitivity analysis

CONTROL PROCUREMENTS (*PMBOK GUIDE®* 12.3)

Summary

Control Procurements evaluates contract progress and results and manages the procurement relationship to improve the likelihood of project success.

Control Procurement focuses on ensuring that both parties meet contractual obligations. This process is used to confirm that the appropriate buyer parties approve seller deliverables and work to settle all conflicts in a positive and fair manner. Any closed procurements will feed directly into final project files and the lessons learned register.

Control Procurements I.T.T.O.

12.3 Control Procurements	Inputs	Tools and Techniques	Outputs
	Project mgt. plan • *Requirements mgt. plan* • *Risk mgt. plan* • *Procurement mgt. plan* • *Change mgt. plan* • *Schedule baseline* **Project documents** • *Assumption log* • *Lessons learned register* • *Milestone list* • *Quality reports* • *Req. documentation* • *Req. traceability matrix* • *Risk register* • *Stakeholder register* **Agreements** **Procurement documentation** **Approved change requests** **Work performance data** **EEFs** **OPAs**	**Expert judgement** **Claims administration** **Data analysis** • *Performance reviews* • *Earned value analysis* • *Trend analysis* **Inspection** **Audits**	**Closed procurements** **Work performance info.** **Procurement doc. updates** **Change requests** **Project mgt. plan updates** • *Risk management plan* • *Procurement mgt. plan* • *Schedule baseline* • *Cost baseline* **Project documents updates** • *Lessons learned register* • *Resource requirements* • *Req. traceability matrix* • *Risk register* • *Stakeholder register* **OPA updates**

Key Outputs

Control Procurements obtains formal verification that the work is completed and generates work performance information and change requests that must be documented in the project management plan and project documents.

CLOSED PROCUREMENTS

The closed procurements are obtained by obtaining formal written notice that the contract has been completed. This is usually provided by authorized procurement administration and must be completed following the terms defined in the contract.

WORK PERFORMANCE INFORMATION

The work performance information will be generated to show how the seller is performing by comparing actual vs. expected performance.

CHANGE REQUESTS

In situations where performance necessitates corrective or preventative actions, **change requests** will be created and addressed by the Perform Integrated Change Control process. Updates to the **procurement management plan** may also be required.

Modifications to baselines will prompt updates to the **schedule baseline** and **cost baseline**.

Along with schedule, cost, and risk performance information, procurement-related performance information is fed back (as an input) to Monitor and Control Project Work.

Before a procurement can be officially closed, formal verification of work completed is required and multiple OPAs must be updated. Closing procurements requires formal written notices that a contract has been completed, and these are usually provided by an authorized procurement administrator. These notices should follow procurement closure terms defined by the contract. The project team should approve all deliverables before written notices are given.

ORGANIZATIONAL PROCESS ASSETS UPDATES

This process results in updates to organizational process assets such as seller performance evaluation documentation. All financial obligations, payment schedules, and requests must be completed.

Other project documents that may need updating include the **lessons learned register** and **resource requirements** documents, as resources will be released upon procurement closure.

Control Procurements ensures that procurement payments are directly linked to the work being completed.

Key Inputs

Project management plans and project documents inform how to monitor contract progress, and data provides the information to evaluate this progress. The **procurement documentation** provides the information necessary to support contract monitoring. **Work performance data** offers information on the status and results of seller activities.

Other key inputs to Control Procurements include the **procurement management plan** and any existing **agreements**.

> Approved change requests feed into Control Procurements, potentially requiring alterations to the procurement SOW.

Key Tools and Techniques

Inspections and **audits** of work progress are required to monitor if deliverables meet the requirements defined in the contract and that schedules are being met. Using work performance data, the project team will conduct data analysis for **performance reviews**, **earned value analysis**, and **trend analysis** to monitor status and directional performance.

Claims administration can be used for contested changes, or when the buyer and seller do not agree on something such as compensation or perceived discrepancies in deliverable requirements. If issues cannot be resolved, the alternative dispute resolution process (ADR) will come into play.

> Negotiations are the optimal method, but the contractually defined ADR processes can be used to handle claims.

MONITOR STAKEHOLDER ENGAGEMENT (*PMBOK GUIDE*® 13.4)

Summary

Much like Monitor Communications, Monitor Stakeholder Engagement constantly gauges stakeholder relationships and should prompt acting on strategies for engagement or modifying existing engagement plans when necessary. Once stakeholders are identified and the engagement plan is in motion, this process should be performed throughout the project.

The project manager's focus should be on improving the effectiveness of stakeholder relationships by

- Collecting work performance data generated by Direct and Manage Project Work (4.3)
- Evaluating to determine if desired engagement levels are obtained
- Delivering on existing engagement plans or generating changes to improve effectiveness

> Monitor Stakeholder Engagement aims to adapt and improve engagement activities as the project progresses.

Monitor Stakeholder Engagement I.T.T.O.

13.4 Monitor Stakeholder Engmt.	Inputs	Tools and Techniques	Outputs
	Project management plan • *Resource mgt. plan* • *Communications mgt. plan* • *Stakeholder engmt. plan* **Project documents** • *Issue log* • *Lessons learned register* • *Project communications* • *Risk register* • *Stakeholder register* **Work performance data** **EEFs** **OPAs**	**Data analysis** • *Alternatives analysis* • *Root cause analysis* • *Stakeholder analysis* **Decision making** • *Multicriteria decision analysis* • *Voting* **Data representation** • *Stakeholder engagement assessment matrix* **Communication skills** • *Feedback* • *Presentations* **Interpersonal and team skills** • *Active listening* • *Cultural awareness* • *Leadership* • *Networking* • *Political awareness* **Meetings**	**Work perf. information** **Change requests** **Project mgt. plan updates** • *Resource mgt. plan* • *Communications mgt. plan* • *Stakeholder engmt. plan* **Project doc. updates** • *Issue log* • *Lessons learned register* • *Risk register* • *Stakeholder register*

Key Outputs

WORK PERFORMANCE INFORMATION

The Monitor Stakeholder Engagement process generates work performance information that must be recorded with project documents updates. Stakeholders typically have no reservations identifying issues or risks that they observe. These interactions facilitate opportunities for **change requests**. Updates to the **issue log** and **risk register** can be born out of this feedback.

PROJECT MANAGEMENT PLAN UPDATES

This is a process used to evaluate and adjust the **stakeholder engagement plan** based on interactions and their effectiveness in achieving project objectives. Any differences between actual and desired engagement levels will require adjusting the stakeholder engagement plan, and changes should flow to the **communication management plan** as well.

Key Inputs

When monitoring stakeholder engagement, **work performance data** and subsequent data analysis yield decision making variables, which spur project documents updates. The following documents may be updated:

- Issue log
- Lessons learned register
- Project communications
- Risk register
- Stakeholder register

> Feedback of work performance data paints the picture of the actual impact of engagement strategies.

PROJECT MANAGEMENT PLAN

While updates to the project management plan are outputs of this process, the plans themselves are inputs. These plans should be referenced as part of assessing the effectiveness of the **stakeholder engagement plan**.

Key Tools and Techniques

INTERPERSONAL AND TEAM SKILLS

Interacting with stakeholders requires good interpersonal and communication skills. The project manager will be sharing information through **presentations**, as well as collecting information through **networking** while demonstrating **active listening** prowess.

> Active listening involves using your own words and interpretations to clarify and confirm the message that you understood.

CLOSING PROCESS GROUP

Closing Process Group Summary

The Closing process group brings closure to all activities across all processes. The Closing process represents the formal completion of the project.

Objectives

The objectives of the Closing process group are to transfer of ownership of the final product, service or result produced by the project and complete the activities to formally close the project. Formal closure involves creating a final report, ensuring all project documents are updated and archived, releasing resources, and asking stakeholders for feedback.

Key Outputs

Closing is part of organizational learning. To become better, an organization strives to continuously improve. An important way to improve is by documenting lessons learned and recording this information into the organization's process assets repository.

The inputs to Closing are accepted deliverables, all the components of the project plan, and all project documents. The key outputs are:

- Final product, service, or result transition
- Final report
- Updated Lessons learned register
- Organizational process assets updates

Close Project or Phase (*PMBOK Guide®* 4.7)

Summary

Close Project or Phase is the formal finalizing process of all groups. Every project should be formally closed and the final project result—a product, service, or process change—must be transitioned to its final owner.

Regardless of the project outcome, all projects should follow the process of Close Project or Phase. Even if the project was cancelled, the lessons learned need to be posted to the lessons learned register, and organizational process assets need to be updated.

> Every project, whether successfully completed or prematurely terminated, should be formally closed.

Close Project or Phase I.T.T.O.

	Inputs	Tools and Techniques	Outputs
13.1 Identify Stakeholders	**Project charter** **Project management plan** • All components **Procurement documents** • *Assumption log* • *Basis of estimates* • *Change log* • *Issue log* • *Lessons learned register* • *Milestone list* • *Project communications* • *Quality control measures* • *Quality reports* • *Requirements documentation* • *Risk register* • *Risk report* **Accepted deliverables** **Business documents** • *Business case* • *Benefits management plan* **Agreements** **Procurement documentation** **OPAs**	**Expert judgement** **Data analysis** • *Document analysis* • *Regression analysis* • *Trend analysis* • *Variance analysis* **Meetings**	**Project documents updates** • *Lessons learned register* **Final product, service, or result transition** **Final report** **OPA updates**

Key Outputs

PROJECT DOCUMENTS UPDATES

In closing the project, the project manager reviews the project management plan and all project documents to ensure that project work is complete and the project has met its objectives. This activity should include reviewing procurement documents and agreements to ensure that all commitments and contracts are brought to closure and all resources are released. The key outputs of Close Process or Phase include project documents updates, particularly the **lessons learned register**, which should be updated and finalized.

FINAL PRODUCT, SERVICE, OR RESULT TRANSITION

The most important output of this process is turning over the final product or output of the project. This is the whole reason for the project and must be conducted formally and professionally.

FINAL REPORT

To accomplish a formal and professional transition, a final report is produced and delivered to the project sponsor and all stakeholders. The final report summarizes project performance elements such as benefit, cost, quality, schedule, etc. The project manager should follow the communication plan to be sure proper dissemination is achieved.

ORGANIZATIONAL PROCESS ASSETS UPDATES

The final report and all project documents updates become the last elements added to the organization's process assets.

Key Inputs

Several outputs of other processes become inputs to Close Project or Phase. These outputs will be critical to making sure that everything the project intended to deliver is finalized.

PROJECT CHARTER

The project charter, which initiated and authorized the project, contains the project objectives and other information that the project manager can reference to deliver the final result to the customer or sponsor.

PROJECT MANAGEMENT PLAN

All components of the project management plan, which includes 12 subsidiary plans and four baselines, should be reviewed and completed.

PROJECT DOCUMENTS

Numerous project documents should be reviewed to address any incomplete items or issues. These documents are essential to revisit during project closure to validate completion and address anything that remains outstanding:

- Assumption log
- Basis of estimates
- Change log
- Issue log
- Lessons learned register
- Milestone list

- Project communications
- Quality control measurements
- Quality reports
- Requirements documentation
- Risk register
- Risk report

ACCEPTED DELIVERABLES

In the Monitoring and Controlling process group and during the Validate Scope process, the project manager was tasked with ensuring that the acceptance criteria were agreed to and approved. To confidently deliver the final product to the customer or sponsor, the project manager should review those accepted deliverables.

> Project deliverables are approved in the Validate Scope process.
> The Close Project process is where the final product is delivered.

PROCUREMENT DOCUMENTATION AND AGREEMENTS

As part of finalizing a project, any contracts, statements of work, service level agreements, or procurement contracts must be brought to closure. All commitments, financial obligations, or resource allocations need to be addressed and completed.

Key Tools and Techniques

DATA ANALYSIS

During the Close Project or Phase process, the project team uses **expert judgement** and focuses on information in project documents, business documents, and the project management plan.

Document analysis is highly leveraged, as well as other analysis techniques such as **trend and variance analyses**. Much of this analysis should take place via **meetings** in a collaborative manner.

Case Study: "Close Project or Phase"

John had called Sara to inform her that the last drawing redesign had been completed and confirmed as an accepted deliverable by the customer. He expected kind words of praise and congratulations, but instead was offered specific direction on how to proceed, "It is great that the project work is done, but don't relax yet. You must apply the same level of detail and effort to closing the project as you did in executing the project plan."

Sara had coached John that in order to officially close the project he must formally transfer the final product to the ownership of the sponsor. Additionally, she explained that the Close Project processes other outputs were a final report and the update and archive of all project documents, most importantly the lessons learned register.

The amount of work required to update and finalize the project documents and create of the final report confirmed an additional point that Sara emphasized. She had strongly advised John not to release the project team until after all of the administrative work was completed saying, "once the team goes back to their jobs, obtaining their assistance will be much more difficult."

John and the team progressively added to the existing lessons learned register through stakeholder interviews and data analysis. By conducting sessions with key stakeholders, they were able to solicit ideas that could be used to improve future performance. The team complemented these ideas by using four types of data analysis techniques; document analysis, regression analysis, trend analysis, and variance analysis. Each technique analyzed the project through a different lens to help identify insights. Scrolling through the 100+ items on the lessons learned register John was confident that the insights would help inform and guide the path of future project leaders.

John followed the completion of the lesson learned register by ensuring all project documents were updated and archived on the project management hub and that the final report was created. The final report was a comprehensive document confirming that the project success and completion criteria were met and that summarized the project's scope, quality, and cost performance.

Armed with physical and digital copies of the final product, the final report, and updated project documents John was now prepared to close the project. He scheduled a meeting with the sponsor to hand over the final product and obtain formal confirmation via signature.

Seeing the project finish line brought John an unexpected level of clarity and hunger. At that moment he made a commitment to himself. "I want to make project management my career and I am going to get my PMP certification. I know I need more experience, but I am going to start studying now."

CASE STUDY QUESTIONS: "CLOSE PROJECT OR PHASE"

Which of the following is not an objective of the Close Project or Phase process?

a) Transfer the finished deliverable to the customer
b) Obtain customer approval of the project deliverables
c) Obtain verification that from the customer that they accept the project deliverables
d) Update and archive all project documents and OPAs

Of the four data analysis techniques used in the Close Project or Phase, which technique is focused on identifying lessons learned and knowledge sharing opportunities to help improve future projects?

a) Document analysis
b) Regression analysis
c) Trend analysis
d) Variance analysis

Sara instructed John that a critical output of the Close Project process was the completion and archive of the Lessons Learned register. Why is ensuring that the register is updating and archived important?

a) To create a means of identifying talented individuals that can assist in improving later projects
b) To identify and make easily available improvement ideas that can be used on comparable projects in the future
c) The project cannot to formally closed until every output is produced
d) To highlight the largest risks and opportunities that were overcome during the project

To complete the Close Project or Phase process the customer must formally confirm that the final deliverables were transferred to his/her ownership. During which process did the customer accept that the deliverables met the acceptance criteria?

a) Control quality
b) Validate scope
c) Control scope
d) Direct and manage project work

CASE STUDY ANSWERS: "CLOSE PROJECT OR PHASE"

Which of the following is not an objective of the Close Project or Phase process?

a) Transfer the finished deliverable to the customer
b) Obtain customer approval of the project deliverables
c) Obtain verification from the customer that they accept the project deliverables
d) Update and archive all project documents and OPAs

Of the four data analysis techniques used in the Close Project or Phase, which technique is focused on identifying lessons learned and knowledge sharing opportunities to help improve future projects?

a) Document analysis
b) Regression analysis
c) Trend analysis
d) Variance analysis

Sara instructed John that a critical output of the Close Project process was the completion and archive of the Lessons Learned register. Why is ensuring that the register is updating and archived important?

a) To create a means of identifying talented individuals that can assist in improving later projects
b) To identify and make easily available improvement ideas that can be used on comparable projects in the future
c) The project cannot be formally closed until every output is produced
d) To highlight the largest risks and opportunities that were overcome during the project

To complete the Close Project or Phase process the customer must formally confirm that the final deliverables were transferred to his/her ownership. During which process did the customer accept that the deliverables met the acceptance criteria?

a) Control quality
b) Validate scope
c) Control scope
d) Direct and manage project work

GLOSSARY

Acceptance Criteria. A set of conditions required to be met before deliverables are accepted.

Accepted Deliverables. Products, results, or capabilities produced by a project and validated by the project customer or sponsor as meeting the specified acceptance criteria.

Accuracy. Within the quality management system, accuracy is an assessment of correctness.

Acquire Resources. The process of obtaining team members, facilities, equipment, materials, supplies, and other resources necessary to complete project work.

Acquisition. Obtaining human and material resources necessary to perform project activities. Acquisition implies a cost of resources, and is not necessarily financial.

Activity. A distinct, scheduled portion of work performed during the course of a project.

Activity Attributes. Multiple attributes associated with each schedule activity that can be included within the activity list. Activity attributes include activity codes, predecessor activities, successor activities, logical relationships, leads and lags, resource requirements, imposed dates, constraints, and assumptions.

Activity Duration. The time in calendar units between the start and finish of a schedule activity. See also **Duration**.

Activity Duration Estimates. The quantitative assessments of the likely number of time periods that are required to complete an activity.

Activity List. A documented tabulation of schedule activities that shows the activity description, activity identifier, and a sufficiently detailed scope of work description so project team members understand what work is to be performed.

Activity-on-Node (AON). See precedence diagramming method (PDM).

Actual Cost (AC). The realized cost incurred for the work performed on an activity during a specific time.

Actual Duration. The time in calendar units between the actual start date of the schedule activity and either the data date of the project schedule if the schedule activity is in progress or the actual finish date if the schedule activity is complete.

Adaptive Life Cycle. A project life cycle that is iterative or incremental.

Affinity Diagrams. A technique that allows large numbers of ideas to be classified for review and analysis.

Agreements. Any document or communication that defines the initial intentions of a project. This can take the form of a contract, memorandum of understanding (MOU), letters of agreement, verbal agreements, email, etc.

Alternatives Analysis. A technique used to evaluate identified options to select the options or approaches to use to execute and perform the work of the project.

Analogous Estimating. A technique for estimating the duration or cost of an activity or a project using historical data from a similar activity or project.

Analytical Techniques. Various techniques used to evaluate, analyze, or forecast potential outcomes based on possible variations of project or environmental variables and their relationships with other variables.

Assumption. A factor in the planning process that is true, real, or certain, without proof or demonstration.

Assumption Log. A project document used to record all assumptions and constraints throughout the project life cycle.

Attribute Sampling. Method of measuring quality that consists of noting the presence (or absence) of some characteristic (attribute) in each of the units under consideration.

Authority. The right to apply project resources, expend funds, make decisions, or give approvals.

Backward Pass. A critical path method technique for calculating the late start and late finish dates by working backward through the schedule model from the project end date.

Bar Chart. A graphic display of schedule-related information. In the typical bar chart, schedule activities or work breakdown structure components are listed down the left side of the chart, dates are shown across the top, and activity durations are shown as date-placed horizontal bars. See also **Gantt Chart**.

Baseline. The approved version of a work product that can be changed only through formal change control procedures and is used as a basis for comparison to actual results.

Basis of Estimates. Supporting documentation outlining the details used in establishing project estimates such as assumptions, constraints, level of detail, ranges, and confidence levels.

Benchmarking. The comparison of actual or planned products, processes, and practices to those of comparable organizations to identify best practices, generate ideas for improvement, and provide a basis for measuring performance.

Benefits Management Plan. The documented explanation defining the processes for creating, maximizing, and sustaining the benefits provided by a project or program.

Bid Documents. All documents used to solicit information, quotations, or proposals from prospective sellers.

Bidder Conference. The meeting with prospective sellers prior to the preparation of a bid or proposal to ensure all prospective vendors have a clear and common understanding of the procurement. Also known as contractor conference, vendor conference, or pre-bid conference.

Bottom-Up Estimating. A method of estimating project duration or cost by aggregating the estimates of the lower-level components of the work breakdown structure (WBS).

Budget. The approved estimate for the project or any work breakdown structure component or any schedule activity.

Budget at Completion (BAC). The sum of all budgets established for the work to be performed.

Buffer. See **Reserve**.

Business Case. A documented economic feasibility study used to establish validity of the benefits of a selected component lacking sufficient definition and that is used as a basis for the authorization of further project management activities.

Business Value. The net quantifiable benefit derived from a business endeavor. The benefit may be tangible, intangible, or both.

Cause and Effect Diagram. A decomposition technique that helps trace an undesirable effect back to its root cause.

Change. A modification to any formally controlled deliverable, project management plan component, or project document.

Change Control. A process whereby modifications to documents, deliverables, or baselines associated with the project are identified, documented, approved, or rejected.

Change Control Board (CCB). A formally chartered group responsible for reviewing, evaluating, approving, delaying, or rejecting changes to the project, and for recording and communicating such decisions.

Change Control System. A set of procedures that describes how modifications to the project deliverables and documentation are managed and controlled.

Change Control Tools. Manual or automated tools to assist with change, configuration management, or both. At a minimum, the tools should support the activities of the change control board (CCB).

Change Log. A comprehensive list of changes submitted during the project and their current status.

Change Management Plan. A component of the project management plan that establishes the change control board, documents the extent of its authority, and describes how the change control system will be implemented.

Change Request. A formal proposal to modify a document, deliverable, or baseline.

Charter. See **Project Charter**.

Checklist Analysis. A technique for systematically reviewing materials using a list for accuracy and completeness.

Check Sheet. A tally sheet that can be used as a checklist when gathering data.

Claim. A request, demand, or assertion of rights by a seller against a buyer, or vice versa, for consideration, compensation, or payment under the terms of a legally binding contract, such as for a disputed change.

Claims Administration. The process of processing, adjudicating, and communicating contract claims.

Close Project or Phase. The process of finalizing all activities for the project, phase, or contract.

Closing Process Group. The processes performed to formally complete or close a project, phase, or contract.

Code of Accounts. A numbering system used to uniquely identify each component of the work breakdown structure (WBS).

Collect Requirements. The process of determining, documenting, and managing stakeholder needs and requirements to meet project objectives.

Colocation. An organizational placement strategy where the project team members are physically located close to one another in order to improve communication, working relationships, and productivity.

Communication Method. A systematic procedure, technique, or process used to transfer information among project stakeholders.

Communication Model. A description, analogy, or schematic used to represent how the communication process will be performed for the project.

Communication Requirements Analysis. An analytical technique to determine the information needs of the project stakeholders through interviews, workshops, study of lessons learned from previous projects, etc.

Communications Management Plan. A component of the project, program, or portfolio management plan that describes how, when, and by whom information about the project will be administered and disseminated.

Communication Styles Assessment. A technique to identify the preferred communication method, format, and content for stakeholders for planned communication activities.

Communication Technology. Specific tools, systems, computer programs, etc., used to transfer information among project stakeholders.

Conduct Procurements. The process of obtaining seller responses, selecting a seller, and awarding a contract.

Configuration Management Plan. A component of the project management plan that describes how to identify and account for project artifacts under configuration control, and how to record and report changes to them.

Configuration Management System. A collection of procedures used to track project artifacts and monitor and control changes to these artifacts.

Conformance. Within the quality management system, conformance is a general concept of delivering results that fall within the limits that define acceptable variation for a quality requirement.

Constraint. A limiting factor that affects the execution of a project, program, portfolio, or process.

Context Diagram. A visual depiction of the product scope showing a business system (process, equipment, computer system, etc.) and how people and other systems (actors) interact with it.

Contingency. An event or occurrence that could affect the execution of the project that may be accounted for with a reserve.

Contingency Reserve. Time or money allocated in the schedule or cost baseline for known risks with active response strategies.

Contingent Response Strategies. Responses provided which may be used in the event that a specific trigger occurs.

Contract. A mutually binding agreement that obligates the seller to provide the specified product or service or result and obligates the buyer to pay for it.

Contract Change Control System. The system used to collect, track, adjudicate, and communicate changes to a contract.

Control. Comparing actual performance with planned performance, analyzing variances, assessing trends to effect process improvements, evaluating possible alternatives, and recommending appropriate corrective action as needed.

Control Account. A management control point where scope, budget, actual cost, and schedule are integrated and compared to earned value for performance measurement.

Control Chart. A graphic display of process data over time and against established control limits which has a centerline that assists in detecting a trend of plotted values toward either control limit.

Control Costs. The process of monitoring the status of the project to update the project costs and manage changes to the cost baseline.

Control Limits. The area composed of three standard deviations on either side of the centerline or mean of a normal distribution of data plotted on a control chart which reflects the expected variation in the data. See also **Specification Limits**.

Control Procurements. The process of managing procurement relationships, monitoring contract performance, making changes and corrections as appropriate, and closing out contracts.

Control Quality. The process of monitoring and recording results of executing the quality management activities to assess performance and ensure the project outputs are complete, correct, and meet customer expectations.

Control Resources. The process of ensuring that the physical resources assigned and allocated to the project are available as planned, as well as monitoring the planned versus actual utilization of resources and performing corrective action as necessary.

Control Schedule. The process of monitoring the status of the project to update the project schedule and manage changes to the schedule baseline.

Control Scope. The process of monitoring the status of the project and product scope and managing changes to the scope baseline.

Corrective Action. An intentional activity that realigns the performance of the project work with the project management plan.

Cost Aggregation. Summing the lower-level cost estimates associated with the various work packages for a given level within the project's WBS or for a given cost control account.

Cost Baseline. The approved version of the time-phased project budget, excluding any management reserves, which can be changed only through formal change control procedures and is used as a basis for comparison to actual results.

Cost-Benefit Analysis. A financial analysis tool used to determine the benefits provided by a project against its costs.

Cost Management Plan. A component of a project or program management plan that describes how costs will be planned, structured, and controlled.

Cost of Quality (CoQ). All costs incurred over the life of the product by investment in preventing nonconformance to requirements, appraisal of the product or service for conformance to requirements, and failure to meet requirements.

Cost Performance Index (CPI). A measure of the cost efficiency of budgeted resources expressed as the ratio of earned value to actual cost.

Cost Plus Award Fee Contract (CPAF). A category of contract that involves payments to the seller for all legitimate actual costs incurred for completed work, plus an award fee representing seller profit.

Cost Plus Fixed Fee Contract (CPFF). A type of cost-reimbursable contract where the buyer reimburses the seller for the seller's allowable costs (allowable costs are defined by the contract) plus a fixed amount of profit (fee).

Cost Plus Incentive Fee Contract (CPIF). A type of cost-reimbursable contract where the buyer reimburses the seller for the seller's allowable costs (allowable costs are defined by the contract), and the seller earns profit if the seller meets defined performance criteria.

Cost-Reimbursable Contract. A type of contract involving payment to the seller for the seller's actual costs, plus a fee typically representing the seller's profit.

Cost Variance (CV). The amount of budget deficit or surplus at a given point in time, expressed as the difference between the earned value and the actual cost.

Crashing. A technique used to shorten the schedule duration for the least incremental cost by adding resources.

Create WBS. The process of subdividing project deliverables and project work into smaller, more manageable components.

Criteria. Standards, rules, or tests on which a judgement or decision can be based or by which a product, service, result, or process can be evaluated.

Critical Path. The sequence of activities that represents the longest path through a project, which determines the shortest possible duration.

Critical Path Activity. Any activity on the critical path in a project schedule.

Critical Path Method (CPM). A method used to estimate the minimum project duration and determine the amount of scheduling flexibility on the logical network paths within the schedule model.

Data. Discrete, unorganized, unprocessed measurements or raw observations.

Data Analysis Techniques. Techniques used to organize, assess, and evaluate data and information.

Data Date. A point in time when the status of the project is recorded.

Data Gathering Techniques. Techniques used to collect data and information from a variety of sources.

Data Representation Techniques. Graphic representations or other methods used to convey data and information.

Decision-Making Techniques. Techniques used to select a course of action from different alternatives.

Decision Tree Analysis. A diagramming and calculation technique for evaluating the implications of a chain of multiple options in the presence of uncertainty.

Decomposition. A technique used for dividing and subdividing the project scope and project deliverables into smaller, more manageable parts.

Defect. An imperfection or deficiency in a project component where that component does not meet its requirements or specifications and needs to be either repaired or replaced.

Defect Repair. An intentional activity to modify a nonconforming product or product component.

Define Activities. The process of identifying and documenting the specific actions to be performed to produce the project deliverables.

Define Scope. The process of developing a detailed description of the project and product.

Deliverable. Any unique and verifiable product, result, or capability to perform a service that is required to be produced to complete a process, phase, or project.

Dependency. See **Logical Relationship**.

Determine Budget. The process of aggregating the estimated costs of individual activities or work packages to establish an authorized cost baseline.

Development Approach. The method used to create and develop the product, service, or result during the project life cycle, such as predictive, iterative, incremental, agile, or a hybrid method

Develop Project Charter. The process of developing a document that formally authorizes the existence of a project and provides the project manager with the authority to apply organizational resources to project activities.

Develop Project Management Plan. The process of defining, preparing, and coordinating all plan components and consolidating them into an integrated project management plan.

Develop Schedule. The process of analyzing activity sequences, durations, resource requirements, and schedule constraints to create the project schedule model for project execution and monitoring and controlling.

Develop Team. The process of improving competences, team member interaction, and overall team environment to enhance project performance.

Diagramming Techniques. Approaches to presenting information with logical linkages that aid in understanding.

Direct and Manage Project Work. The process of leading and performing the work defined in the project management plan and implementing approved changes to achieve the project's objectives.

Discrete Effort. An activity that can be planned and measured and that yields a specific output. Discrete effort is one of three earned value management (EVM) types of activities used to measure work performance.

Discretionary Dependency. A relationship that is established based on knowledge of best practices within a particular application area or an aspect of the project where a specific sequence is desired.

Documentation Reviews. The process of gathering a corpus of information and reviewing it to determine accuracy and completeness.

Duration. The total number of work periods required to complete an activity or work breakdown structure component, expressed in hours, days, or weeks. Contrast with **Effort**.

Early Finish Date (EF). In the critical path method, the earliest possible point in time when the uncompleted portions of a schedule activity can finish based on the schedule network logic, the data date, and any schedule constraints.

Early Start Date (ES). In the critical path method, the earliest possible point in time when the uncompleted portions of a schedule activity can start based on the schedule network logic, the data date, and any schedule constraints.

Earned Value (EV). The measure of work performed expressed in terms of the budget authorized for that work.

Earned Value Management. A methodology that combines scope, schedule, and resource measurements to assess project performance and progress.

Effort. The number of labor units required to complete a schedule activity or work breakdown structure component, often expressed in hours, days, or weeks. Contrast with **Duration**.

Emotional Intelligence. The ability to identify, assess, and manage the personal emotions of oneself and other people, as well as the collective emotions of groups of people.

Enterprise Environmental Factors. Conditions not under the immediate control of the team that influence, constrain, or direct the project, program, or portfolio.

Estimate. A quantitative assessment of the likely amount or outcome of a variable, such as project costs, resources, effort, or durations.

Estimate Activity Durations. The process of estimating the number of work periods needed to complete individual activities with the estimated resources.

Estimate Activity Resources. The process of estimating team resources and the type and quantities of material, equipment, and supplies necessary to perform project work.

Estimate at Completion (EAC). The expected total cost of completing all work expressed as the sum of the actual cost to date and the estimate to complete.

Estimate Costs. The process of developing an approximation of the monetary resources needed to complete project work.

Estimate to Complete (ETC). The expected cost to finish all the remaining project work.

Execute. Directing, managing, performing, and accomplishing the project work; providing the deliverables; and providing work performance information.

Executing Process Group. Those processes performed to complete the work defined in the project management plan to satisfy the project requirements.

Expert Judgement. Judgement provided based upon expertise in an application area, knowledge area, discipline, industry, etc. as appropriate for the activity being performed. Such expertise may be provided by any group or person with specialized education, knowledge, skill, experience, or training.

Explicit Knowledge. Knowledge that can be codified using symbols such as words, numbers, and pictures.

External Dependency. A relationship between project activities and non-project activities.

Fallback Plan. An alternative set of actions and tasks available in the event that the primary plan needs to be abandoned because of issues, risks, or other causes.

Fast Tracking. A schedule compression technique in which activities or phases normally done in sequence are performed in parallel for at least a portion of their duration.

Fee. Represents profit as a component of compensation to a seller.

Finish Date. A point in time associated with a schedule activity's completion. Usually qualified by one of the following: actual, planned, estimated, scheduled, early, late, baseline, target, or current.

Finish-to-Finish (FF). A logical relationship in which a successor activity cannot finish until a predecessor activity has finished.

Finish-to-Start (FS). A logical relationship in which a successor activity cannot start until a predecessor activity has finished.

Firm Fixed Price Contract (FFP). A type of fixed price contract where the buyer pays the seller a set amount (as defined by the contract) regardless of the seller's costs.

Fishbone Diagram. See **Cause and Effect Diagram**.

Fixed Price Contract. An agreement that sets the fee that will be paid for a defined scope of work regardless of the cost or effort to deliver it.

Fixed Price Incentive Fee Contract (FPIF). A type of contract where the buyer pays the seller a set amount (as defined by the contract), and the seller can earn an additional amount if the seller meets defined performance criteria.

Fixed Price with Economic Price Adjustment Contract (FPEPA). A fixed-price contract, but with a special provision allowing for predefined final adjustments to the contract price due to changed conditions, such as inflation changes or cost increases (or decreases) for specific commodities.

Float. Also called slack. See **Total Float** and **Free Float**.

Flow Chart. The depiction in a diagram format of the inputs, process actions, and outputs of one or more processes within a system.

Focus Group. An elicitation technique that brings together prequalified stakeholders and subject matter experts to learn about their expectations and attitudes about a proposed product, service, or result.

Forecast. An estimate or prediction of conditions and events in the project's future based on information and knowledge available at the time of the forecast.

Forward Pass. A critical path method technique for calculating the early start and early finish dates by working forward through the schedule model from the project start date or a given point in time.

Free Float. The amount of time that a schedule activity can be delayed without delaying the early start date of any successor or violating a schedule constraint.

Functional Organization. An organizational structure in which staff is grouped by areas of specialization and the project manager has limited authority to assign work and apply resources.

Funding Limit Reconciliation. The process of comparing the planned expenditure of project funds against any limits on the commitment of funds for the project to identify any variances between the funding limits and the planned expenditures.

Gantt Chart. A bar chart of schedule information where activities are listed on the vertical axis, dates are shown on the horizontal axis, and activity durations are shown as horizontal bars placed according to start and finish dates.

Grade. A category or rank used to distinguish items that have the same functional use but do not share the same requirements for quality.

Ground Rules. Expectations regarding acceptable behavior by project team members.

Histogram. A bar chart that shows the graphical representation of numerical data.

Historical Information. Documents and data on prior projects including project files, records, correspondence, closed contracts, and closed projects.

Identify Risks. The process of identifying individual risks as well as sources of overall risk and documenting their characteristics.

Identify Stakeholders. The process of identifying project stakeholders regularly and analyzing and documenting relevant information regarding their interests, involvement, interdependencies, influence, and potential impact on project success.

Implement Risk Responses. The process of implementing agreed-upon risk response plans.

Imposed Date. A fixed date imposed on a schedule activity or schedule milestone, usually in the form of a "start no earlier than" and "finish no later than" date.

Incentive Fee. A set of financial incentives related to cost, schedule, or technical performance of the seller.

Incremental Life Cycle. An adaptive project life cycle in which the deliverable is produced through a series of iterations that successively add functionality within a predetermined time frame. The deliverable contains the necessary and sufficient capability to be considered complete only after the final iteration.

Independent Estimates. A process of using a third party to obtain and analyze information to support prediction of cost, schedule, or other items.

Influence Diagram. A graphical representation of situations showing causal influences, time ordering of events, and other relationships among variables and outcomes.

Information. Organized or structured data, processed for a specific purpose to make it meaningful, valuable, and useful in specific contexts.

Information Management Systems. Facilities, processes, and procedures used to collect, store, and distribute information between producers and consumers of information in physical or electronic format.

Initiating Process Group. Those processes performed to define a new project or a new phase of an existing project by obtaining authorization to start the project or phase.

Input. Any item, whether internal or external to the project, which is required by a process before that process proceeds. May be an output from a predecessor process.

Inspection. Examination of a work product to determine whether it conforms to documented standards.

Interpersonal and Team Skills. Skills used to effectively lead and interact with team members and other stakeholders.

Interpersonal Skills. Skills used to establish and maintain relationships with other people.

Interviews. A formal or informal approach to elicit information from stakeholders by talking to them directly.

Invitation for Bid (IFB). Generally, this term is equivalent to request for proposal. However, in some application areas, it may have a narrower or more specific meaning.

Issue. A current condition or situation that may have an impact on the project objectives.

Issue Log. A project document where information about issues is recorded and monitored.

Iterative Life Cycle. A project life cycle where the project scope is generally determined early in the project life cycle, but time and cost estimates are routinely modified as the project team's understanding of the product increases. Iterations develop the product through a series of repeated cycles, while increments successively add to the functionality of the product.

Knowledge. A mixture of experience, values and beliefs, contextual information, intuition, and insight that people use to make sense of new experiences and information.

Lag. The amount of time whereby a successor activity will be delayed with respect to a predecessor activity.

Late Finish Date (LF). In the critical path method, the latest possible point in time when the uncompleted portions of a schedule activity can finish based on the schedule network logic, the project completion date, and any schedule constraints.

Late Start Date (LS). In the critical path method, the latest possible point in time when the uncompleted portions of a schedule activity can start based on the schedule network logic, the project completion date, and any schedule constraints.

Lead. The amount of time whereby a successor activity can be advanced with respect to a predecessor activity.

Lessons Learned. The knowledge gained during a project which shows how project events were addressed or should be addressed in the future for the purpose of improving future performance.

Lessons Learned Register. A project document used to record knowledge gained during a project so that it can be used in the current project and entered into the lessons learned repository.

Lessons Learned Repository. A store of historical information about lessons learned in projects.

Level of Effort (LOE). An activity that does not produce definitive end products and is measured by the passage of time.

Life Cycle. See **Project Life Cycle**.

Log. A document used to record and describe or denote selected items identified during execution of a process or activity. Usually used with a modifier, such as issue, change, or assumption.

Logical Relationship. A dependency between two activities, or between an activity and a milestone.

Make-or-Buy Analysis. The process of gathering and organizing data about product requirements and analyzing them against available alternatives including the purchase or internal manufacture of the product.

Make-or-Buy Decisions. Decisions made regarding the external purchase or internal manufacture of a product.

Manage Communications. The process of ensuring timely and appropriate collection, creation, distribution, storage, retrieval, management, monitoring, and the ultimate disposition of project information.

Management Reserve. An amount of the project budget or project schedule held outside of the performance measurement baseline (PMB) for management control purposes which is reserved for unforeseen work that is within scope of the project.

Management Skills. The ability to plan, organize, direct, and control individuals or groups of people to achieve specific goals.

Manage Project Knowledge. The process of using existing knowledge and creating new knowledge to achieve the project's objectives and contribute to organizational learning.

Manage Quality. The process of translating the quality management plan into executable quality activities that incorporate the organization's quality policies into the project.

Manage Stakeholder Engagement. The process of communicating and working with stakeholders to meet their needs and expectations, address issues, and foster appropriate stakeholder involvement.

Manage Team. The process of tracking team member performance, providing feedback, resolving issues, and managing team changes to optimize project performance.

Mandatory Dependency. A relationship that is contractually required or inherent in the nature of the work.

Master Schedule. A summary-level project schedule that identifies the major deliverables and work breakdown structure components and key schedule milestones. See also **Milestone Schedule**.

Matrix Diagram. A quality management and control tool used to perform data analysis within the organizational structure created in the matrix. The matrix diagram seeks to show the strength of relationships between factors, causes, and objectives that exist between the rows and columns that form the matrix.

Matrix Organization. Any organizational structure in which the project manager shares responsibility with the functional managers for assigning priorities and for directing the work of persons assigned to the project.

Methodology. A system of practices, techniques, procedures, and rules used by those who work in a discipline.

Milestone. A significant point or event in a project, program, or portfolio.

Milestone Schedule. A type of schedule that presents milestones with planned dates. See also **Master Schedule**.

Mind Mapping. A technique used to consolidate ideas created through individual brainstorming sessions into a single map to reflect commonality and differences in understanding and to generate new ideas.

Monitor. Collect project performance data, produce performance measures, and report and disseminate performance information.

Monitor and Control Project Work. The process of tracking, reviewing, and reporting overall progress to meet the performance objectives defined in the project management plan.

Monitor Communications. The process of ensuring that the information needs of the project and its stakeholders are met.

Monitoring and Controlling Process Group. Those processes required to track, review, and regulate the progress and performance of the project; identify any areas in which changes to the plan are required; and initiate the corresponding changes.

Monitor Risks. The process of monitoring the implementation of agreed-upon risk response plans, tracking identified risks, identifying and analyzing new risks, and evaluating risk process effectiveness throughout the project.

Monitor Stakeholder Engagement. The process of monitoring project stakeholder relationships, and tailoring strategies for engaging stakeholders through the modification of engagement strategies and plans.

Monte Carlo Simulation. An analysis technique where a computer model is iterated many times, with the input values chosen at random for each iteration driven by the input data, including probability distributions and probabilistic branches. Outputs are generated to represent the range of possible outcomes for the project.

Multicriteria Decision Analysis. A technique that utilizes a decision matrix to provide a systematic analytical approach for establishing criteria, such as risk levels, uncertainty, and valuation, to evaluate and rank many ideas.

Network. See **Project Schedule Network Diagram**.

Network Logic. All activity dependencies in a project schedule network diagram.

Network Path. A sequence of activities connected by logical relationships in a project schedule network diagram.

Networking. Establishing connections and relationships with other people from the same or other organizations.

Node. A point at which dependency lines connect on a schedule network diagram.

Nominal Group Technique. A technique that enhances brainstorming with a voting process used to rank the most useful ideas for further brainstorming or for prioritization.

Objective. Something toward which work is to be directed, a strategic position to be attained, a purpose to be achieved, a result to be obtained, a product to be produced, or a service to be performed.

Opportunity. A risk that would have a positive effect on one or more project objectives.

Organizational Breakdown Structure (OBS). A hierarchical representation of the project organization which illustrates the relationship between project activities and the organizational units that will perform those activities.

Organizational Learning. A discipline concerned with the way individuals, groups, and organizations develop knowledge.

Organizational Process Assets. Plans, processes, policies, procedures, and knowledge bases that are specific to and used by the performing organization.

Output. A product, result, or service generated by a process. May be an input to a successor process.

Overall Project Risk. The effect of uncertainty on the project as a whole, arising from all sources of uncertainty including individual risks, representing the exposure of stakeholders to the implications of variations in project outcome, both positive and negative.

Parametric Estimating. An estimating technique in which an algorithm is used to calculate cost or duration based on historical data and project parameters.

Path Convergence. A relationship in which a schedule activity has more than one predecessor.

Path Divergence. A relationship in which a schedule activity has more than one successor.

Percent Complete. An estimate expressed as a percent of the amount of work that has been completed on an activity or a work breakdown structure component.

Performance Measurement Baseline (PMB). Integrated scope, schedule, and cost baselines used for comparison to manage, measure, and control project execution.

Performance Reviews. A technique that is used to measure, compare, and analyze actual performance of work in progress on the project against the baseline.

Perform Integrated Change Control. The process of reviewing all change requests; approving changes and managing changes to deliverables, organizational process assets, project documents, and the project management plan; and communicating the decisions.

Perform Qualitative Risk Analysis. The process of prioritizing individual project risks for further analysis or action by assessing their probability of occurrence and impact as well as other characteristics.

Perform Quantitative Risk Analysis. The process of numerically analyzing the combined effect of identified individual project risks and other sources of uncertainty on overall project objectives.

Phase. See **Project Phase**.

Phase Gate. A review at the end of a phase in which a decision is made to continue to the next phase, to continue with modification, or to end a project or program.

Plan Communications Management. The process of developing an appropriate approach and plan for project communication activities based on the information needs of each stakeholder or group, available organizational assets, and the needs of the project.

Plan Cost Management. The process of defining how the project costs will be estimated, budgeted, managed, monitored, and controlled.

Planned Value (PV). The authorized budget assigned to scheduled work.

Planning Package. A work breakdown structure component below the control account with known work content but without detailed schedule activities. See also **Control Account**.

Planning Process Group. Those processes required to establish the scope of the project, refine the objectives, and define the course of action required to attain the objectives that the project was undertaken to achieve.

Plan Procurement Management. The process of documenting project procurement decisions, specifying the approach, and identifying potential sellers.

Plan Quality Management. The process of identifying quality requirements or standards for the project and its deliverables, and documenting how the project will demonstrate compliance with quality requirements or standards.

Plan Resource Management. The process of defining how to estimate, acquire, manage, and utilize physical and team resources.

Plan Risk Management. The process of defining how to conduct risk management activities for a project.

Plan Risk Responses. The process of developing options, selecting strategies, and agreeing on actions to address overall project risk exposure, as well as to treat individual project risks.

Plan Schedule Management. The process of establishing the policies, procedures, and documentation for planning, developing, managing, executing, and controlling the project schedule.

Plan Scope Management. The process of creating a scope management plan that documents how the project and product scope will be defined, validated, and controlled.

Plan Stakeholder Engagement. The process of developing approaches to involve project stakeholders, based on their needs, expectations, interests, and potential impact on the project.

Plurality. Decisions made by the largest voting bloc in a group, even if a majority is not achieved.

Policy. A structured pattern of actions adopted by an organization such that the organization's policy can be explained as a set of basic principles that govern the organization's conduct.

Portfolio. Projects, programs, subsidiary portfolios, and operations managed as a group to achieve strategic objectives.

Portfolio Management. The centralized management of one or more portfolios to achieve strategic objectives.

Practice. A specific type of professional or management activity that contributes to the execution of a process and that may employ one or more techniques and tools.

Precedence Diagramming Method (PDM). A technique used for constructing a schedule model in which activities are represented by nodes and are graphically linked by one or more logical relationships to show the sequence in which the activities are to be performed.

Precedence Relationship. A logical dependency used in the precedence diagramming method.

Predecessor Activity. An activity that logically comes before a dependent activity in a schedule.

Predictive Life Cycle. A form of project life cycle in which the project scope, time, and cost are determined in the early phases of the life cycle.

Preventive Action. An intentional activity that ensures the future performance of the project work is aligned with the project management plan.

Probability and Impact Matrix. A grid for mapping the probability of occurrence of each risk and its impact on project objectives if that risk occurs.

Procedure. An established method of accomplishing a consistent performance or result. A procedure typically can be described as the sequence of steps that will be used to execute a process.

Process. A systematic series of activities directed towards causing an end result such that one or more inputs will be acted upon to create one or more outputs.

Procurement Audits. The review of contracts and contracting processes for completeness, accuracy, and effectiveness.

Procurement Documents. The documents used in bid and proposal activities that include the buyer's invitation for bid, invitation for negotiations, request for information, request for quotation, request for proposal, and seller's responses.

Procurement Documentation. All documents used in signing, executing, and closing an agreement. Procurement documentation may include documents predating the project.

Procurement Management Plan. A component of the project or program management plan that describes how a project team will acquire goods and services from outside of the performing organization.

Procurement Statement of Work. Describes the procurement item in sufficient detail to allow prospective sellers to determine if they are capable of providing the products, services, or results.

Procurement Strategy. The approach by the buyer to determine the project delivery method and the type of legally binding agreement(s) that should be used to deliver the desired results.

Product. An artifact that is produced, is quantifiable, and can be either an end item in itself or a component item. Additional words for products are material and goods. See also **Deliverable**.

Product Analysis. For projects that have a product as a deliverable, product analysis is a tool to define scope that generally means asking questions about a product and forming answers to describe the use, characteristics, and other relevant aspects of what is going to be manufactured.

Product Life Cycle. The series of phases that represent the evolution of a product, from concept through delivery, growth, maturity, and to retirement.

Product Scope. The features and functions that characterize a product, service, or result.

Product Scope Description. The documented narrative description of the product scope.

Program. Related projects, subsidiary programs, and program activities that are managed in a coordinated manner to obtain benefits not available from managing them individually.

Program Management. The application of knowledge, skills, and principles to a program to achieve the program objectives and obtain benefits and control not available by managing program components individually.

Progressive Elaboration. The iterative process of increasing the level of detail in a project management plan while greater amounts of information and more accurate estimates become available.

Project. A temporary endeavor undertaken to create a unique product, service, or result.

Project Calendar. A calendar that identifies working days and shifts that are available for scheduled activities.

Project Charter. A document issued by the project initiator or sponsor that formally authorizes the existence of a project and provides the project manager with the authority to apply organizational resources to project activities.

Project Communications Management. Includes the processes required to ensure timely and appropriate planning, collection, creation, distribution, storage, retrieval, management, control, monitoring, and ultimate disposition of project information.

Project Cost Management. Includes the processes involved in planning, estimating, budgeting, financing, funding, managing, and controlling costs so the project can be completed within the approved budget.

Project Funding Requirements. Forecast project costs to be paid that are derived from the cost baseline for total or periodic requirements, including projected expenditures plus anticipated liabilities.

Project Governance. The framework, functions, and processes that guide project management activities to create a unique product, service, or result to meet organizational, strategic, or operational goals.

Project Initiation. Launching a process that can result in the authorization of a new project.

Project Integration Management. Includes the processes and activities to identify, define, combine, unify, and coordinate the various processes and project management activities within the project management process groups.

Project Life Cycle. The series of phases that a project passes through from its start to its completion.

Project Management. The application of knowledge, skills, tools, and techniques to project activities to meet the project requirements.

Project Management Body of Knowledge. A term that describes the knowledge within the profession of project management. The project management body of knowledge includes proven traditional practices that are widely applied as well as innovative practices that are emerging in the profession.

Project Management Information System. An information system consisting of the tools and techniques used to gather, integrate, and disseminate the outputs of project management processes.

Project Management Knowledge Area. An identified area of project management defined by its knowledge requirements and described in terms of its component processes, practices, inputs, outputs, tools, and techniques.

Project Management Office (PMO). A management structure that standardizes the project-related governance processes and facilitates the sharing of resources, methodologies, tools, and techniques.

Project Management Plan. The document that describes how the project will be executed, monitored and controlled, and closed.

Project Management Process Group. A logical grouping of project management inputs, tools and techniques, and outputs. The project management process groups include initiating processes, planning processes, executing processes, monitoring and controlling processes, and closing processes. Project management process groups are not project phases.

Project Management System. The aggregation of the processes, tools, techniques, methodologies, resources, and procedures to manage a project.

Project Management Team. The members of the project team who are directly involved in project management activities. See also **Project Team**.

Project Manager (PM). The person assigned by the performing organization to lead the team that is responsible for achieving the project objectives.

Project Organization Chart. A document that graphically depicts the project team members and their interrelationships for a specific project.

Project Phase. A collection of logically related project activities that culminates in the completion of one or more deliverables.

Project Procurement Management. Includes the processes necessary to purchase or acquire products, services, or results needed from outside the project team.

Project Quality Management. Includes the processes for incorporating the organization's quality policy regarding planning, managing, and controlling project and product quality requirements, in order to meet stakeholders' expectations.

Project Resource Management. Includes the processes to identify, acquire, and manage the resources needed for the successful completion of the project.

Project Risk Management. Includes the processes of conducting risk management planning, identification, analysis, response planning, response implementation, and monitoring risk on a project.

Project Schedule. An output of a schedule model that presents linked activities with planned dates, durations, milestones, and resources.

Project Schedule Management. Includes the processes required to manage the timely completion of the project.

Project Schedule Network Diagram. A graphical representation of the logical relationships among the project schedule activities.

Project Scope. The work performed to deliver a product, service, or result with the specified features and functions.

Project Scope Management. Comprises the processes required to ensure that the project includes all the work required, and only the work required, to complete the project successfully.

Project Scope Statement. The description of the project scope, major deliverables, assumptions, and constraints.

Project Stakeholder Management. Includes the processes required to identify the people, groups, or organizations that could impact or be impacted by the project, to analyze stakeholder expectations and their impact on the project, and to develop appropriate management strategies for effectively engaging stakeholders in project decisions and execution.

Project Team. A set of individuals who support the project manager in performing the work of the project to achieve its objectives. See also **Project Management Team**.

Project Team Directory. A documented list of project team members, their project roles, and communication information.

Proposal Evaluation Techniques. The process of reviewing proposals provided by suppliers to support contract award decisions.

Prototype. A method of obtaining early feedback on requirements by providing a working model of the expected product before building it.

Quality. The degree to which a set of inherent characteristics fulfills requirements.

Quality Audit. A structured, independent process to determine if project activities comply with organizational and project policies, processes, and procedures.

Quality Checklist. A structured tool used to verify that a set of required steps has been performed.

Quality Control Measurements. The documented results of control quality activities.

Quality Management Plan. A component of the project or program management plan that describes how applicable policies, procedures, and guidelines will be implemented to achieve the quality objectives.

Quality Management System. The organizational framework whose structure provides the policies, processes, procedures, and resources required to implement the quality management plan. The typical project quality management plan should be compatible to the organization's quality management system.

Quality Metrics. A description of a project or product attribute and how to measure it.

Quality Policy. A policy specific to the Project Quality Management knowledge area that establishes the basic principles that should govern the organization's actions as it implements its system for quality management.

Quality Report. A project document that includes quality management issues, recommendations for corrective actions, and a summary of findings from quality control activities and may include recommendations for process, project, and product improvements.

Quality Requirement. A condition or capability that will be used to assess conformance by validating the acceptability of an attribute for the quality of a result.

Questionnaire. Written set of questions designed to quickly accumulate information from many respondents.

RACI Chart. A common type of responsibility assignment matrix that uses responsible, accountable, consult, and inform statuses to define the involvement of stakeholders in project activities.

Regression Analysis. An analytical technique where a series of input variables are examined in relation to their corresponding output results to develop a mathematical or statistical relationship.

Regulations. Requirements imposed by a governmental body. These requirements can establish product, process, or service characteristics, including applicable administrative provisions that have government-mandated compliance.

Request for Information (RFI). A type of procurement document whereby the buyer requests a potential seller to provide various pieces of information related to a product or service or seller capability.

Request for Proposal (RFP). A type of procurement document used to request proposals from prospective sellers of products or services. In some application areas, it may have a narrower or more specific meaning.

Request for Quotation (RFQ). A type of procurement document used to request price quotations from prospective sellers of common or standard products or services. Sometimes used in place of request for proposal and, in some application areas, it may have a narrower or more specific meaning.

Requirement. A condition or capability that is necessary to be present in a product, service, or result to satisfy a business need.

Requirements Documentation. A description of how individual requirements meet the business need for the project.

Requirements Management Plan. A component of the project or program management plan that describes how requirements will be analyzed, documented, and managed.

Requirements Traceability Matrix. A grid that links product requirements from their origin to the deliverables that satisfy them.

Reserve. A provision in the project management plan to mitigate cost and/or schedule risk. Often used with a modifier (e.g., management reserve, contingency reserve) to provide further detail on what types of risk are meant to be mitigated.

Reserve Analysis. An analytical technique to determine the essential features and relationships of components in the project management plan to establish a reserve for the schedule duration, budget, estimated cost, or funds for a project.

Residual Risk. The risk that remains after risk responses have been implemented.

Resource. A team member or any physical item needed to complete the project.

Resource Breakdown Structure. A hierarchical representation of resources by category and type.

Resource Calendar. A calendar that identifies the working days and shifts when each specific resource is available.

Resource Histogram. A bar chart showing the amount of time that a resource is scheduled to work over a series of time periods.

Resource Leveling. A resource optimization technique in which adjustments are made to the project schedule to optimize the allocation of resources and which may affect critical path. See also **Resource Optimization Technique** and **Resource Smoothing**.

Resource Management Plan. A component of the project management plan that describes how project resources are acquired, allocated, monitored, and controlled.

Resource Manager. An individual with management authority over one or more resources.

Resource Optimization Technique. A technique in which activity start and finish dates are adjusted to balance demand for resources with the available supply. See also **Resource Leveling** and **Resource Smoothing**.

Resource Requirements. The types and quantities of resources required for each activity in a work package.

Resource Smoothing. A resource optimization technique in which free and total float are used without affecting the critical path. See also **Resource Leveling** and **Resource Optimization Technique**.

Responsibility. An assignment that can be delegated within a project management plan such that the assigned resource incurs a duty to perform the requirements of the assignment.

Responsibility Assignment Matrix (RAM). A grid that shows the project resources assigned to each work package.

Result. An output from performing project management processes and activities. Results include outcomes (e.g., integrated systems, revised process, restructured organization, tests, trained personnel, etc.) and documents (e.g., policies, plans, studies, procedures, specifications, reports, etc.). See also **Deliverable**.

Rework. Action taken to bring a defective or nonconforming component into compliance with requirements or specifications.

Risk. An uncertain event or condition that, if it occurs, has a positive or negative effect on one or more project objectives.

Risk Acceptance. A risk response strategy whereby the project team decides to acknowledge the risk and not take any action unless the risk occurs.

Risk Appetite. The degree of uncertainty an organization or individual is willing to accept in anticipation of a reward.

Risk Audit. A type of audit used to consider the effectiveness of the risk management process.

Risk Avoidance. A risk response strategy whereby the project team acts to eliminate the threat or protect the project from its impact.

Risk Breakdown Structure (RBS). A hierarchical representation of potential sources of risks.

Risk Categorization. Organization by sources of risk (e.g., using the RBS), the area of the project affected (e.g., using the WBS), or other useful category (e.g., project phase) to determine the areas of the project most exposed to the effects of uncertainty.

Risk Category. A group of potential causes of risk.

Risk Data Quality Assessment. Technique to evaluate the degree to which the data about risks is useful for risk management.

Risk Enhancement. A risk response strategy whereby the project team acts to increase the probability of occurrence or impact of an opportunity.

Risk Escalation. A risk response strategy whereby the team acknowledges that a risk is outside of its sphere of influence and shifts the ownership of the risk to a higher level of the organization where it is more effectively managed.

Risk Exploiting. A risk response strategy whereby the project team acts to ensure that an opportunity occurs.

Risk Exposure. An aggregate measure of the potential impact of all risks at any given point in time in a project, program, or portfolio.

Risk Management Plan. A component of the project, program, or portfolio management plan that describes how risk management activities will be structured and performed.

Risk Mitigation. A risk response strategy whereby the project team acts to decrease the probability of occurrence or impact of a threat.

Risk Owner. The person responsible for monitoring the risks and for selecting and implementing an appropriate risk response strategy.

Risk Register. A repository in which outputs of risk management processes are recorded.

Risk Report. A project document developed progressively throughout the Project Risk Management processes that summarizes information on individual project risks and the level of overall project risk.

Risk Review. A meeting to examine and document the effectiveness of risk responses in dealing with overall project risk and with identified individual project risks.

Risk Sharing. A risk response strategy whereby the project team allocates ownership of an opportunity to a third party who is best able to capture the benefit of that opportunity.

Risk Threshold. The level of risk exposure above which risks are addressed and below which risks may be accepted.

Risk Transference. A risk response strategy whereby the project team shifts the impact of a threat to a third party, together with ownership of the response.

Role. A defined function to be performed by a project team member, such as testing, filing, inspecting, or coding.

Rolling Wave Planning. An iterative planning technique in which the work to be accomplished in the near term is planned in detail, while the work in the future is planned at a higher level.

Root Cause Analysis. An analytical technique used to determine the basic underlying reason that causes a variance or a defect or a risk. A root cause may underlie more than one variance or defect or risk.

Schedule. See **Project Schedule** and **Schedule Model**.

Schedule Baseline. The approved version of a schedule model that can be changed using formal change control procedures and is used as the basis for comparison to actual results.

Schedule Compression. A technique used to shorten the schedule duration without reducing the project scope.

Schedule Data. The collection of information for describing and controlling the schedule.

Schedule Forecasts. Estimates or predictions of conditions and events in the project's future based on information and knowledge available at the time the schedule is calculated.

Schedule Management Plan. A component of the project or program management plan that establishes the criteria and the activities for developing, monitoring, and controlling the schedule.

Schedule Model. A representation of the plan for executing the project's activities including durations, dependencies, and other planning information used to produce a project schedule along with other scheduling artifacts.

Schedule Network Analysis. A technique to identify early and late start dates, as well as early and late finish dates, for the uncompleted portions of project activities.

Schedule Performance Index (SPI). A measure of schedule efficiency expressed as the ratio of earned value to planned value.

Schedule Variance (SV). A measure of schedule performance expressed as the difference between earned value and planned value.

Scheduling Tool. A tool that provides schedule component names, definitions, structural relationships, and formats that support the application of a scheduling method.

Scope. The sum of the products, services, and results to be provided as a project. See also **Project Scope** and **Product Scope**.

Scope Baseline. The approved version of a scope statement, work breakdown structure (WBS), and its associated WBS dictionary, that can be changed using formal change control procedures and is used as a basis for comparison to actual results.

Scope Creep. The uncontrolled expansion to product or project scope without adjustments to time, cost, and resources.

Scope Management Plan. A component of the project or program management plan that describes how the scope will be defined, developed, monitored, controlled, and validated.

Secondary Risk. A risk that arises as a direct result of implementing a risk response.

Self-Organizing Team. A team formation where the team functions in the absence of centralized control.

Seller. A provider or supplier of products, services, or results to an organization.

Seller Proposals. Formal responses from sellers to a request for proposal or other procurement document specifying the price, commercial terms of sale, and technical specifications or capabilities the seller will do for the requesting organization that, if accepted, would bind the seller to perform the resulting agreement.

Sensitivity Analysis. An analysis technique to determine which individual project risks or other sources of uncertainty have the most potential impact on project outcomes, by correlating variations in project outcomes with variations in elements of a quantitative risk analysis model.

Sequence Activities. The process of identifying and documenting relationships among the project activities.

Service Level Agreement (SLA). A contract between a service provider (either internal or external) and the end user that defines the level of service expected from the service provider.

Simulation. An analytical technique that models the combined effect of uncertainties to evaluate their potential impact on objectives.

Source Selection Criteria. A set of attributes desired by the buyer which a seller is required to meet or exceed to be selected for a contract.

Specification. A precise statement of the needs to be satisfied and the essential characteristics that are required.

Specification Limits. The area on either side of the centerline, or mean, of data plotted on a control chart that meets the customer's requirements for a product or service. This area may be greater than or less than the area defined by the control limits. See also **Control Limits**.

Sponsor. A person or group who provides resources and support for the project, program, or portfolio and is accountable for enabling success.

Sponsoring Organization. The entity responsible for providing the project's sponsor and a conduit for project funding or other project resources.

Stakeholder. An individual, group, or organization that may affect, be affected by, or perceive itself to be affected by a decision, activity, or outcome of a project, program, or portfolio.

Stakeholder Analysis. A technique of systematically gathering and analyzing quantitative and qualitative information to determine whose interests should be taken into account throughout the project.

Stakeholder Engagement Assessment Matrix. A matrix that compares current and desired stakeholder engagement levels.

Stakeholder Engagement Plan. A component of the project management plan that identifies the strategies and actions required to promote productive involvement of stakeholders in project or program decision making and execution.

Stakeholder Register. A project document including the identification, assessment, and classification of project stakeholders.

Standard. A document established by an authority, custom, or general consent as a model or example.

Start Date. A point in time associated with a schedule activity's start, usually qualified by one of the following: actual, planned, estimated, scheduled, early, late, target, baseline, or current.

Start-to-Finish (SF). A logical relationship in which a successor activity cannot finish until a predecessor activity has started.

Start-to-Start (SS). A logical relationship in which a successor activity cannot start until a predecessor activity has started.

Statement of Work (SOW). A narrative description of products, services, or results to be delivered by the project.

Statistical Sampling. Choosing part of a population of interest for inspection.

Successor Activity. A dependent activity that logically comes after another activity in a schedule.

Summary Activity. A group of related schedule activities aggregated and displayed as a single activity.

SWOT Analysis. Analysis of strengths, weaknesses, opportunities, and threats of an organization, project, or option.

Tacit Knowledge. Personal knowledge that can be difficult to articulate and share, such as beliefs, experience, and insights.

Tailoring. Determining the appropriate combination of processes, inputs, tools, techniques, outputs, and life cycle phases to manage a project.

Team Charter. A document that records the team values, agreements, and operating guidelines, as well as establishing clear expectations regarding acceptable behavior by project team members.

Team Management Plan. A component of the resource management plan that describes when and how team members will be acquired and how long they will be needed.

Technique. A defined systematic procedure employed by a human resource to perform an activity to produce a product or result or deliver a service, and that may employ one or more tools.

Template. A partially complete document in a predefined format that provides a defined structure for collecting, organizing, and presenting information and data.

Test and Evaluation Documents. Project documents that describe the activities used to determine if the product meets the quality objectives stated in the quality management plan.

Threat. A risk that would have a negative effect on one or more project objectives.

Three-Point Estimating. A technique used to estimate cost or duration by applying an average or weighted average of optimistic, pessimistic, and most likely estimates when there is uncertainty with the individual activity estimates.

Threshold. A predetermined value of a measurable project variable that represents a limit that requires action to be taken if it is reached.

Time and Material Contract (T&M). A type of contract that is a hybrid contractual arrangement containing aspects of both cost-reimbursable and fixed-price contracts.

To-Complete Performance Index (TCPI). A measure of the cost performance that is required to be achieved with the remaining resources to meet a specified management goal, expressed as the ratio of the cost to finish the outstanding work to the remaining budget.

Tolerance. The quantified description of acceptable variation for a quality requirement.

Tool. Something tangible, such as a template or software program, used in performing an activity to produce a product or result.

Tornado Diagram. A special type of bar chart used in sensitivity analysis for comparing the relative importance of the variables.

Total Float. The amount of time that a schedule activity can be delayed or extended from its early start date without delaying the project finish date or violating a schedule constraint.

Trend Analysis. An analytical technique that uses mathematical models to forecast future outcomes based on historical results.

Trigger Condition. An event or situation that indicates that a risk is about to occur.

Unanimity. Agreement by everyone in the group on a single course of action.

Update. A modification to any deliverable, project management plan component, or project document that is not under formal change control.

Validate Scope. The process of formalizing acceptance of the completed project deliverables.

Validation. The assurance that a product, service, or result meets the needs of the customer and other identified stakeholders. Contrast with **Verification**.

Variance. A quantifiable deviation, departure, or divergence from a known baseline or expected value.

Variance Analysis. A technique for determining the cause and degree of difference between the baseline and actual performance.

Variance At Completion (VAC). A projection of the amount of budget deficit or surplus, expressed as the difference between the budget at completion and the estimate at completion.

Variation. An actual condition that is different from the expected condition that is contained in the baseline plan.

Verification. The evaluation of whether or not a product, service, or result complies with a regulation, requirement, specification, or imposed condition. Contrast with **Validation**.

Verified Deliverable. Completed project deliverable that has been checked and confirmed for correctness through the Control Quality process.

Virtual Team. Group of people with a shared goal who fulfill their roles with little or no time spent meeting face to face.

Voice of the Customer. A planning technique used to provide products, services, and results that truly reflect customer requirements by translating those customer requirements into the appropriate technical requirements for each phase of project product development.

WBS Dictionary. A document that provides detailed deliverable, activity, and scheduling information about each component in the work breakdown structure.

What-If Scenario Analysis. The process of evaluating scenarios in order to predict their effect on project objectives.

Work Breakdown Structure (WBS). A hierarchical decomposition of the total scope of work to be carried out by the project team to accomplish the project objectives and create the required deliverables.

Work Breakdown Structure Component. An entry in the work breakdown structure that can be at any level.

Work Package. The work defined at the lowest level of the work breakdown structure for which cost and duration are estimated and managed.

Work Performance Data. The raw observations and measurements identified during activities being performed to carry out the project work.

Work Performance Information. The performance data collected from controlling processes, analyzed in comparison with project management plan components, project documents, and other work performance information.

Work Performance Report. The physical or electronic representation of work performance information compiled in project documents, intended to generate decisions, actions, or awareness.

INDEX